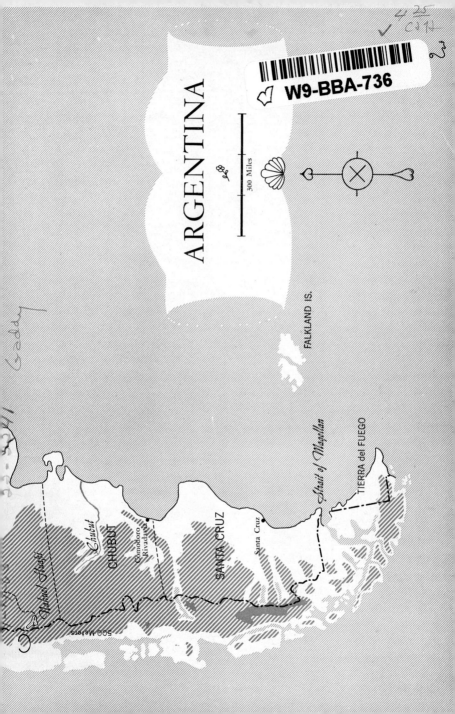

ARGENTINA

300 Miles

FALKLAND IS.

CHUBUT

Comodoro Rivadavia

SANTA CRUZ

Santa Cruz

Strait of Magellan

TIERRA del FUEGO

500 Meters

The United States and Argentina

THE AMERICAN FOREIGN POLICY LIBRARY

DONALD C. MCKAY, EDITOR

THE
UNITED STATES
AND
Argentina

By
Arthur P. Whitaker

HARVARD UNIVERSITY PRESS
Cambridge, Massachusetts
1954

Distributed in Great Britain by
GEOFFREY CUMBERLEGE
OXFORD UNIVERSITY PRESS
LONDON

MAPS BY R. L. WILLIAMS

LIBRARY OF CONGRESS CATALOG CARD NUMBER 55-5541

PRINTED IN THE UNITED STATES OF AMERICA

CONTENTS

20312

Part II: Under Perón

Contents

INTRODUCTION

The Perón regime in Argentina has been the subject of almost endless vituperation and of substantial misunderstanding, both public and official, in the United States. It has been denounced in season and out as "Nazi-Fascist," "authoritarian," "totalitarian." Let there be no mistake: this is a full-blown authoritarian regime, which has altered the Constitution, purged the Supreme Court and the Universities, brought the press under rigorous control, and employed the usual instruments of terror and violence. Perón had studied the fascist dictatorships, and his borrowings are obvious. But there is one significant difference — this regime, preserving the outward trappings of democracy, apparently commands majority support of the Argentine people, coming largely from underprivileged workers in town and country, the *descamisados,* "the shirtless ones." To this large group Perón has, however cynically, promised and delivered social reforms which have improved their standard of living. His regime apparently has a solid base both in the workers and in the army, from which he emerged.

Mr. Whitaker has skillfully developed another central aspect of the Perón regime: it is deeply anchored in Argentina's history and geographic position. The sense of isolation, the attraction of Europe, the preference for Spanish-Americanism as against Pan-Americanism, Perón's deep-going preferences for bilateralism as opposed to multilateralism, the hypersensitive nationalism, the suspicion of Yankee power and "imperialism" — all of these attitudes are very old indeed. And the present volume devotes nearly half of its pages to a broad consideration of the history that lies behind Perón and that goes far to explain why his regime has taken the course it has.

In terms of the interests of the United States, Argentina has come to occupy a very special position. Until the turn of the century, the relations of the two countries were relatively unimportant. Then persistent Argentine neutrality during the first world war occasioned widespread misgivings and criticism in the United States, although the best evidence suggests that the Argentines were following a policy which was logically self-interested and quite traditional. Perón has strengthened this trend of half a century and has managed to make of Argentina our most important and difficult Latin American problem. It is relevant also that the United States has now displaced Britain in the top position in Argentina's economic foreign relations.

Official American reaction to the new regime in these postwar years has taken, successively, two forms. In the first stage, we revealed our profound distaste for the dictatorship by openly intervening in such events as the presidential elections of February 1946. When this policy of overt opposition failed, we turned to one of "intermittent conciliation for limited objectives," seeking to promote our economic interests and to forge more effective military defenses for the free world. For the present, Perón seems more friendly, or, to speak more precisely, the pendulum-swing has come some little distance in our direction. But this policy is still one identifiably traditional and Argentine-centered: Perón's so-called "Third Position" is at once an attempt to find his way, on the domestic front, between collectivism (communism) and capitalism, and, in the international field, between the "perils" of Moscow and Washington. Despite reverses, to date the dictator has had considerable success in both directions.

With its recency and all the characteristic difficulties of documenting the life story of any dictatorship, Perón's regime offers inevitable and serious pitfalls for the historian. Mr. Whitaker has brought to his task exceptionally sound equipment and wide experience in scholarship, travel, and public service (he is the author of the volume on the Bolivarian Republics in this same series). And he has, it seems to me, approached this thorny and much debated subject with an unusually objective temper. His book will be of interest and significance for many added reasons. The dramatic account of the rise of the dictator and his seizure of power is an instructive case history in how revolutions are made. The author puts his finger on certain of the pathological symptoms in the Argentine body social, which invited Perón's action. The dictator's consort, Evita, with her beginnings as a burlesque girl, her extraordinary grass-roots sensitivity, and her ostensible concern for the masses, adds a gaudy but important note to this bizarre cavalcade.

Nor is Mr. Whitaker timorous about discussing the future. He sees nothing threatening the continuance of the dictatorship in the coming years, and alas, predicts that even if the Radicals should in some unforeseen circumstances succeed Perón, the United States would still face serious problems with Argentina, and that in some respects indeed, for all that they are sound practicing democrats, the Radicals would prove even more "recalcitrant" than the present dictator.

Donald C. McKay

PREFACE

Since Juan Perón began his rise to power in 1943, Argentina has been the most important and difficult of all the Latin American countries from the point of view of the United States. In both respects the Perón period has only strengthened a trend that had been in progress for half a century. During those years Argentina became increasingly important to the United States as she won and consolidated an outstanding position among the twenty Latin American states in wealth, foreign trade, culture, and international prestige. Simultaneously, the complex Argentine problem became one of increasing difficulty for the United States as the two countries developed economies and foreign policies which were largely competitive, not complementary, for while the United States sought to develop Western Hemisphere regionalism, Argentina took on a more and more pronounced orientation — economic, cultural, and political — towards Britain and Western Europe.

A decade of domination by Perón increased the importance and difficulty of the problem by giving Argentina more dynamic leadership in the execution of a more nationalistic policy; by destroying a democratic system largely modeled upon that of the United States and replacing it with a quasi-totalitarian tyranny; and by maintaining a "Third Position" or middle way between communism and capitalism, between the Soviet Union and the United States, in such a manner as to constitute his government the chief trouble-maker for the United States in all Latin America.

The Perón regime has been in power so long and has used its wide powers with such thoroughgoing ruthlessness that, even if it should fall tomorrow, it could not fail to leave an enduring mark on the nation and its role in world affairs. Consequently, even a long-range examination of relations between the United States and Argentina, such as this volume attempts, must be focused upon the Perón regime. That focus is accordingly taken in this volume, more than half of which deals with the Perón regime from its beginning in 1943 to the end of 1953.

I have tried, however, to avoid the twin error of treating that regime as an isolated and a static phenomenon. The view taken here is that it is a part of the stream of Argentine history and that it is no exception to the universal law of change. No one would be likely to question either proposition; but I believe that I have given both of them a fuller application than they have hitherto had. At any rate, the following pages stress the Argentine rather than (as has been customary) the European background of Peronismo. They also point out some significant but little-noticed (or, at any rate, little discussed) symptoms of change in the economic, social, and political character of the regime, especially since Eva Perón's death in 1952 — a change which, if it continues, may conceivably lead to a long-range improvement in the relations between Washington and Buenos Aires.

Believing that the Perón regime cannot be understood apart from the Argentine historical background, I have devoted not far from half the present volume to sketching that background from colonial times to 1943.

In the following pages stress will be laid upon the international aspects of the story, especially from the point of view of the United States. This stress seems proper not only because the present volume belongs to a series called the American Foreign Policy Library, but also because Argentina's international relations have long been important both to that country and to the rest of the world — exceptionally so, in the past decade, to the United States.

Since there is a good deal of misapprehension in the United States about the accenting of derivatives of "Perón," it may not be amiss to state here that the correct forms of the true derivatives are "Peronista" and "Peronismo," without the accent. Space does not permit an explanation of why this is so; I shall add only that, on this analogy, I have also thought it proper to omit the accent in such Anglicized derivatives as "Peronization." It should also be pointed out that, in order to avoid the excessive use of italics, Spanish words such as *gaucho* and *descamisado* are italicized only the first time they occur in the text.

I am much indebted to two experts in this field, both old friends, George Wythe and Miron Burgin, for aid of various kinds; to Donald B. Easum for the loan of his excellent manuscript study of the triangular relations between Argentina, Great Britain, and the United States; and to many Argentines, who shall be nameless, who likewise aided me in many ways, particularly while I was in their country in 1952 gathering material for this book.

Philadelphia, July 1954   Arthur P. Whitaker

... that is good, and which permeating in the whole. I think
better, that the elevation of enlightened ... Nature. It may not
also seem to high ... the mind of man. I begin at the first of the
present. Economics and Production, will at the same time ... ...
I do not wish any explanation of why this is so. I am, I shall also
only point out ... section. I have also thought it proper to omit
the aspect in such Analytical sharpness as Economics, it
should also be pointed out that in order to avoid the same use
use of value which works such as goods and documents are
are followed only the first describes them in the text.

I feel much indebted to two experts in this field, Prof. O.
Brandt, of the ... and Mr. ... Batista, for aid of various
kinds, to Donald B. Blanco for the loan of his excellent monographs ... of the first useful relation between Argentine, Chili,
Brazil and the United States, and to Isidor Argentina, who
shall be anxious, who likewise aided me in many ways parties
help which I was in this country in 1923, ... procured for
this book.

Philadelphia, July, 1924.   Arthur L. M. Hagerty

1. Argentina: Land and People

Argentina and Iran lie far apart on the map, but for several years past they have been close together on the issue which, next to communism, is mainly responsible for the troubled state of the world today. This is the fervent nationalism and rabid anti-imperialism of the underdeveloped countries.

In two respects, however, Argentina differs from most of the other countries in this category. In the first place, it is more highly developed than the great majority of them and has a large urban proletariat and also a large but amorphous and uneasy middle class. In the second place, the Argentine ferment, besides exacerbating the international relations of that country with the great powers, and particularly with the United States, has also brought about a domestic social and political revolution in the name of the Argentine masses.

However laudable the objectives may have been, this revolution produced an authoritarian regime which has employed democratic procedures only to make a mockery of them. To most observers in the United States, the establishment of such a regime in Argentina was one of the most unexpected and disturbing developments that had taken place in Latin America in the twentieth century, for until recently Argentina had seemed to be setting the pace for all Latin America in the evolution of a stable and responsible democratic system of government. Feeling on this score was a major cause of the ten-year crisis in relations between the two countries after 1943. It still persists among many people in the United States despite the reconciliation begun in 1953 between the two governments and it seems likely to continue to color their relations with each other for a long time to come.

Since their relations in recent years have been more deeply affected by developments in Argentina than in the United States, we shall begin with an examination of the former country — the land, the people, and the evolution of the Argentine nation down to the advent of its present regime in 1943. We shall have much to say about the part played by foreign influences in this evolution from the eighteenth century on, for they were so strong and varied that in the end they profoundly altered the character of the Argentine people and the use they made of their land.

1. THE LAND

In area, Argentina is the eighth largest country in the world and second among the twenty Latin American states. It is only a third as large as Brazil, but larger by a fourth than the next Latin American country, Mexico. Argentina is also only a third as large as the United States, but in comparable latitudes its length from north to south is greater. A map of Argentina superimposed upon one of North America in these latitudes reaches from a point almost as far south as Mexico City to a point well north of Winnipeg, Canada.

Except for the Falkland Islands, which Argentina claims but which Britain holds, and a slice of Antarctica, which it has yet to develop, Argentina lies wholly in South America and very largely in the south temperate zone, though its extremities reach from the tropics to the frozen south. Its shape has inspired someone to describe Argentina as a dagger pointed at the heart of the Antarctic. In more prosaic terms, its shape is roughly that of an elongated triangle. The base, which runs roughly from east to west, is formed by the boundary between northern Argentina and Brazil, Paraguay, and Bolivia. Far to the south, below the Strait of Magellan, lies the apex of the triangle, which is formed by the Argentine segment of Tierra del Fuego; the rest of that big, bleak island belongs to Chile. The western side of the triangle is formed by the watershed of the towering Andes, west of which lies

Chile. The eastern side runs along the Atlantic Ocean as far north as the estuary called the Río de la Plata (or, in English, the Plata River or River Plate) and then passes inland through the Plata basin until, in the tropics, it meets the base of the triangle.

Northern Argentina consists mainly of the Andes, which widen out here, and the hot Chaco plain, which continues northward through Paraguay into Brazil. From this region come semitropical products and most of the nation's scanty mineral production. Central Argentina contains one of the finest farming areas in the world — the broad, fertile prairie land called the pampas, which made modern Argentina one of the world's great food-producing countries. The pampas have a temperate climate and, normally, adequate rainfall. Watercourses are few, however, except for the Plata system along its eastern fringe, and the country is almost treeless. The southern fourth of Argentina, Patagonia, is ever cool and wind-swept. Outside the Comodoro Rivadavia oil field on the Atlantic coast and the Bariloche lake region in the west, which has become a vacation land, only sheep-raising has flourished in Patagonia, and that only in recent times.

Between the two chief tributaries of the Plata, the Uruguay and Paraná rivers, lies Argentina's Mesopotamia, which contains the historically important provinces of Entre Ríos and Corrientes. These, together with the even more important province of Buenos Aires, form the bulk of the region called by Argentines the *Litoral*. The rest of the area of effective occupation down to the late nineteenth century — the area west and northwest of the Litoral — is called the Interior. Here lie the oldest cities in Argentina, one of which, Córdoba, was the country's first city during most of the colonial period and is still its second city. Here also, until the nineteenth century, was concentrated the greater part of the population and wealth of Argentina.

Though extraordinarily rich in agricultural and pastoral resources, Argentina has always been comparatively poor in the mineral resources most highly prized by western man at various periods of history. From the names of the nation and its principal "river" or estuary, the Río de la Plata, one might infer that Argentina was once rich in one of the precious metals most eagerly sought after in the colonial period, for Argentina is a Latinized form of the Spanish word *plata,* meaning "silver." In fact, however, the original use of the name was a product of wishful thinking on the part of the early conquistadores which was not justified by the event; Argentina has never produced silver on any but a small scale. The country has so far proved almost equally deficient in the minerals required by the modern age. The two most important of all, coal and iron, were until very recently conspicuous by their absence. Only lead, zinc, and petroleum have been produced in large quantities over a considerable period, and the production of petroleum has always lagged so far behind consumption that heavy imports have been essential at all times. Hence it was that the stoppage of shipments from Iran in 1951 immediately produced a shortage of fuel oil and gasoline in Argentina. Even the sources of hydroelectric power are in the wrong places, for they lie in northern and western Argentina, far away from the main centers of population and industry, which are in the east.

The Perón regime has redoubled the search for minerals and has come up with some startling announcements of its discoveries, which include coal, iron, and uranium, as well as more petroleum. Even if all the claims turn out to be true, their significance lies in the future. The Argentina with which we have to deal in this volume is one poor in minerals but rich in pastoral and agricultural resources and in the flourishing commerce to which, in the nineteenth century, new forms of exploitation of soil and livestock gave rise under the ministrations of foreign investors, entrepreneurs, and technicians. How the Argentines' use of their land was altered and extended in the process will appear in later chapters.

2. THE PEOPLE

In 1953, on the four hundredth anniversary of the first permanent settlement by the Spaniards in what is now Argentina, that country had a population of about 18,500,000. It ranked third in Latin America in this respect, with only one-third as many inhabitants as Brazil and two-thirds as many as Mexico, but with more than half again as many as the fourth country, Colombia.

More important than the differences in numbers are the differences in kind which set the Argentines apart from the other peoples of Latin America. One of the most important facts about the divergence between the two is that the Argentines are a comparatively new people, for they are mainly the product of economic, social, and demographic changes that took place in Argentina between 1880 and 1930. So rapid and far-reaching were these changes that their profoundly unsettling effect is still felt there today. As a result, while the traditional preponderance of the Spanish language, the Roman Catholic religion, and a pastoral-agricultural economy are still maintained in Argentina, these familiar landmarks now have the appearance of islands in an encroaching sea of change.

The Argentines differ from most other Latin American peoples in many respects and from all of them in some important respects. Except for the people of little Uruguay, the Argentines are the whitest and culturally the most Europeanized people in Latin America. Their literacy rate (about 90 per cent) is the highest without exception, and appreciably higher than that of Uruguay (about 70 per cent). Until the Perón blight descended upon the country, it had the highest per capita income in Latin America, the best schools, universities, and newspapers, and, in Buenos Aires, the largest and best publishing center. For two or three generations before the 1930's the degree of social mobility in Argentina was probably the highest in Latin America, and though it has diminished since then, it is still above the average. The Argentine middle class is one of the oldest and largest in Latin America; its emergence dates from about 1900 and by the 1940's it included half the population of the country.

One of the most distinctive and important characteristics of Argentine society is that it is one of the most highly urbanized in Latin America. This is a phenomenon one would hardly expect to find in a country whose economy is basically agricultural-pastoral and whose population density was still only 17 persons per square mile in 1953. Yet the fact is that by 1938 half the people of Argentina were already living in communities of more than 10,000 inhabitants, and the urban trend has continued since that date. In Mexico the corresponding figure in 1940 was only 22 per cent; and even excluding the city of Buenos Aires, which contained over one-fifth of the total national population, Argentina still had a higher proportion of urban dwellers than Mexico including Mexico City.

To most observers an even more striking idiosyncrasy of Argentina is that the overwhelming majority of its people are white. As already noted, the only other Latin American nation that matches it (or, indeed, approximates it) in this respect is neighboring Uruguay, whose population is only about one-sixth as large. In 1940 both countries had populations that were about 90 per cent white, and in both most of the balance, about 8 per cent, was mestizo (mixed white and Indian). The scant remainder of 1 or 2 per cent was negroid in Uruguay and Indian in Argentina.

To this extent the efforts made by Domingo Sarmiento and other nineteenth-century Argentine leaders to Europeanize or North Americanize their country has been crowned with success. By comparison, the highest white percentages in the other Latin American countries in 1940 were 48 in faraway Costa Rica and 39 in contiguous Brazil. As for Argentina's other immediate neighbors, the bulk of their populations were either mestizo (66 per cent in Chile) or Indian (57 per cent in Bolivia, 65 in Paraguay).

If this is one of the respects in which the Argentines of today differ most widely from other Latin American peoples, it is also one in which they themselves have changed most radically since 1880. Analyzing the national census taken a decade earlier (1869), the Argentine sociologist José Ingenieros concluded that at that time the whites made up only a small minority of the total population, being outnumbered nearly four to one by the mestizos and outnumbering the Negroes and mulattoes less than three to one.

The racial revolution of the next half century is accounted for largely by the tidal wave of immigration from Italy and Spain that swept over the country for several decades after 1880. It is also accounted for, however, by the Argentine (and generally Latin American) definition of "white," which is broader than the one prevailing in the United States, since it classifies as white all those who are not obviously non-white and reflects a cultural (in the anthropological sense) rather than a racial criterion.

3. THE CULTURE

In this sense the Argentine people have become overwhelmingly white, for their culture is almost wholly European or creole (the Argentine variant of European). The Indianism of such countries as Mexico and Peru has no real counterpart in modern Argentina; still less does the Negro influence, which is so strong in the folk culture of Brazil and several Caribbean countries.

The description of Argentine culture as European and creole requires a gloss. The core of both these aspects of Argentine culture is Spanish, but in both cases the core has been modified by other elements. In its European aspect, the Spanish core, which had always been peripheral in the mother country, was drawn closer to the central stream of European culture by a variety of influences which played upon it in Argentina. Among these we may note the heavy preponderance of Italians in the immigrant flood of the late nineteenth and early twentieth centuries, and the prestige long enjoyed by France in Argentine social and literary circles, by Germany in military circles, and by Britain in business and politics.

Recently a new major influence has appeared — that of the United States, which "in the last two decades . . . has increased tremendously." So, at any rate, we are assured by James Bruce, ambassador of the United States to Argentina from 1947 to 1949, who cultivated the society of Argentines assiduously, visited many parts of the country, and was aided in his observations by a large and alert embassy staff and an experienced North American journalist. According to Bruce, the influence of the United States on Argentina is apparent in many ways — in soap and soap opera (Palmolive's "daily serial gave Evita Perón one of her early radio jobs"); in the extensive use that Argentines have

made of United States news services, not only for reports from
Europe as well as the United States on politics, economics,
science, and art, but also for syndicated columns of beauty hints,
advice to the lovelorn, and comic strips such as "Flash Gordon"
and "Terry and the Pirates," all in translation of course; in the
increasing informality and different "desires, ambitions, and outlook" of the Argentine youth; and above all in "the realization
. . . that this is the age of business and industrialization, of science and technology, of chemistry and medicine, in all of which
the United States is the leader."

The influence of the United States has grown at the expense of
that of Europe; but in any long-range view of history the two are
more in harmony than in conflict, and both alike have stimulated
the further differentiation of Argentina from the many Latin
American countries in which Indian and African elements are
strong.

The creole culture of Argentina, which survives today mainly
in the provinces, likewise has a Spanish core modified by other
elements — in this case, by geography and the Indian. The fusion
is embodied in the *gaucho*, or cowboy, long celebrated in song
and story as the symbol of creole culture, for the typical gaucho
was a mestizo and a product of Argentina's wide-open spaces
teeming with wild cattle and infested by "bad" Indians (*ma-
lones*). The true gaucho has long since disappeared, replaced by
the cowhand, as his wild cattle have been replaced by blooded
stock; and the nationalistic Perón's efforts to revive gaucho ways
have not met with much success among the now highly urbanized people of Argentina.

The whole creole complex is breaking down. Again the gaucho
provides the clue. A recent writer credits him with four major
contributions to Argentine life: the drinking of *mate* (a kind of
tea, rich in vitamins), the *asado* (a lamb or ox barbecued whole),
the tango, and the theme of Argentina's best literature. As to the
tango we have some reservations, since its origin is disputed by
experts and it did not take its present form until the end of the
nineteenth century, when the true gaucho had already disappeared. And what of his other contributions today? Mate, once a

universal, round-the-clock beverage, has given way with many who can afford it to coffee in the morning and a cocktail in the afternoon. Most city-dwelling Argentines do not see a real asado from one year's end to the next. The gaucho was indeed the theme of much of the best creative writing in Argentina when the way of life that it celebrated was gone but not forgotten; but in the past quarter century the vein seems to have been worked out.

There are many other ways in which the gradual but inexorable disintegration of the creole way of life could be illustrated. The Argentines' "universal passion for riding," noted by the North American traveler Brackenridge in 1817, had by the end of the century become a universal passion for going to the races and playing the ponies — a passion which still prevails. In the 1920's Ricardo Rojas, loving and eloquent interpreter of the history of the Argentine people, recorded with regret that the traditional guitar had already been widely supplanted by the Italian immigrant's accordion. Today, the symbol of power of the common man is no longer the lone gaucho's deadly knife, but the strike and the organized mass demonstration of the kind that brought Perón definitively to power on the now famous October 17, 1945; and the passionate individualism of a century ago has given way to the quest for social security.

The reader may think by now that we have labored the point excessively; but Perón has so often been compared to the Argentine tyrant and gaucho's hero of a hundred years ago, Juan Manuel de Rosas, that the North American reader at any rate should be warned against identifying Perón's following with that of Rosas. The comparison between the two leaders is apt, if only because there is always a family likeness between one tyrant and another; but there is a world of difference between Rosas' gaucho hordes and Perón's phalanx of *descamisados*.

4. SOCIAL CLASSES

And who are these descamisados? They are for the most part the members of the Argentine lower classes — a fact suggested by the literal meaning of the term, "the shirtless ones," which recalls the *sans-culottes* of the French Revolution and which Perón used to dramatize his bid for popular support through the promise of a social revolution for the benefit of the "oppressed masses" of Argentina. At the outset, the descamisados were largely an amorphous mass, of whom not more than 10 per cent were members of labor unions, and these unions were in most respects independent of government control — so much so that just before the advent of Perón, though the government was Conservative, communism had made heavy inroads in the Argentine labor movement. Since then, the bulk of the descamisados (who now number about six million) have been regimented in labor unions, both urban and rural, which are under the government's thumb. Conversely, the descamisados are one of the regime's two main sources of strength and an indispensable counterpoise to the other, the armed forces.

The strength of the descamisado element in the Perón regime has no precedent in the history of Argentina and little in that of any other Latin American country. Only the Mexico of the 1920's and 1930's approximated it, and since 1940, Mexico has moved towards a more bourgeois type of regime. There have quite recently been some indications that a similar shift from left to center may have begun in Argentina; but so far the evidence is inconclusive. At the present writing the Perón regime represents a unique form of the social revolution which has been gaining force in most of Latin America during the past generation. Somewhat similar regimes have subsequently been established in Bolivia, Chile, Ecuador, and Guatemala, but all of these differ from the Argentine in important respects. One of the most striking differences consists in the great strength developed by the communists in Guatemala in the early 1950's. In Argentina, on the other hand, Perón's rise crippled the previously flourishing communist movement. It probably did so by offering the Argentine malcontents an acceptable native alternative. Rightly or wrongly, the Argentine masses were convinced that Perón's government was of and for, if not by, the descamisados. If the problem of the Western World today is to defeat communism at all costs, then Perón has provided it with one successful solution by developing his version of the dictatorship of the descamisados.

At the opposite end of the social scale from the descamisados is the Argentine oligarchy. In the stream of Argentine history, the oligarchy came first. It had been under fire from the liberal sector long before Perón strengthened the attack and made it one of the two main targets of his assault on the existing order, the other being foreign imperialism as represented mainly by Great Britain and the United States. These two, foreign imperialism and the native oligarchy, so the charge runs, have long been leagued together in an unholy alliance which dominated and exploited Argentina until Perón broke their power.

Though now shorn of power, the oligarchy has not been destroyed. For reasons that will appear below, there has been no wholesale liquidation or expulsion of the members of this former ruling class remotely resembling the one carried out in Bolshevik Russia after 1917 or even the less thoroughgoing one in Mexico after the Revolution of 1910. At least potentially, therefore, the oligarchy remains an important factor in present-day Argentina, and since it was actually, as its critics charge and its friends admit, a dominant factor in Argentine life throughout most of the nation's history before the rise of Perón, it must be given a prominent place in any but the most superficial account of the state of that nation.

Despite the many evidences of its power, the Argentine oligarchy is difficult to define or to describe in terms of parallels in the other Latin American countries or the United States. Even Perón, who sets himself up as an expert on the subject, could give no better definition of the oligarchy than that it consists of three groups, to wit, "powerful associations accustomed to rule from behind the scenes, their henchmen who serve in all sorts of positions, and men with talents but without honor." All are agreed that its core has always been made up of great landowners, particularly of those engaged in stock-raising, the *estancieros*. All are also agreed that the inner core of this group consisted, from its founding in 1866, of the exclusive Argentine Rural Society (*Sociedad Rural Argentina*). This society was undoubtedly one of the "powerful associations" Perón had in mind in his definition, for a leading authority on Argentine rural life has described it as "probably the most powerful farmers' organization in the Western Hemisphere" and as exercising "immeasurable" influence.* Yet the Rural Society cannot be described as constituting the oligarchy, for two reasons: first, because, as the same authority declares, it has never operated as a political pressure group; and second, because the great political influence which, before the rise of Perón, its members exercised as individuals was increasingly offset by that of leaders in other walks of life, such as business and banking. In the twentieth century these two have likewise developed their "powerful associations," in the form of chambers of commerce and industry.

Moreover, the Argentine oligarchy is larger than the nation's patrician class, which does not make up the whole of even the Rural Society, where it is strongest; and this patrician class, like its colonial forebears, has never been a feudal aristocracy, but rather an uncommonly successful and durable group of ranchers and farmers. As the newer elements were added to the estancieros, the Argentine oligarchy became increasingly a plutocracy rather than an aristocracy, and a counterpart for it was easier to find in the United States than in other Latin American countries. Yet the contrast even with the United States is striking, for the latter's "oligarchy" has generally been pictured by its critics as led by the economic royalists whose citadel is Wall Street, whereas the core of the Argentine oligarchy has continued to be formed by the estancieros, whose way of life recalls not that of Wall Street, but rather that of a Virginia or South Carolina plantation in the antebellum South.

Politically, the oligarchy has been so deeply divided that it is a question whether one is justified in calling it an oligarchy in the strict sense of the term. Most of its members have been conservatives, but the opposition to the latter has included outstanding members of the Argentine élite, from Bartolomé Mitre in the late nineteenth century to Honorio Pueyrredón and Marcelo T. de

* Carl C. Taylor, *Rural Life in Argentina* (Baton Rouge, 1948), p. 396.

Alvear, both Radicals, in the 1920's and 1930's, and Federico
Pinedo, a Socialist in the 1920's and today a recently converted
Peronista. The Perón thesis has it that both groups differed only
in nonessentials and that at bottom both were equally devoted
to the maintenance of an economic and social system that served
the interests of the oligarchy. To an outsider, this thesis has the
air of a convenient fiction. Whether it has been converted into
fact by a natural defensive reaction against Perón's demagogic
assault is a question that it will not be possible to answer with
assurance until freedom of political expression is restored in
Argentina.

The third and last of the major social groups in Argentina is
the middle class, which, as already noted, is one of the oldest
and largest middle classes in Latin America and by the 1940's
included about half the population of Argentina. So Argentine
sociologists tell us, but the reader should keep constantly in mind
their warning that this so-called middle class is not in fact a
united, coherent class, but rather an aggregation of disparate
groups and individuals who have little in common beyond the
fact that they occupy a middle position between the oligarchy
above and the descamisados beneath.

To begin with, the authorities distinguish between two sectors
which developed at different periods and have never coalesced —
the old middle class, which was largely creole and in which the
small independent farmers bulked large, and the new middle
class, which was recruited mainly from the Spanish and Italian
immigrants and their descendants and from the rapidly growing
white-collar groups of shopkeepers, clerks, and bureaucrats. A
distinction is also made between the upper middle class, which
has clung tenaciously to the individualism once characteristic of
Argentine society at all levels, and the lower middle class which,
in order to defend its more precarious position, has tended more
and more to develop group action, but has done so in unrelated
occupational groups, not as a class. We are further told that ever
since the great depression of the 1930's the members of both
sectors of the middle class have been increasingly haunted by

the specter of insecurity as they feel themselves ground beneath the upper and nether millstones of the oligarchy and the descamisados.

The situation of the Argentine middle class has deteriorated sharply under the Perón regime. The galloping inflation of recent years has done its greatest injury to this class; its members have time and again been pilloried by Perón himself on the ground that their "selfish individualism" is out of place in the fraternal, coöperative atmosphere of his "New Argentina"; and many of those who compose its lower fringe have been enticed or dragooned into captive unions, thus swelling the ranks of the descamisados. Yet for all its incoherence and lack of morale, a middle class of sorts still forms one of the two major segments of Argentine society.

Since the Army has played so important a part in the history of Argentina, especially since 1930, it should be noted that most of the army officers have been recruited from this amorphous and unstable middle class; Perón himself is an example. This may help to explain the otherwise puzzling affinity that the officer class of an essentially creole-Spanish-Italian nation have exhibited for the German military training and ideals to which they were systematically exposed for three decades after the first German mission arrived in Argentina in 1911. Perhaps it would not be fanciful to regard affinity for German discipline and authoritarianism as an overcompensation for the insecurity and excessive individualism of that middle class from which the Argentine officers were sprung and were, so to speak, refugees.

5. NATIONAL CHARACTER

We have spoken with some assurance of traits of particular groups in Argentina, and for a long time past there has been general agreement among observers, both native and foreign, regarding the existence of certain Argentine traits which are so widespread that they can be called national. Foremost among these is an ebullient patriotism, which has on the reverse side of the shield an excessive sensitivity to criticism that easily becomes resentment and xenophobia. Argentines do not have a well-developed sense of humor and are not very witty. They have never produced a Mark Twain, a *New Yorker*, or a *Punch*, and of the many kinds of laughter, theirs seems most often to be of the kind described by Hobbes as "thorns crackling under a pot."

Otherwise, however, they are a versatile people. In the nineteenth century they produced not only distinguished generals, statesmen, and writers, such as José de San Martín, Bartolomé Mitre, Domingo Sarmiento, and Juan Bautista Alberdi, but also artists of exceptional merit, including two of the three best painters in all Latin America, Prilidiano Pueyrredón and Juan Manuel Blanes. In the twentieth century, Argentines have gained worldwide renown in a variety of fields: in the social sciences, José Ingenieros, who was at one time the most widely read of all writers in the Spanish language; in the natural sciences, Bernardo Houssay, who was awarded the Nobel Prize for Medicine and Physiology in 1947; and in international affairs, Carlos Saavedra Lamas, who in 1936 was both president of the League of Nations Assembly and winner of the Nobel Peace Prize. Argentines are also, by common consent, regarded as the most energetic people in Latin America, the "Yankees of the South," though some Argentine students make a distinction between the original creole stock, whom they find easygoing, and the immigrant horde of the half century after 1880, who came seeking their fortune and spared no pains to win it. Argentines also like to think of themselves as an exceptionally peace-loving people and point as proof to the fact that they have not fought a foreign war since 1870 nor a civil war since 1880, and to the many international disputes that they have settled by arbitration or other peaceful means.

Yet all these agreed national traits, and others which we have not mentioned, do not add up to a national character. One may have been taking shape in the first half of the nineteenth century, but if so, it was all but obliterated by the immigrant flood of later years and the accompanying economic revolution. In 1912, a third of a century after the transformation began, James Bryce found on a visit to Argentina that its people "are beginning to show a character different from that of the other [South American] peoples" but that "their mental and moral type . . . is not yet fully formed" — "as is natural," he added, "in a country rapidly growing and deluged with immigrants." Another third of a century after Bryce, an Argentine observer made a similar report. He made it in even more emphatic terms, possibly because by this time Argentina had produced a phenomenon which no observer of 1912, no matter how pessimistic, would have predicted. That was the demagogic dictatorship of Juan Perón, whose popularity showed many of Argentina's leading intellectuals how little they understood their fellow-countrymen. This observer, José Luis Romero, was one such intellectual, and accordingly he confessed in 1946 that: "It would be difficult to say what we Argentines are like, what our predominant characteristics are, and what the traits we have in common . . . The soul of Argentina is an enigma, for the collective personality of the country is still in process of formation."

6. THE PROVINCES

No discussion of this subject, however brief, should fail to take account of Argentina's provinces and of the deep dichotomy which has always existed between them and their now overgrown and all-conquering capital city, Buenos Aires. Cosmopolitan Buenos Aires is not Argentina, and the capital's traits and character are not the nation's, though some otherwise well-informed visitors have written as though both propositions were true. For example, one of them, an American ambassador who had spent several years in Argentina and who liked its people and had studied them as he saw them in the capital and on their estancias outside it, could bring himself to assert in 1939 that Argentine culture is "essentially French." By some stretch of the imagination that might have been said of the upper-class and literary culture of the capital about the time his book was written. It could not have been said of the culture of the provinces at any time.

Generally speaking, their culture was Spanish and creole, though each province had — and still has — a character of its own and in some cases still other elements have gone into their making, such as the Indians in times long past, or more recently the Italian, German, Swiss, or Irish immigrants. Consider a few of the varieties: populous Córdoba, called "the learned" (*la docta*) because of its famous university, the first founded in Argentina (1624), has a strong Catholic and conservative tradition, but by the twentieth century had developed a democratic society and initiated the university reform movement that soon spread to Buenos Aires. In neighboring Entre Ríos, where mestizos are numerous, the creole culture is so strong that even the European immigrants who came here in large numbers were assimilated by it; and its Normal School (*Escuela Normal*) at Paraná, established by Sarmiento in 1870, was long a center from which the lay spirit and the Argentine variety of positivism irradiated throughout Argentina. Contiguous Santa Fe became the nation's most cosmopolitan province after Buenos Aires under the impact of systematic, large-scale European immigration which made it a major center of wheat production. Tucumán, a center of sugar production since colonial times and now one of the most densely populated areas in the republic, has likewise attracted many foreigners, including three who played a notable part in the cultural development of Argentina: Paul Groussac (French), Paolo Mantegazza (Italian), and Germán Burmeister (German); but, thanks to the exceptional vigor of its creole stock, Tucumán has retained its traditional character, and its rapid development since 1880 has been carried out mainly by native capital and enterprise.

Still another type, that of the provinces of the northwest that have decayed since the rise of Buenos Aires transformed Argentina from a "Mediterranean" into a maritime country, is represented by Catamarca. Like Córdoba, Catamarca has a strong Spanish Catholic element, but unlike Córdoba, it also has a strong Indian element, with the result that, as Ricardo Rojas puts it, the culture of the province is a combination of Spanish hagiography and Calchaquí (Indian) folklore; and until quite recently it was governed by a patriarchal oligarchy stemming from the colonial period.

The provinces have contributed greatly to the formation of modern Argentina. The historical tradition in which the Argentine's ebullient patriotism finds nourishment is largely provincial. The decisive battle of the war of independence, Argentina's Yorktown, was fought at Salta; Argentina's declaration of independence (1816) was made at Tucumán; her great liberator, José de San Martín, was born in Corrientes and organized his famous liberating expedition to Chile in Mendoza; and the Constitution of 1853, under which, as extensively amended in 1860 and 1949, Argentina is still governed, was adopted at Santa Fe. The provinces were also mainly responsible for three crucial events in the nation's development: in 1820, the rejection of monarchical in favor of republican government; in 1852, the overthrow of the long-entrenched tyrant Rosas; and in 1880 the conversion of the city of Buenos Aires from the capital of the province of that name into the capital of the nation.

Likewise, many of the nation's greatest generals, statesmen, and writers have been provincials. To mention only a few, these include, in addition to San Martín, just mentioned as born in Corrientes, Julio A. Roca and Nicolás Avellaneda (Tucumán), the former the hero of Argentina's last Indian war and both presidents of the republic; Domingo Sarmiento (San Juan), also a president and, in addition, a great writer and educator; Juan Bautista Alberdi (Tucumán), the father of the Constitution of 1853; Joaquín Gonzalez (La Rioja), another great writer and educator; and Ricardo Rojas (Santiago del Estero), the "prince of Argentine letters" today. Some of the classics of Argentine literature are books that these and other provincials have written about their respective provinces, such as Sarmiento's *Recuerdos de provincia*, Gonzalez' *Mis montañas*, and Rojas' *El país de la selva*. And of course the whole enormous body of gaucho literature, to which we have already referred, is provincial in theme if not always in authorship.

Opinions regarding the role of the provinces in Argentina vary according to one's point of view; those emanating from Buenos Aires have tended to minimize its importance. To an outsider, however, it would seem that the best estimate is that made a quarter of a century ago by Ricardo Rojas, a provincial long resident in Buenos Aires, who has garnered the best of both worlds. He believes that the provinces have, on balance, strengthened the forces of democracy and a healthy "federalism" (in the sense of regionalism or localism) in the nation at large; that as Buenos Aires has served as a channel for the Europeanization of the provinces, so the latter have been the source of the Americanization of Buenos Aires; and that from the fruitful interplay of these two forces has resulted "the complex originality of our still formative culture."

When that was written a generation ago, it was part of an appeal to the Argentine people to save their precious provincial heritage, which was threatened with destruction by the Buenos Aires leviathan. In the early years of the Perón regime the almost universal trend towards centralization made the danger even more acute; recently, official policy has decreed a reversal of the trend in the interest of the provinces as the custodians of true "Argentinity," but it is still too early to say what the result will be.

7. THE SOUTH AMERICAN UNITED STATES?

"We must North Americanize ourselves" was the advice dinned into his fellow countrymen by Argentina's great statesman, educator, and man of letters, Domingo Sarmiento, from his first visit to the United States in 1847 until the end of his life some forty years later. Argentina has in fact been North Americanized to a considerable extent, in the sense that its people have passed through experiences and have developed institutions and traits similar to those of the United States.

Like her neighbor to the north, Argentina within the past century has terminated her centuries-long Indian wars and eliminated the Indians as a major factor in her national life; she has revolutionized her economy through the application of modern technology and heavy capital investments; she has become one of the world's great food-exporting nations; she has attracted a horde of immigrants from Europe; and she has developed a high standard of living (until very recently the highest in Latin America). Argentina is as white a nation as the United States and her rates of literacy and urban concentration are only slightly lower. From 1853 to 1949 the country was governed under a constitution so closely modeled upon that of the United States that Argentine courts repeatedly based their interpretations of it on court decisions and constitutional commentaries emanating from their North American model. When one adds that the Argentines are an exceptionally energetic and enterprising people, it should be easy to understand why they are often called the Yankees of the South and their country the South American United States.

Yet observers who know both countries well are usually more impressed by the differences than by the resemblances between them. Some of the most important differences are also the most obvious. The language of Argentina is Spanish, its religion Roman Catholic, and its cultural and racial origins lie mainly in Latin Europe. Whereas the United States is situated in the Northern Hemisphere, where most of the world's affairs are carried on, Argentina lies so far down in the Southern Hemisphere that the distance between Buenos Aires and New York is 6000 miles by sea and over 5000 miles by air. The United States exceeds Argentina threefold in area and ninefold in population; a much larger proportion of the latter's area is waste land, and four-fifths of its population and wealth are concentrated within three hundred miles of Buenos Aires. Far from enjoying a preponderance in South America like that of the United States in North America, Argentina is overshadowed by contiguous Brazil in both area and population. The nearest Argentine equivalent of the Mississippi River is the Plata System, which, though the second largest in the world (only the Amazon is larger), is peripheral to all of Argentina except its northeastern corner and is shared with four other nations (Uruguay, Paraguay, Brazil, and Bolivia).

One of the most important differences between the two countries consists in the fact that Argentina contains no counterpart of the heavily industrialized region stretching from Illinois to

Massachusetts. Hence, while Argentina is about the same size as the United States east of the Mississippi, a truer equivalent would be obtained by substituting for the northeastern United States some of the states lying west of the Mississippi — Kansas, Nebraska, and Iowa for their wheat and corn, part of Texas for its cattle, and Colorado for its high plains suddenly springing up into its Rocky Mountains. No part of the United States can provide an equivalent for the southern fourth of Argentina, bleak, wind-swept Patagonia.

The imbalance that has existed since the late nineteenth century between Argentina's highly developed pastoral-agricultural system and its tardily and only partially developed industrial system has differentiated it in yet another way from the United States by making Argentina far more dependent upon foreign trade. It could be said with almost as much truth of modern Argentina as it has recently been said of Great Britain, that the country must export or die. Most of its huge foreign trade has been carried on through the port of Buenos Aires and with Western Europe, especially Great Britain. As a result, Argentina developed closer and more exclusive ties with Europe than the United States has had since the early years of the republic, and Buenos Aires has grown to a size which, in proportion to the national total, has no parallel in the United States. The city contains one-fifth of the nation's population, and the city and province together contain nearly half of it. The remaining half is unequally distributed among the other fifteen provinces and the seven national territories, and, with only an occasional exception, thins out progressively as the distance from Buenos Aires increases. The great urban centers of the Middle West and Pacific Coast of the United States have no counterpart in Argentina.

Though we cannot undertake to catalogue all the differences between the two peoples, there is one more which should not be omitted in any listing. This involves a political trait of fundamental importance in a democracy: the willingness to abide by the results of a free election. In the United States such a willingness has been demonstrated unbrokenly since the end of the Civil War in 1865; its existence has been attributed to general agreement on fundamental issues. In Argentina such a willing-ness has almost never been demonstrated. Whether its absence is to be attributed to lack of agreement on fundamentals or to some other cause, the fact is written across the whole history of Argentina for all to see. Perón has made some important innova-tions, but his use of force and fraud to win and hold political power is not one of them, for the nation's record is replete with precedents for both fraud and force.

PART I. BEFORE PERÓN

2. Economic and Social Development

The first permanent Spanish settlement in the present limits of Argentina was made at Santiago del Estero in 1553. Santiago lies in the interior of northern Argentina and for the next two and a half centuries this region (which local writers call "Mediterranean") contained the bulk of the population, wealth, and culture of civilized Argentina. Buenos Aires, though founded in 1580,* still had a population of only 2200 a century and a half later, and did not become the country's metropolis until the nineteenth century. During this long Mediterranean period, civilized Argentina was a precarious corridor stretching from the Plata estuary to the Andes, with hostile Indians on both sides. The population of the corridor was made up mainly of tame Indians, mestizos, and Negro slaves, ruled over by a white minority. The economy was primitively pastoral and agricultural, and insofar as it was not self-sufficient, its orientation was towards Chile, Peru, and Paraguay, from which Argentina's first settlers came. It remained one of Spain's least prized and most undeveloped possessions in America until the last half century of the colonial period.†

* The first settlement at Buenos Aires was made in 1535, but soon abandoned.

† Recently some Argentine historians (notably Ricardo Levene, *Las Indias no eran colonias*, Buenos Aires, 1950) have supported the thesis

The present chapter will show briefly how Mediterranean Argentina took shape; how it was transformed into maritime Argentina, which eliminated the Indians, became one of the two whitest nations in Latin America, and led all Latin America in overseas trade, commercialized agriculture, and per capita wealth; and how, nevertheless, this modern Argentina developed pathological symptoms which, in retrospect, help to explain the rise of Perón's socially revolutionary and xenophobe regime.

1. THE FOUNDING OF ARGENTINA

The Spaniards were late in settling Argentina, and they never settled any but the northern third of it. They had established themselves in the West Indies between 1492 and 1510, in Panama in the next decade, in Mexico and on the northern fringe of South America in the 1520's, and in the Andean region of Colombia, Ecuador, and Peru in the 1530's. Even landlocked Paraguay and Chile, the remotest country from Spain in all South America, were settled before Argentina, and were indeed, with Peru, the sources from which all the early settlements in Argentina were made. From Chile came the founders not only of Santiago del Estero (1553), but also of San Juan and Mendoza (both 1562) and San Luis (1596); from Paraguay, those of Corrientes and Paraná (both 1558), Santa Fe (1573), and Buenos Aires (1580); and from Peru, those of Salta (1562), Tucumán (1565), Córdoba (1573), and La Rioja (1591). Nearly a century had passed since the discovery of America before the Spaniards were firmly seated in northern Argentina; the occupation was carried out not from Spain but by the overflow from older colonies in the neighborhood; and to the end of the colonial period both Spaniards and colonists left untouched the whole of the vast region lying south of Buenos Aires, which includes most of the fertile pampas.

This tardiness and neglect cannot be explained by ignorance. Argentina was discovered by the Spaniards twenty years before

that the Spanish possessions in America were not colonies but dominions of the crown. Without taking sides on this question, we shall nevertheless use "colony" and "colonial" here, since there is no satisfactory alternative in English.

Peru, yet its occupation began twenty years later. In 1513 Juan Díaz de Solís explored the Plata estuary, where the Indians killed and probably ate him.* In 1519 Magellan's great voyage, on which he lost his life, carried him down the coast of Argentina to and through the strait which bears his name. By 1535 Argentina was so well known that a large expedition, commanded by a member of the distinguished Mendoza family, was sent out from Spain to settle it, and tried to do so at Buenos Aires, but failed. Mendoza, broken in spirit and health, returned to Spain to die.

The gloomy record of these early ventures may help to explain the Spaniards' lack of enthusiasm for Argentina, but most of the explanation is to be found in the motive forces of the conquest and the character of the country and its Indians. Without subscribing to the "black legend" of Spanish greed, cruelty, and other assorted vices, we may nevertheless record the fact that the *conquistadores* were mainly interested in finding gold, silver, and Indians to convert or exploit. These requirements were met in the greatest degree by Mexico and Peru, with their wealth of precious metals and their highly developed Maya-Aztec and Inca civilizations; and Mexico and Peru were from first to last the main centers of the Spanish empire in America. Argentina, on the other hand, was almost as deficient in these respects as the United States, and after the early Spanish explorers had sampled both countries and found them wanting, subsequent generations largely neglected both.

Argentina was somewhat the more attractive of the two. While most of its sparse Indian population consisted of "hunting and gathering" tribes too intractable and in too low a stage of cultural development to be satisfactory either as laborers or as converts to Christianity, there were in the north some communities of Guaraní- and Quechua-speaking Indians who were more civilized, more sedentary, and more adaptable to Spanish needs. Here almost all the early Spanish settlements were established. This region also had the double advantage of serving as

* Amerigo Vespucci discovered the Río de la Plata in 1502, but he was then in the service of Portugal.

a bulwark against the Portuguese in Brazil on the east, and as a source of foodstuffs and mules for the mining communities of Upper Peru (Bolivia) in the barren Andes to the west. Buenos Aires was perched on the southeastern tip of a Mediterranean colony, whose orientation was towards the west until it was gradually reversed by the commercial and political revolutions of the eighteenth and nineteenth centuries.

South of Buenos Aires there was nothing in the resources, climate, or native population to lure the conquistadores and their descendants, and much to repel them. In the far south the Indians were among the most primitive to be found anywhere in America. Nearer at hand, the Araucanians, a branch of the group made famous by its fierce and tenacious resistance to the Spaniards in Chile, became expert horsemen and harried the southern frontier of white settlement with increasing intensity well on into the nineteenth century. Their constant forays, which sometimes came close to the southern cities of Buenos Aires and Córdoba and frequently cut communications between them, were one of the reasons why most of the rich pampas were left uncultivated throughout the whole Spanish colonial period and the first half century after the establishment of Argentine independence. But there was also an economic reason: like the world's other great grasslands, the pampas had to wait until the nineteenth century before their exploitation was rendered feasible and profitable by technological improvements and the markets created by the rapid growth of industrial and urban centers.

Except for the native corn, all the chief farm products of the colonial period were introduced from Europe, either directly or by way of the neighboring Spanish colonies and Brazil. Most of them were introduced at an early stage: horses in 1535, hogs in 1542, sheep in 1550, cattle in 1555, wheat possibly as early as 1535 and certainly no later than 1556, and sugar cane in 1542. In addition, by 1600 there were flourishing vineyards in Córdoba and Mendoza, and cotton production was well established in several northern centers, including Tucumán, which was exporting to the big mining city of Potosí large quantities of cotton textiles handmade by Indian artisans. The mining area of upper Peru provided almost the only outlet for other Argentine products as well. The demand for mules and cattle was particularly heavy, and this helped to fix upon Argentina from the start the predominantly pastoral character that it retained until the twentieth century. Stock-raising flourished in all parts of the country — a fact which is symptomatic of the colonial economy of Argentina, for regional specialization had only a rudimentary development and the colony was a mere aggregation of largely self-sufficient regions united mainly by the political ties of their common subjection to the king of Spain and his viceroy in Lima.

In the eighteenth century a number of factors combined to bring about extensive economic and social changes in Argentina, greatly to the benefit of Buenos Aires. The decline of the mining area in Upper Peru reduced its demand for Argentine products. The commercial revolution in Europe increased the threats to the Spanish empire in America, both in the form of smuggling and of armed aggression; and the close ties which from the beginning of the century united Portugal and Britain, both hereditary enemies of Spain, made the River Plate area, bordering on Portuguese Brazil, one of the chief danger-zones. Finally, the new Bourbon dynasty in Spain, best represented by that typical "benevolent despot," Charles III (1759–1788), instituted a number of reforms which, while conceived primarily in the interest of the crown, stimulated the economic development of various parts of Spanish America, including Buenos Aires and the rest of the Argentine litoral. In 1777 the Viceroyalty of the Río de la Plata (embracing not only modern Argentina, but Uruguay, Paraguay, and southern Bolivia as well) was carved out of the Viceroyalty of Peru. Buenos Aires was made the capital of the new viceroyalty and thrown open to trade with Spain, and by way of Spain, with Britain, France, and the rest of Europe.

Vigorous use was made of the new viceregal authority to foment the growth of the River Plate area and particularly its capital city. Buenos Aires supplanted Lima as the port through which Upper Peru exported its gold and silver and received its returns in European goods. Traffic between Buenos Aires and the interior was protected against Indian attacks by the establishment of armed patrols and a string of blockhouses; the frontier thus fixed by one of the first and best of the viceroys, Juan José de Vertiz (1778–1783), remained unaltered until the national period. Vertiz also sought to promote both stock-raising and agriculture by establishing them in separate zones, and to meet the labor shortage both by stimulating the importation of Negro slaves and by requiring urban workers (such as those in the brick and tile factories of Buenos Aires) to labor in the fields at harvest time. Encouragement was given to the growing export trade in salt meat and hides, as also to the exportation of wheat. In the latter case, however, careless harvesting and handling proved a serious handicap and in any case Argentina remained on balance an importer of wheat for a century to come. Either Vertiz or his successors also fomented the production of indigo, established regular mail services to other places in the viceroyalty and to Chile and Peru, created a *consulado* (a kind of chamber of commerce) and a *proto-medicato* (medical examining board) in Buenos Aires, and brought about a great improvement in the policing and street lighting and cleaning of this now rapidly growing city.

Although two-thirds of the population of Argentina still lived in the interior at the end of the eighteenth century, the shift to Buenos Aires had already begun by that time. The total population had increased only twofold in the past hundred years, from about 300,000 in 1700 to 600,000 in 1800, whereas in only half a century from 1726 to 1778 Buenos Aires had grown fifteenfold from 2200 to 33,500, and by the end of the century its population was estimated at about 45,000.

2. INDEPENDENCE AND COLONIAL SURVIVALS

By this time Buenos Aires had taken on the character and proportions that it was to retain during the independence movement, which began in 1810. A visitor from the United States, H. M. Brackenridge, who saw the city a few years later through good republican eyes, described it as follows:

[Buenos Aires] stretches along a high bank about two miles; its domes and steeples, and heavy masses of building, give it an im-

posing, but somewhat gloomy aspect. Immense piles of dingy brown
coloured brick, with little variety, heavy and dull, showed that it
did not take its rise under the patronage of liberty. Compared to
Philadelphia or New York, it is a vast mass of bricks piled up without taste, elegance, or variety.

He was better pleased with the people of Buenos Aires than
with its architecture:

> I saw nothing but the plainness and simplicity of republicanism; in
> the streets, there were none but plain citizens, and citizen soldiers
> . . . In fact, I could almost have fancied myself in one of our own
> towns, judging by the dress and appearance of the people whom I
> met . . . The mixture of negroes and mulattoes is by no means
> remarkable, not as great, perhaps, as in Baltimore . . . But . . .
> other figures . . . give a different cast to the whole from anything
> I have seen . . . Great numbers of *gauchos,* and other country
> people, are seen in the streets, and always on horseback; and as
> there prevails a universal passion for riding, the number of horses
> is very great.

Except for his too great readiness to identify plainness with
republicanism, Brackenridge accurately sketched some of the
main features of this imposing metropolis of a nation on horse-
back whose horseman par excellence, the gaucho, was now in his
heyday. Brackenridge also showed prescience in his prediction,
made in another passage, that "the pampas," then considered
"unpromising," would be "found deserving of a better character"
when they came to be better known. Another half century passed,
however, before his prophecy was fulfilled.

The political history of these fifty years was filled with great
events, from the completion of the wars of independence,
through the long dictatorship of Juan Manuel de Rosas, to the
formation of a new union, all of which will be discussed in their
place. Economically and socially, however, the Argentina of the
1850's had changed remarkably little since late colonial times.
The winning of independence had not produced either a social
revolution or a mass migration of loyalists comparable even to
that from the United States at the time of the American Revolution. Social and economic reforms attempted by early republican
leaders were wiped out by the reactionary Rosas, and even under

his tyranny there was still no mass migration — the famous
exiles of that period, mostly intellectuals, were only a handful
of the total population. Nor was there any considerable immigration, either before or under Rosas.

The drift towards Buenos Aires continued, but its progress was
slow, although it was favored by the war of independence and
the ensuing civil strife, from which the interior suffered more
than Buenos Aires. The nation was now free to trade with all the
world, and did trade with a good part of it, above all with the
world's greatest trading nation, Britain, whose unsuccessful
effort of 1806–07 to wrest the River Plate from Spain by force
of arms had proved no bar to her gaining an economic preponderance in Argentina once the independence of that country
had been established. Yet the volume of Argentine foreign
commerce increased no more rapidly than in the late colonial
period, and its character changed hardly at all. Hides were still
the principal export item, and still, as in the eighteenth century,
outsiders noted wonderingly how the Argentines slaughtered
droves of cattle for their hides and horns alone and threw the
carcasses away. And there was still the same reason for this
apparent wastefulness: the cattle were wild, the meat poor, and
it could be exported only on a small scale in the form of salted or
jerked meat which Brazilian and Cuban planters fed to their
slaves.

Landownership was still concentrated in a few hands, as in
colonial times, and as new lands were opened up the old Spanish
system of large land grants was still followed — an effort to
democratize the system had been made by the government of
Bernardino Rivadavia in the 1820's, but had failed almost completely. Finally, as we have already pointed out, the Argentine
racial pattern of the late colonial period — preponderantly mestizo, with substantial minorities of Negroes and Indians as well
as whites — persisted through the 1860's.

3. THE EMERGENCE OF MODERN ARGENTINA

Modern Argentina began to take shape only after the overthrow of Rosas' tyranny in 1852. Slow at first, the pace of

economic and social change soon accelerated so rapidly that by the end of the century Argentina had been revolutionized in both respects.

The new economy was one of scientific stock-raising and commercialized agriculture, aimed mainly at the production of meat and cereals for Britain and Continental Europe. It was integrated by a railway network comparable to that in our own Middle West, financed largely by British capital, and centered in Chicago's Argentine counterpart, the booming megalopolis of Buenos Aires.

The emergence of this new economy was due to a remarkable coincidence of favorable developments both abroad and at home. As the capitalist-industrial system matured in Europe, its rapidly growing urban population created a demand for the kind of foodstuffs that a modernized Argentina could produce, and the accumulation of surplus European (mainly British) capital provided the means for modernizing it with the aid of technological improvements recently made in Europe and the United States. At just the right time, Argentina's ejection of Rosas threw the country wide open to this European impact. During the next sixty years Argentina was governed by a class which was eager to develop its resources with the aid of foreign capital, business enterprise, technology, and immigrants, and whose watchword in economic policy was *laissez faire*.

The resultant release of energy was discharged first and foremost upon the rich pampas region. Here the ancient Indian barrier was swept aside in a series of campaigns culminating in 1879. The veterans were rewarded with large land grants, and other land grants were made to railway builders. In one way or another, most of the rich pampas lands were soon concentrated in the hands of some three hundred owners, and cheap labor was provided by the stream of immigrants, which, starting as a trickle in 1856, became a torrent in the 1880's. Thanks to this combination of large landholdings and cheap labor with the fertility of the pampas, Argentina had fully developed by the end of the century that system of large-scale, low-cost farm production that was the secret of her resounding success as a competitor in the world market.

Yet even this was by no means all. The pampas lacked surface water; the deficiency was made good by artesian wells and steel windmills (introduced about 1890). The almost riverless pampas lacked natural highways; transportation was provided by the construction of the most complete network of railways in any part of America south of the United States. The total railway mileage of Argentina increased from 1434 in 1880 to 9254 in 1890, 20,805 in 1913, and 27,000 in 1930, by which time Argentina had not only much the largest railway system in Latin America, but also the seventh largest in the world; and most of it served the pampas. The native livestock of Argentina found no favor in foreign markets; it was replaced by high-grade cattle and sheep imported from England. The diet of native grasses did not produce meat suited to foreign palates; alfalfa was introduced and became one of the largest of all Argentine crops. In order to maintain the new breeds and keep the cattle out of the corn and wheat fields, it was necessary to fence them in, but the treeless, stoneless pampas provided no fencing material. To meet this need, the newfangled barbed wire, borrowed from the United States, was used on a large scale after 1876. The equally novel device of refrigeration was introduced in 1877 to preserve the meat on its long journey to the European market (the French ship that carried it was appropriately named the *Frigorifique*), and the first freezing plant (*frigorífico*) was built in 1882.

This economic revolution was first pastoral, then agricultural. Reapers and threshers came into general use in the 1870's, but even in 1876 the whole country produced only 7000 bushels of wheat. By 1890 the figure had shot up to 31 million, and in 1912 it reached 187 million. As a result, while, in 1880, pastoral products accounted for 94 per cent of all Argentine exports and agricultural products for less than 2 per cent, by 1908 the roles had been reversed, only 30 per cent of the exports being pastoral and 65 per cent agricultural.

In the meanwhile, meat-packing plants and grain elevators had sprung up along the River Plate, mainly at or near Buenos Aires and Rosario. Multiplying fleets of British, German, French, and Italian ships took away cargoes of meat and wheat, largely to Britain, and brought back cargoes of immigrants, largely from Italy and Spain.

By 1940 the pampas contained 62 per cent of the nation's total population of just under 14,000,000 and produced 82 per cent of the nation's wealth. But the economic revolution had spread to every part of the country and its general effect was to stimulate regional specialization and at the same time to tie the regions more closely to Buenos Aires. The north and west, formerly oriented towards Chile and Peru, now faced their own national capital. The rapidly growing industries of wine in the Mendoza district and sugar around Tucumán supplied the domestic market, which for them was largely the Buenos Aires market. The tannic acid extracted from the Chaco's incredibly hard wood, *quebracho* ("break-ax" in Spanish), the linseed oil made from the flax of Entre Ríos and Corrientes, and the mutton and wool obtained from the herds of sheep that now range the once waste spaces of Patagonia — all these are products of peripheral areas that have achieved commercial importance since the close of the nineteenth century, and most of them find their markets in or through Buenos Aires.

4. INDUSTRIALIZATION AND URBANIZATION

In the face of many serious handicaps, beginning with the lack of coal and iron deposits, the industrial economy of Argentina had developed by 1943 to such a point that it exceeded the pastoral-agricultural sector in the number of workers employed and was not far behind it in the value of its products. The factories were heavily concentrated in the city and province of Buenos Aires. Only light industries had developed, such as food processing, the manufacture of textiles, shoes, matches, and books, and repair shops for the nation's extensive railway system. An infant iron industry, however, had just been established, and hopeful Argentine economists were arguing that this could be developed on a large scale by the use of imported scrap iron, as had already happened in Japan, even if the exploitation of the very recently discovered iron deposits in remote Jujuy should not prove feasible. By 1943 Argentine industry had already become a major factor both in the national economy and in the nation's thinking.

Industry first achieved appreciable importance in Argentina in the 1890's and the first measure of its status was provided by the census of 1895. Its development in the next 48 years falls into three clearly defined periods. From 1895 to 1918 it enjoyed a steady and fairly rapid growth, which was greatly accelerated during the last four years, when World War I favored Argentine manufacturers by reducing the volume of imports from Europe. The next period, however, from 1918 to 1930, was one of general stagnation and, in some respects, decline. Argentina's industrialists had not taken full advantage of the war period to consolidate their gains on the basis of long-range planning. Her wealthy landowning class clung to their traditional preference for investing their money in land rather than in industry, and were encouraged to do so by the generally satisfactory prices obtained for their farm products on the world market in the 1920's. After the war the great industrial nations redoubled their efforts to conquer markets in the less highly developed countries, of which Argentina was one of the most attractive to them; and the Argentine government failed to give home industry adequate protection against this cutthroat competition.

In the third period, from 1930 to 1943, Argentine industry resumed its growth, and flourished mightily, thanks mainly to the world-wide economic depression that began in 1929. The explanation of this seeming paradox is quite simple; Argentine economists have explained it fully.* The sharp reduction of Argentina's purchasing power abroad (the combined result of the devaluation of the *peso* and a 50 to 60 per cent decline in Argentine exports) forced Argentines to buy at home or not at all. World prices of manufactured goods remained at a much higher level than prices of farm products throughout the decade of the 1930's, with the result that Argentine investors were at

* See particularly Adolfo Dorfman, *Evolución industrial argentina* (Buenos Aires, 1942), pp. 73–102.

last persuaded to put their money into industry rather than land. Additional capital came from abroad in the form of the establishment of Argentine branches of North American and European firms, which thus not only found employment for capital, machines, executives, and technicians rendered idle by the depression at home, but also escaped from many of the difficulties created by the exchange controls, quotas, and rising tariff walls of an increasingly nationalistic world. Moreover, an abundant urban labor supply existed in Argentina in the 1930's, for the continuing agricultural-pastoral depression in that country reduced both the scale of rural operations and the opportunity of farm laborers and tenants to rise in the social scale; and the result was an acceleration of the trend of population from the countryside to the cities. Last but by no means least, from 1931 on, the Argentine government gave substantial protection to domestic industry, mainly by increasing import duties and establishing quotas.

The rapid growth of industry in Argentina and the importance of the position it had gained by 1940 in the nation's economy are shown by the accompanying figures.

DISTRIBUTION OF ARGENTINE WORKING POPULATION, 1914–1940 *

	1914	1933	1940	% of Increase 1914 to 1940
Industries	1,246,000	2,156,000	2,770,000	122.3
Agriculture and live-stock	880,000	1,137,000	1,050,000	19.3
Commerce	349,000	603,000	750,000	114.9
Transport	111,000	151,000	160,000	44.1
Other professions	647,000	971,000	1,000,000	54.6
Total occupied	3,223,000	5,018,000	5,730,000	77.8

Moreover, Argentina's fuel position had been strengthened since 1913 as a result of the fact that, like most other countries, its relative consumption of coal (which it did not produce) had

* Adapted by Donald B. Easum from Alejandro E. Bunge, *Una nueva Argentina* (Buenos Aires: Kraft, 1940), p. 165.

declined greatly, and its consumption of petroleum (which it did produce, to the extent of about half its needs) had risen correspondingly.

Though industrialization and the consequent rise of domestic commerce diminished somewhat the nation's dependence upon foreign trade, Argentina still retained the leadership in the foreign commerce of Latin America which she had won in the late nineteenth century. In 1913, she accounted for one-third of the exports and imports of all Latin America. In 1938, the last full year before the trade of the whole area was upset by the outbreak of World War II, her share had been reduced to one-forth of the combined total (28 per cent of the imports, 22 per cent of the exports), but she still led her nearest rival, Brazil, by a comfortable margin.

The industrialization of Argentina was paralleled by the rapid growth of its cities. Buenos Aires provided the most conspicuous, but by no means the only, example. Although there was an extraordinarily rapid increase in the area of land under cultivation in Argentina — from five million acres in 1880 to 30 million in 1905 and 64 million in 1923 — the metropolis grew even more rapidly than the rest of the nation. From 1852 to 1938, the total population of Argentina increased from 1,200,000 to 13,130,000, or in a ratio of 11 to 1, whereas in the same period the population of the city of Buenos Aires (excluding its suburbs) increased from 90,000 to 2,500,000, or in a ratio of over 25 to 1. The population of the whole metropolitan area now numbered 3,114,000, which was nearly one-fourth of the total population of Argentina.

In all America and Europe this concentration was exceeded in only one country, Uruguay, where Montevideo contained one-third of the nation's population, and it was equaled in only two, Chile and Great Britain. By comparison, New York City proper contained only 6 per cent of the population of the United States, and even Greater New York, including adjacent parts of New Jersey and Connecticut, only 10 per cent.

The same urban pattern was reproduced on a smaller scale in most parts of Argentina, particularly in its most populous area, the pampas, where four-fifths of the people lived in towns and

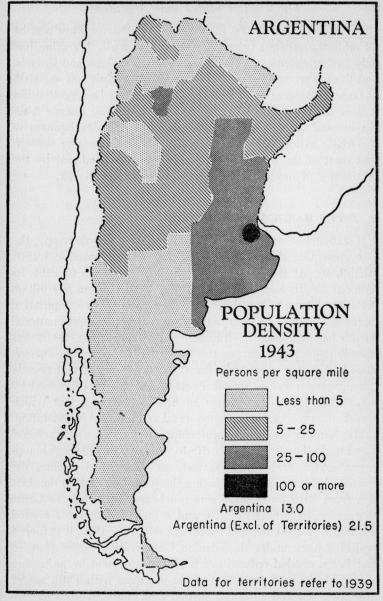

ARGENTINA

POPULATION
DENSITY
1943

Persons per square mile

Less than 5

5 – 25

25 – 100

100 or more

Argentina 13.0
Argentina (Excl. of Territories) 21.5

Data for territories refer to 1939

Adapted from *Argentina, Summary of Biostatistics*, prepared by the Bureau of the Census in coöperation with the Coördinator of Inter-American Affairs.

cities of more than 10,000 inhabitants. Yet Buenos Aires was by all odds the greatest urban concentration of all. Argentina had only two other cities of considerable size, Córdoba and Rosario, and these were respectively only about one-eighth and one-sixth as large as Buenos Aires. This fact should never be forgotten, for it goes far to explain why, in modern Argentina, Buenos Aires has exerted so powerful an influence upon the development of the whole nation. And it was amidst this city's teeming millions that most of the tensions and maladjustments produced by the emergence of modern Argentina were most keenly felt.

5. PATHOLOGICAL SYMPTOMS

If statistics of national wealth could make a people happy, the new Argentina should have been a terrestrial paradise for its inhabitants. At the height of the boom, from 1886 to 1914, its national wealth increased in a ratio of 15 to 1 (from one billion dollars to fifteen billion dollars), as compared with a population increase of only 3 to 1, so that on paper the per capita national wealth had increased fivefold in a single generation. Yet it was already apparent as early as the 1890's that the Argentine success story had a very seamy side, for at the beginning of that decade a temporary recession set off a revolt, and this was followed by two others in the brief span of fifteen years — a fact which reveals the existence of a serious social and political fermentation.

The ferment continued uninterruptedly for half a century and was a major factor in Perón's rise to power in the 1940's. Though begun under, and aimed against, an oligarchical regime, the ferment did not cease even during the period of Radical domination from 1916 to 1930. It was quickened again by the Great Depression beginning in 1929, and contributed to the army-led revolution of 1930, the first successful one since 1852. It gathered explosive force under the ensuing Conservative Restoration, so that Perón needed only to touch off the explosion by promising to replace the new Argentina of the oligarchs with a still newer Argentina devoted to social justice and national economic independence.

Even today there are still wide differences of opinion among informed observers as to what went wrong with the new Argentina of the oligarchs, and why. Tentatively, however, we may suggest that the four economic and social factors discussed below were the most important; political factors will be discussed in a later chapter.

(1) There was a growing disparity between the wealthy few and the needy masses, which was accentuated by the widening gap between employer and employee and between landlord and farm laborer or tenant. It is true that the standard of living was higher in Argentina than in the neighboring countries, but the average Argentine seldom if ever saw his poorer foreign counterpart, whereas he was a daily witness of the increasingly opulent way of life in the élite in his own country. This élite was composed mainly of two groups — the old landowning aristocracy and the new commercial, financial, industrial plutocracy — and members of both groups were the chief beneficiaries under modern Argentina's expanding economy. Its expansion therefore widened the existing gap between the élite and the masses, both in the city and the country. In both cases this widening of the social gap was primarily a function of that growth of the scale of enterprise which was the hallmark of modern Argentina. In 1937, one-fifth of all the land in Argentina was owned by two thousand landlords, individual and corporate, and the industrial expansion of the 1930's was marked by a sharp increase in the relative strength of large-scale enterprise.

(2) No effective defense of the interests of the masses was built up, either through labor unions or political parties or otherwise. Efforts were made in that direction through various parties, especially the Socialist and Radical, during the generation beginning with the ferment of the 1890's. They had their best chance of success in the period 1916–1930, when the Radical party, led by Hipólito Irigoyen, was in power; but for reasons that will be explained in a later chapter, little use was made of the opportunity.

Although the organized labor movement in Argentina dates from the 1880's, it developed slowly and rather obscurely until

1916, for legislation and law enforcement, then in the hands of the conservatives, were unfriendly. By a natural reaction, extremism flourished, as evidenced by the formation in 1901 of the anarchist federation known as F.O.R.A. (*Federación Regional Obrera Argentina,* or Argentine Regional Labor Federation).

From 1916 to 1930, the more propitious climate created by the national Radical administration both stimulated the labor movement and made it more moderate. The climax came in 1930 with the formation of a new federation, the C.G.T. (*Confederación General del Trabajo,* or General Confederation of Labor), which has always been much the largest group in Argentina from that day to this. Yet down to the eve of Perón's rise, the great majority of Argentine workers remained unorganized. In 1939 the C.G.T. had only 263,000 members, and all the other unions combined had 119,000, so that there were only 382,000 organized workers in a total population of about 13,000,000. By comparison, in Mexico at the same time there were four times as many labor union members (1,511,000) in a total population only half again as large (19,478,000). For the most part, the Argentine unions represented the "aristocracy" of labor and left the masses untouched even in the urban centers.

This was not so much because an unfriendly conservative government was in power again after 1930 as because labor's own leadership became bureaucratized and complacent.* As a result, there was a decline of vitality in the unions after 1936, as reflected both in the number of union meetings and in the attendance. Extremism flourished again, particularly in the form of a small but vigorous communist movement led by Victorio Codovilla. In 1942 this state of affairs, aggravated by wartime pressures, led to a split of the C.G.T. into two wings, one "orthodox" and moderate, the other made up of communists and left-wing socialists. The schism occurred just in time to facilitate the coup of June 1943 and the rise of Perón.

Though the Conservative restoration of the 1930's did not suppress the labor movement, it did nothing important to alleviate the rising tide of popular discontent. The contrast with the

* Robert J. Alexander, *The Perón Era* (New York, 1951), pp. 9–10.

contemporaneous New Deal Administration in the United States is striking, and the difference goes far to explain the disaster that befell the Conservatives in the 1940's. To most Argentines, however, an even more vivid and disturbing contrast was offered by the progress that social and labor legislation was making at this time in three of their country's immediate neighbors, Uruguay, Brazil, and Chile.

(3) The extremely heavy tide of European immigration that poured into Argentina between 1856 and 1930 brought about a great change in the racial composition of the population and built up a large minority element which did not possess the same political and social background as the native Argentine majority. In this period the proportion of Argentines with Indian and Negro blood, which had been high at the beginning, was reduced almost to the vanishing point; but simultaneously the proportion of European-born Argentines increased threefold, from 7 per cent of the total population in 1852 (173,000, in a total of 2,500,000) to 20 per cent in 1935 (2,500,000, in a total of 12,280,000).

In proportion to population, Argentina has received more permanent immigrants than any other country in the world. In comparison with the United States, whose net immigration (26,180,000) from 1820 to 1930 was three times as large as its total population in 1820, Argentina's net immigration (4,118,600) from 1857 to 1930 was four times as large as its population in 1857. The proportion of foreign-born to total population (30 per cent) revealed by the Argentine census of 1914 was twice as high as it has ever been in the widely heralded "melting-pot" of the United States. Immigration was severely restricted after 1930, but that came too late to change the situation greatly by 1943.

Of the many far-reaching results of this mass immigration, three stand out for our present purpose: (1) It made possible that economic revolution just described, by greatly augmenting the labor force. (2) It gave a great stimulus to the development of both the middle class and the proletariat. (3) It added greatly to the social and cultural diversity of Argentina. Eighty per cent of the immigrants between 1857 and 1930 were Italians and Spaniards. The Italians were an almost entirely new element and the Spaniards were aliens in everything but language. Neither group acquiesced in the rule of the Argentine oligarchy, as the creole masses had learned to do.

One pathological detail of this development should be emphasized. In Argentina the middle class is large (it was said by an expert to include 45 per cent of the population in 1945), but it does not provide that stabilizing influence which most people in the United States seem to expect this class to provide automatically wherever it grows up. The reason seems to be that the Argentine middle class is itself unstable. It lacks coherence and self-confidence. One Argentine writer, José Luis Romero, believes that from the start it has suffered from the imperfect fusion of its two chief component elements, the energetic immigrant and the easy-going creole. Another, Sergio Bagú, points out that while this class has gained greatly in numbers through the industrialization of Argentina since 1930, its morale has simultaneously been weakened by a growing sense of insecurity arising out of the fact that its members typically cling to a rugged individualism which leaves them defenseless in a society increasingly characterized by large-scale enterprise, group action, and mass movements. Still another, Gino Germani, differentiates the Argentine middle class sharply from the European middle classes that have sought protection in fascism against the revolt of the masses; but he, too, points out the incoherence of the Argentine middle class, the growth of rifts within it since 1930, and the increasing concern of the upper middle class over the "pretensions" of labor.

(4) Foreign economic penetration gave an indispensable stimulus to the development of modern Argentina, but it also placed the control of key sectors of the nation's economy in foreign hands. Down to World War II this control was concentrated to a high degree in the hands of a single foreign country, Great Britain, which held about 60 per cent of all foreign investments in Argentina and was that country's best customer. As a result, Argentina came to be called, half in jest, Britain's fifth dominion. British investments in that country began to be made on a considerable scale in the 1870's and by 1913 amounted to $1500

million. They reached their all-time peak of $2250 million in 1936, at which time they made up 54 per cent of Britain's total investments in Latin America. More than 60 per cent of the British capital in Argentina was in railways, and nearly 70 per cent of the Argentine railways were British-owned.

The United States, together with other countries — notably Germany and France — made much smaller but still substantial investments in Argentina. Whether as investors or not, United States firms began to enter the country at the turn of the century. The first large investment was made in 1907, when Swift and Company purchased one of the principal *frigoríficos;* but other North American enterprises had already begun to do business in Argentina by this time — General Electric in 1899, the United Shoe Machinery Company in 1903, and the Singer Sewing Machine Company in 1905. After World War I the United States stood second only to Britain in Argentine investments and trade. As late as 1938, its investments amounted to only $320 million; but, like the British, they were concentrated in key sectors of the Argentine economy, especially in meat-packing plants and public utilities. As a market for Argentine exports, the United States still lagged far behind Britain and Continental Europe; but since 1914 it had gained a firm hold on second place in Argentine imports and at times even forged into first place, ahead of great Britain. Whichever of the two was in the lead, these two countries supplied most of the imports essential to the Argentine economy, such as fuel, vehicles, and machinery, as well as assorted manufactures.

Consequently, while Argentina made considerable progress in the formation of domestic capital and the development of internal commerce during the inter-war years from 1919 to 1939, at the end of that period her national economy was still dependent to a high degree upon foreign capital, business enterprise, and trade. This state of affairs caused increasing dissatisfaction among her people in the atmosphere of superheated nationalism generated after 1929 by the Great Depression. Naturally, the two main targets of this dissatisfaction were Great Britain and the United States.

Britain was Argentina's best customer, and yet the relationship became a galling one to many Argentines as it took on the aspect of dependency in the depression years. A case in point was the famous Roca-Runciman Agreement of 1933. Argentina, which was under a conservative government at that time, entered into the agreement mainly to protect its British beef market against the threat of the imperial preference system adopted at the Ottawa Conference of 1932. The desired protection was obtained, but on terms which did not even benefit the whole oligarchy, much less the nation at large, but only the beef barons, and which threatened to cripple the growing industrial sector by encouraging imports from Britain. Though the threat did not materialize, the whole arrangement was anathema to Argentine anti-imperialists, who were further incensed by the monopoly of public transportation in Buenos Aires obtained by British interests in 1935.

In the case of the United States, too, economic considerations nourished a growing antipathy. Imports from the northern republic consisted in large part of competitive manufactures and the balance of trade was consistently "unfavorable" to Argentina. It was never more unfavorable in peacetime than in the years 1925–1929, when Argentina bought more than two and one half times as much from the United States as she sold to it. This was bad enough in Argentine eyes when the multilateral system of international trade was in vogue; when that system was broken down by the Great Depression, it became intolerable, all the more so because Argentine beef was excluded from the United States after 1927 on the ground of the existence of the hoof-and-mouth disease in Argentina.

The nature of Argentina's relations with Britain and the United States helps to explain why, although by 1943 Argentine investors and businessmen were already in control of many domestic enterprises, the Argentine people were more than ever impatient to reach the goals of industrialization and economic independence. The answer probably lies in the common human propensity to put forth the most strenuous effort when the goal comes in sight. A useful analogy is suggested by political revolutions, which often occur, not when a people are most oppressed, but when they have already begun to break their chains; thus, the American Revolution of 1776 was, in Carl Becker's phrase, a rebellion of "the freest people on earth." It is, therefore, no occasion for surprise that Argentina, which was economically the farthest advanced of all the Latin American countries in 1943, put itself in the vanguard of the Latin American struggle for economic independence during the next decade.

Argentine opinion was deeply divided, however, on the questions of what "economic independence" meant and how it should be achieved. If economic independence meant upsetting the relationship with Britain which the beef barons had found so profitable, then the barons were against it. They made their position clear by supporting the Roca-Runciman agreement; so did the rising industrial group, by opposing it; and thus Argentine society was divided at the top.

On almost every other public question as well, opinion was deeply divided, though often in different ways. The best illustration is provided by the case of *laissez faire,* which had been the basic principle of the new Argentina. Now the new Argentina was taking on the aspect of an *ancien régime,* fresh winds of doctrine were astir in the country, and by the 1930's there was general agreement that laissez faire must give way to national controls. It had already done so on a small scale under the Radicals, and the scale was now greatly increased under the Conservatives; but the appearance of national unity that these facts give is deceptive, for there was deep disagreement as to the kinds of controls that were to be set up and the purposes for which they were to be used. The divisions cut now horizontally between classes, now vertically across class lines, depending upon the nature of the issues at stake. Among these issues, probably the most controversial were those relating to economic foreign policy and social justice at home.

The result was a confusion which was intensified to the point of chaos by a new series of economic and ideological impacts from abroad just before and during World War II. Crippled by dissension, the country's established power groups failed to take decisive action along any consistent line. The situation was made to order for the new power group headed by Perón, whose stand on the two major issues of economic independence and social justice won it wider and more enthusiastic support than any of the older groups had had for many years past.

3. Political Development

In many respects the political development of Argentina in the four centuries from its first settlement by the Spaniards to 1943 paralleled its economic and social development as described in the preceding chapter. There was the same initial preponderance of the interior and orientation towards the Pacific, followed by the same slow shift to Buenos Aires and an orientation towards the Atlantic; the same displacement of the influence of Spain by that of Britain, France, and other countries; and the same gradual fusion of many local diversities into national unity. Likewise, in modern Argentina the economic liberalism of laissez faire was matched by the political liberalism of the Constitution of 1853, until, in the second quarter of the twentieth century, both fell victims to a mounting reaction which culminated in the combined economic and political regimentation of the Perón regime.

1. THE COLONIAL CENTURIES

The colonial centuries left a deep imprint upon the Argentine people, but as a political entity Argentina was largely a creation of the secessionist movement which disrupted Spain's American empire in the early nineteenth century. The contrast with the rest of Spanish America in this respect is striking. Most of the other new states corresponded to long-established colonial units of the Spanish Empire; many of them (such as Chile, Peru, Guatemala, and Mexico) continued to call themselves by their colonial names; and while the exact extent of their boundaries was often a matter of dispute, almost all the disputed areas were either uninhabited or, at most, thinly settled by white men.

Argentina, on the other hand, had no close political counterpart in the colonial period. For more than two hundred years after its first settlement in 1553 it was an aggregation of local governments subject to the viceroy of Peru at Lima. When in 1777 the River Plate area was at last freed from this dependency by the erection of a viceroyalty with its capital at Buenos Aires, the new viceroyalty embraced present-day Uruguay, Paraguay, and southern Bolivia; and, on the other hand, it contained no administrative subdivision corresponding to Argentina. Finally, the very word "Argentina" was a neologism in the sense that, before independence, it had never been the official name of any part of the River Plate area; in the colonial period, its usage had been exclusively literary and it was applied generally to the whole area.

Colonial Argentina had no metropolis, but various cities successively achieved a certain preëminence, politically as well as economically and culturally. The first was Santiago del Estero, which was soon supplanted by Tucumán, a city favored by its proximity to the fountain of authority and wealth in Peru. The prestige of Tucumán is reflected in the fact that its name was applied to a region extending from Jujuy, Salta, and Chaco in the far north to Córdoba in the south. Córdoba in turn supplanted Tucumán as the movement of population to the southeast gave centrally located Córdoba the advantage of position, which was fortified by the establishment of the first *audiencia* (a kind of court of appeals) and the first university in Argentina.

Finally, in the last generation of the colonial period, preëminence passed to Buenos Aires as the capital of the new viceroyalty. This was a signal honor, since there were only three other viceroyalties in the whole vast dominion of Spain stretching from Florida and California to Cape Horn, and the honor carried with it many practical benefits to the capital city. Yet even at the end of the colonial period Córdoba was still a serious rival to Buenos Aires, and there were other cities which did not lag far behind these two, at least in the estimation of the people in the surrounding areas. Regionalism was so strong throughout the country, and so sharply focused on the chief city of each region, that at the beginning of the independence movement it seemed not unlikely that the component parts of Argentina would either not unite at all or else would become a nation of city states, as did nineteenth-century Colombia.

The task of making a nation out of these materials was a formidable one, and Spain's colonial regime was such as to provide the people with little training for political tasks of any kind. It probably never gave them less training than in the last colonial century, when the Spanish trend towards centralization and absolutism reached its peak. By this time the *cabildo* (a kind of town council), the only institution that gave the colonials practice in self-government, had lost the representative character and most of the powers that it had once had. Even as servants of the crown, whether in the secular government or in the Church (which, in Spanish America, was closely controlled by the crown), colonials were seldom employed in the higher posts. Authoritarianism, an all-powerful executive, a union of church and state, an administrative system shot through with fraud and favoritism — these were leading items in Spain's political bequest to Argentina. There was also another major item — the viceregal tradition, which stemmed from the colonial Viceroyalty of the Río de la Plata and had two aspects: the political unity of the whole area, and the preëminence of Buenos Aires in that area. Long after independence this tradition continued to play an important and often troublesome part in the relations of ambitious Buenos Aires with the rest of the country, and of Argentina with the neighboring countries that had formed a part of the viceroyalty.

2. INDEPENDENCE AND TYRANNY

There was an interval of half a century between the political and economic revolutions that produced modern Argentina. The political revolution — the winning of independence from Spain — came first. It was the result of a more or less concerted movement in many parts of Spanish America which came out into the open in 1810. An event that gave the movement a strong impulse in Argentina was the British invasion of the country in 1806 and 1807, and the repulse of the British by Argentine forces without the aid of Spain. The event was celebrated in a poem entitled "The Argentine Victory" (*El triunfo argentino*) which gave popular currency to the term "Argentine" and thus prepared the way for its adoption (a good many years later) as one of the names of the new republic.

In Argentina, as in the rest of continental Spanish America, however, the independence movement was the product of many factors, domestic and foreign, including the example of colonial revolt set by the United States. The immediate occasion for its launching was Napoleon's intervention in Spain in 1808, where he forced the abdication of the ruling house and set his own brother on the throne. The response in Spanish America was first to set up autonomous "caretaker" governments in the, principal colonial capitals, and later to make these fully independent. Such a caretaker government was set up at Buenos Aires on May 25, 1810, by the famous *cabildo abierto,* a sort of New England town meeting; and independence was declared on July 9, 1816, by an assembly held at Tucumán, representing most parts of the country.

While patricians quarreled with democrats, and most of the country's domestic problems remained unsolved, the government of Argentina hastened to the aid of the hard-pressed patriots in Chile. Strongly supported by the patrician leader Juan Martín de Pueyrredón, and carefully organized and brilliantly commanded by José de San Martín, native of Corrientes and veteran of the campaign in Spain against the forces of Napoleon, an Argentine army made its way over the high Andes from Mendoza to Chile in a march often compared to Hannibal's crossing of the Alps.

The Spanish royalists were soon driven from Chile and San Martín, supported by a Chilean naval force under a cashiered British admiral, Lord Cochrane, thereupon began the liberation of Peru. This task he never completed. Unable to obtain the indispensable coöperation of the liberator from the north, the Venezuelan Simón Bolívar, San Martín magnanimously withdrew in favor of Bolívar and retired to private life. This action was typical of his whole career. He was one of Spanish America's great liberators and one of its great men, a "knight of the sword" (*caballero de la espada*), in the words of his best biographer, Ricardo Rojas. Subsequent generations of Argentines have heaped merited praise upon him, though they have more than once forgotten his solemn injunction that the army should serve, not rule, the nation and should keep out of politics.

Turmoil characterized the domestic history of Argentina from the beginning of independence until, in 1880, an acceptable solution was at last found for the stubborn problem of the relationship of the city of Buenos Aires to the rest of the country.

Buenos Aires was the logical capital of the new state, but the ingrained particularism of the colonial period survived in such strength that during these seventy years the country had its full share of the anarchy, despotism, and civil war from which all the new states of Spanish America suffered in some degree. In Argentina, besides the Buenos Aires question, the subjects of controversy included almost everything from the extent of the country and the form of its government to its very name. The problem of its extent is best illustrated by the effort to hold the old viceroyalty together. The effort failed at an early date through the establishment of the independence of Paraguay (1814), Bolivia (1825), and Uruguay (1828), but was not abandoned on that account. The unity of Argentina itself hung in the balance for many years. Controversy raged over the form of government — first, whether it should be republican or monarchical, then, whether the republic should be centralized ("unitary") or decentralized ("federal"), democratic or oligarchical — and local *caudillos* (chieftains) waxed strong without bothering their heads about political theory.

In ways that cannot be discussed here, the controversy over the form of government gave meaning to the long conflict over the alternative names proposed for the country, such as Provincias Unidas del Río de la Plata, Confederación Argentina, and Nación Argentina. Suffice it to say that the name Argentina was first popularized in 1806 * and first made official in 1826, but then

* See above, p. 50.

dropped, and not definitively adopted until 1860, by a constitutional amendment. In an effort to keep everybody happy, however, that amendment adopted other names, too, and these are still enshrined in the Constitution as amended by Perón in 1949. Usage rather than law gave "Argentina" the final victory in this war of names.

The most famous product of the turmoil in Argentina was the dictatorship (1829–1852) of Juan Manuel de Rosas. Though Argentine to his finger tips, Rosas differed sharply from all the previous leaders of his country. Born in Buenos Aires in 1793, he took no part in the revolution of 1810 and had no sympathy for the patrician leadership which it ushered in for the next decade, though he himself came of a patrician family. The popular revolt of 1820 against a pro-monarchist government was no less distasteful to him, for his motto was "order and discipline." Finally, he incarnated the creole reaction against the unitarist, liberal, and cosmopolitan innovations promoted by Bernardino Rivadavia after 1820 in an effort to Europeanize Argentina.

At an early age Rosas left Buenos Aires, took up the gauchos' way of life, and soon excelled most of them in the handling of horses and cattle, the lariat, bola, and knife, and tough language. His courage and prowess as an Indian fighter won him the gauchos' support and started him on his rise to power as the caudillo of the province of Buenos Aires. The chaos following Rivadavia's fall in 1826 enabled him to extend his control, first over the city of Buenos Aires, and then over the whole country.

Once in power, Rosas enforced "order and discipline" ruthlessly with the aid of a kind of Ku Klux Klan or strong-arm gang called the Mazorca. He thereby won the support of the many Argentines who preferred order to liberty. Churchmen applauded his reversal of the earlier anticlerical trend. His resolute defense of Argentine rights and honor against French and British interventions between 1838 and 1850 excited admiration even among those who otherwise thought ill of his regime; one such was the liberator San Martín, now living in voluntary exile in France. For a time, Rosas was also greatly aided by his Amazonian wife, Encarnación, but she died early and her popularity with the masses never approached that of the late Eva Perón, to whom she has been compared.

To liberals and intellectuals, Rosas was anathema. First at home, then from the exile into which they were driven, such men as Domingo Sarmiento, Esteban Echeverría, Juan Bautista Alberdi, and Bartolomé Mitre waged an unflagging "literary war" against him. Its most famous product is Sarmiento's classic, *Facundo, or the Conflict between Civilization and Barbarism*, published in Chile in 1845, which pilloried the caudillo type represented by Rosas and the Facundo Quiroga of the title, and which equated the rural gauchos, who were the caudillo's main support, with barbarism, and the cities with civilization. Yet, no matter how devastating these literary attacks were, they availed little against Rosas. What finally overthrew him in 1852 was a combination of a revolt in his own army, led by General Justo José de Urquiza, and an invasion from Brazil and Uruguay provoked by Rosas' prolonged intervention in the latter country.

On balance, Rosas' regime was a thoroughly bad one, but it was hardly "sterile," as a noted Argentine historian has called it. For better or for worse, it arrested the disintegration of Argentina, preserved national unity, fortified the spirit of nationalism, helped the provinces to fit themselves to become "self-governing units of a future federal state," forced his opponents to clarify their own ideas about Argentina's political needs, and created an authentically Argentine tradition of authoritarian leadership which was to emerge as a vital force in the next century.

3. LIBERALISM, LAISSEZ FAIRE, AND OLIGARCHY

On General Urquiza's initiative, but without interference from him, a new Argentine constitution was drawn up by a convention at Santa Fe in 1853, which, as extensively amended in 1860 and 1949, is still in effect. Since Argentina had failed to solve her political problem in her own way, the framers of the constitution drew heavily from foreign sources, especially the Constitution of the United States. But there was no slavish imitation; Argentine precedent, too, was followed, and the whole was designed to conciliate so far as possible the country's various contending factions.

As a result, while Argentina's new constitution resembled that of the United States in most respects, there were important differences. There was the same federal system based upon a division of powers between the central government and the provinces; the same separation of powers into executive, legislative, and judicial; the same provision for a president, chosen by an Electoral College, who was also commander-in-chief, and for a bicameral Congress and a federal judiciary headed by a Supreme Court; and the article on the judiciary was virtually a verbatim translation of the North American original. On the other hand, the president was limited to one six-year term, after which he was not eligible for reëlection until another six years had passed; state support of the Roman Catholic Church was provided for (though freedom of conscience and public worship was also stipulated); and congress was given more extensive powers in regard to commerce and certain other matters.

Even when the provisions of the two constitutions were substantially the same, wide differences sometimes developed in practice. The most striking illustration is provided by the provisions relating to federal intervention in the states or provinces. In the United States, this power has never been used except during the period of Reconstruction following the Civil War. In Argentina, its frequent use became a normal feature of the nation's political life almost from the start; by 1943 there had been 142 such interventions. Their cumulative effect was to convert Argentina's nominally federal government into one of a centralized, national type — a process which was complete long before Perón came to power.

Despite the conciliatory spirit in which the constitution of 1853 was drawn up, its adoption was followed by another twenty-seven years of turmoil. The province of Buenos Aires at first refused to join the union, and finally did so (1860) only after it had been defeated in a civil war and mollified by extensive alterations in the constitution. Soon thereafter the conflict was renewed over the question whether the city of Buenos Aires should be the national capital, and on what terms. This, too, was settled only after another civil war. The settlement (1880) federalized the city, making it a kind of District of Columbia, with the important difference that the city was given representation in both the national Congress and the Electoral College. And all the while the insubordination of the still powerful provincial caudillos kept a large part of the country in an uproar, despite the best-intentioned efforts of such talented presidents as Bartolomé Mitre and Domingo Sarmiento.

Peace and stability came at last with the settlement of the Buenos Aires question and the opening of the rich pampas by the campaign of 1879 in which General Julio A. Roca, "the last of the conquistadores," inflicted a crushing and definitive defeat upon the Indians. The next generation was one of vertiginously rapid economic growth. Though it was also a generation of serious social and political discontent, which broke out in revolts in 1890, 1893, and 1905, none of these was successful or prolonged. From 1880 to 1930 Argentina was on the whole a model of political good behavior, at least as compared with most of the other Latin American countries in that half century and with her own record both before and after it. Indeed, believers in progress found much in the history of Argentina during this golden period to confirm them in their faith, for, starting from a low level, the country's political behavior improved steadily until by the 1920's its government was generally regarded as the most stable and democratic in Latin America.

During the first third of a century after 1880, the Argentine government was dominated by the new conservative oligarchy, less patrician than plutocratic, which battened on a system of unrestricted laissez faire. Its best representative was General Roca, hero of the Indian campaign of 1879 and twice president after that date. Roca himself was an honest as well as an able and devoted public servant; but in the get-rich-quick atmosphere of this boom period, even during Roca's administrations the oligarchical regime reminded one of the Gilded Age of the Grant Administration in the United States.

Former President Mitre, an oligarch, but one of the old school, was so disgusted by the brazen corruption and crass selfishness of the new-rich who were now in control and who kept themselves in control by stolen elections, that in 1890 he joined in forming a new party, the Civic Union. The new party sought to organize itself along the lines of political parties in the United States as described in James Bryce's recently published *American Commonwealth*; but this did not deter it from having a hand in the revolt of 1890.

In the next thirty years Argentina developed the best political party system in Latin America. After the failure of the revolt of 1890, the Civic Union split. One wing formed in 1892 the Radical Party, under the leadership first of Leandro Além and later of Hipólito Irigoyen; in the same year the Radicals held the first national political convention in the history of Argentina. Most of those in the other wing ultimately rejoined the Conservatives, who took the name National Democratic Party. Still another new party, the Socialist, was founded in 1894; among its early leaders were some of Argentina's outstanding intellectuals — Juan B. Justo, José Ingenieros, and Alfredo L. Palacios.

In the early decades of the twentieth century hopeful signs began to multiply. For courage, intelligence, and responsible leadership, Argentina never produced a better politician than Lisandro de la Torre, a former Radical who, unable to tolerate Irigoyen's iron rule of that party, formed an agrarian party of his own, which was rooted mainly in cosmopolitan Santa Fe. Immigrants were active in politics and sometimes rose to positions of power. For example, Enrique Dickmann, who was born in Russia in 1874 and emigrated to Argentina in 1890 as one of a group of Jews sent there by the Jewish Colonization Association, helped to found the Argentine Socialist Party, represented it in congress seven times between 1914 and 1943, and at various periods was the editor of its organ, the newspaper *La Vanguardia*.

Down to 1912 the elections were rigged by the dominant Conservatives, and on that ground the Radicals, the largest opposition party, adopted a policy of "abstention and revolution." This was a pathological condition that cried out for correction and some members of the ruling class itself were already convinced that the time had come to correct it by bowing to the popular clamor for honest elections and democratic suffrage. The ablest exponent of this view was Carlos Pellegrini, son of an Italian immigrant (painter and engineer). Except that he rose to be president, the younger Pellegrini was the Alexander Hamilton of Argentina, and he won enormous prestige by steering Argentina safely through the grave political and financial crisis of the early 1890's. The following sketch of him, drawn by a British diplomat in 1902, tells us something about the oligarchy as well as about Pellegrini:

Dr. Pellegrini is certainly about the most prominent personality in this country [in which] politics are essentially personal in character . . . On him may perhaps be said to depend the future of his country. A man of very superior intelligence, an orator of great eloquence, and, like most South Americans, a gambler to the core, he now holds a position to which no other Argentine can aspire and one to which neither General Mitre nor General Roca in the days of their ascendancy and popularity ever attained. His law practice, investments, and speculations in the stock exchange would have made him rich but for his spendthrift and generous habits and a passion for gambling . . . he is, to a certain extent, a man of pleasure, and his tall figure is noticeable at all social functions, at all race meetings, and at all club gatherings.

In 1906 Pellegrini devoted what was to prove his last and most famous speech to warning his fellow oligarchs that "the floodgates must be opened" to the people. That same year he died, at the age of fifty-nine, as did Mitre, at eighty-six.

4. RADICAL REGIME: IRIGOYEN

The floodgates were opened by the Electoral Law of 1912, often known by the name of the Conservative president, Roque Sáenz Peña, who, in the spirit of Pellegrini, carried it through Congress over strong opposition offered by many of his own party. They might well oppose it, for while the law merely made voting secret and compulsory and provided for minority representation and a new and honest registration of voters, it was virtually certain to bring the Radicals to power — provided the elections were honest. Assured that they would be, the Radicals gave up their intransigent policy of "abstention and revolution" and won the next national election (1916), though by a narrow margin. This ended the oligarchy's thirty-five-year monopoly of power and ushered in fourteen years of Radical rule. A revolution had taken place, but it was the work of ballots, not bullets. Argentina had come of age politically, it seemed.

The new president was the Radical party's chief, Hipólito Irigoyen. As the first "people's choice" ever elected to that office, he has been called the Andrew Jackson of Argentina. The comparison is far from perfect, but it does suggest the importance of the break with the past. Irigoyen signalized the break by riding to his inauguration in a streetcar. There was no affectation about this. All his life he lived simply, in many ways austerely, the better to serve the people's cause. To be sure, he could rule them with a rod of iron, as he did in breaking a longshoremen's strike that paralyzed the port of Buenos Aires in 1919. Some writers have seen in this and other actions of Irigoyen's more than a touch of Rosas. Yet there can be no doubt about his apostolic zeal for the democratic cause as he understood it. Now for the first time the plain people were made to feel welcome in the presidential palace, the Casa Rosada, and held high government office. Even in the sacrosanct Ministry of Foreign Affairs, Irigoyen had as his second in command the son of an Italian immigrant — a day-laborer, and not, like Pellegrini's father, an engineer and artist. This was Diego Luis Molinari, who was to hold high office again under Perón.

The masses responded by idolizing Irigoyen — until adversity struck in 1930. After his death they veered about again and canonized him; and since 1943 Perón and the Radical opposition have fought for possession of his mantle.

How then are we to explain the meager achievements of the fourteen-year Radical domination, first under the famous Irigoyen, then under the worthy Marcelo T. de Alvear, and finally, for two years, under Irigoyen again? For they were meager — a few bits of social and labor legislation that did not compare with what had already been done with less fanfare just across the

River Plate in Uruguay, and a beginning of state control in the production of oil (through the Y.P.F. monopoly) and the marketing of meat. All sorts of explanations have been given, beginning with the narrowness of Irigoyen's margin of victory in 1916 and the distractions of the war period. The three most important, however, seem to be the heterogeneous character of the Radical party, which, though middle-class at the core, contained such widely different elements that sustained action in any direction was difficult; the early split of the party into two factions, the larger led by Irigoyen, the smaller and more conservative (called Anti-Personalist) by Alvear, who was a scion of the oligarchy; and above all, Irigoyen's defects of leadership.

His defects were many and they were decisive because he was more than a party boss — he was a political caudillo and the Radical party was only an extension of his personal leadership. That he had no program is admitted even by his sympathetic biographer, the gifted Manuel Gálvez. He conceived of democracy in political terms, not in the social and economic terms that the Argentina of the 1920's called for; he never stopped fighting the last war — the war for political democracy won by the electoral reform of 1912. Yet in his intransigent Radicalism he himself corrupted the democratic process by continuing the old abuse of intervention in the provinces for party advantage. He was not a good administrator, partly because he could not bring himself to delegate authority and did not trust his subordinates; in his later years he became pathologically suspicious of everyone.

The last-named trait proved his undoing, and that of his party, in the political crisis brought on by the depression of 1929. Because of the nature of her economy, Argentina was one of the first to feel the impact of the depression; but the seventy-five-year-old Irigoyen, not knowing what to do and trusting no one to act for him, did nothing. As early as June 1930 the American chargé d'affaires in Buenos Aires, J. C. White, was reporting "hard times," "partial paralysis of the . . . government," the "exceptionally refractory temper" of labor, and general agreement that Irigoyen's government was "exceptionally dictatorial and extraordinarily inactive" and that his continuation in office was "if not problematical, at any rate a serious problem."

As an Argentine writer has pointed out, the personalist cult so conspicuously represented by Irigoyen has two sides: when all goes well, the caudillo is the nation's hero; when things go badly, he is its handiest scapegoat. This was now to be Irigoyen's role.

5. ARMY COUP, 1930

On September 4, 1930, an Army group revolted under the leadership of General José E. Uriburu, firm believer in the new doctrine of the Army's mission to regenerate the nation. One member of the group was thirty-five-year-old Captain Juan Perón. A host of civilians rallied to their support — Conservatives, Anti-Personalist Radicals, and dissident Socialists alike. Even the orthodox Socialists, who did not support the coup, though they had helped to bring it on by their bitter attacks on the Radical regime's administrative corruption and stolen elections, raised no hand in defense of Irigoyen. Against these odds, his followers had no heart for a fight. On September 6 he resigned, and the fourteen-year-old Radical regime vanished with hardly a whiff of grapeshot to speed its disappearance.

Superficially, the revolt was spontaneous, nearly unanimous, and essentially civilian, with the Army serving only as the agent of an aroused citizenry. This view was reflected in Ambassador Robert Woods Bliss's report to Washington from Buenos Aires a week after the event: "The overthrow of Irigoyen may justly be described as restoration rather than revolution. It is unquestionably civilian or popular rather than military, a constitutionalist movement unconstitutionally born."

Actually, the revolt had been carefully prepared at least several months in advance; it was the work of a small group of army officers and civilians dominated by the former; there was wide disagreement between the two elements on fundamental questions; and all these were settled by the army officers. Said General Uriburu to the civilian conspirators: "I took part in one revolution [1890] that was botched by the civilians, and I am not going to let that happen again. This show will be run by the Army."

General Uriburu was the leader both before and after the revolt. As soon as it was over, he set up a dictatorship thinly disguised as a Provisional Government. By promising respect for the Constitution and a quick return to political normality, he obtained the Supreme Court's recognition of his regime as a *de facto* government. The court's reasoning was curious, and its decision was deeply regretted in the next decade; but it strengthened Uriburu's position greatly, for the court then enjoyed great prestige. At first the impression he made was generally favorable. A British visitor at this time, Philip Guedalla, looked with friendly eyes on this "darkish military man with kindly manners and a charming smile."

His manner was authoritative [continued Guedalla], with the slight touch of brusqueness that comes from training with the German Army; but, unlike his teachers, he did not forget to smile . . . He was what not all Dictators are, brave and unpretentious. For I have seen him, conspicuous in the red band on his General's cap, shouldering his way through a football crowd.

Soon, however, Uriburu reneged his promises. A better soldier than politician, he revealed in a speech on December 14, 1930 what he really had in mind. In it he denounced the minimum wage law, universal and equal suffrage, and the whole democratic regime, in place of which he proposed the establishment of a corporative system and government by a select minority. In the months that followed, he canceled a Buenos Aires election that went against him, suppressed hostile newspapers, made arbitrary arrests, and deported critics whom it was not convenient to keep in jail.

As the nature of his plans for setting up a quasi-Fascist state became clear, civilian opposition increased and the Army itself was divided. One large segment of the latter, headed by General Agustín P. Justo, an Anti-Personalist Radical, remained loyal to the Argentine tradition of a nonpolitical Army. The opposition of the Justo Army group was decisive, for Uriburu was unable to offset it by an appeal to the masses; no popular support was to be won by his unpopular doctrine of government by an élite. After a year of frustration Uriburu acknowledged defeat and meekly ordered an election, which gave Justo the presidency and relegated Uriburu to obscurity. Here was a lesson to Uriburu's young subordinate, Juan Perón, in how not to make a revolution.

6. CONSERVATIVE RESTORATION

Justo, supported by a conservative coalition (called the *Concordancia*) of National Democrats and Anti-Personalists, won easily the election of November 1931 because the chief opposition candidate, Alvear (now returned to the Radical fold) was declared constitutionally ineligible. The declaration was amply justified, for much less than the constitutional six years had elapsed since the end of his presidential term (1928). Yet the Radicals stubbornly refused to make another nomination, and reverted for the next four years to their intransigent policy of abstention.

Justo's administration (1932–1938) partially fulfilled the Conservatives' dream of a return to the good old days of the oligarchy. Yet there were important differences. In the first two years there seemed to be a greater awareness of social responsibilities, as illustrated by the adoption of income and inheritance tax laws; but thereafter the regime reverted to the Gilded Age practices of the 1880's. More lasting was the break with the laissez-faire doctrines so dear to the hearts of the old oligarchy. Under the leadership of Justo's able Minister of Finance from 1933 to 1935, Federico Pinedo (a former Socialist), the government established controls over foreign exchange, crops, and prices, and made its control of banking more effective through the establishment of a Central Bank. The national government was strengthened at the expense of the provinces by these and other measures, notably an act of 1934 unifying internal taxes, which ended the increasing use of these to build up what amounted to protective tariff walls between one province and another. In Pinedo's phrase, the act thereby "completed the economic unification of Argentina."

Though Argentina made a substantial recovery from the depression during Justo's term, and though his administration deserves some of the credit for the recovery, social and political discontent nevertheless continued to increase. A major complaint was that his "sound" economic policy benefited only the oligarchy and left the middle and lower classes worse off than ever. The administration handled the complaint ineptly. Thus, one critic asserted in Congress that the concentration of wealth in Argentina had reached so high a point that there were now more large fortunes in that country than in much wealthier and more populous England, and asked rhetorically, "Does that accord with the principles of Christian morality?" To which the spokesman for the Justo administration replied bluntly, "Christian morality has nothing to do with the case." There were many Argentines who thought that it did.

Discontent grew as the government offended the rising spirit of economic nationalism in ways that have already been noted.* But perhaps the most ominous development was the creeping paralysis that afflicted all parties, those of the opposition as well as of the government coalition, the Concordancia. The leadership of the chief opposition party, the Radical, became bureaucratized, developed a kind of oligarchy of its own, and lost contact both with the party rank and file and still more with the general public. Much the same thing happened to the Socialist party, too; its young men complained that the oldsters kept a death grip on the party. As for the Concordancia, it suffered from the weakness of all coalitions, and matters were made worse as Justo used his great powers as president to build up his wing, the Anti-Personalist, at the expense of the larger National Democratic wing. The organized political groups were falling into a state verging on anarchy; the stage was being set for Perón's appeal to the masses to follow his lead to the New Jerusalem over the ruins of all the old parties.

In the national election of 1938 the Concordancia made a barefaced steal reminiscent of the worst days of the old oligarchy. For a brief time, however, it appeared that better days were at

* See above, Chapter 2.

hand, for the new president, Roberto M. Ortiz, was one of the more liberal Anti-Personalists, and many expected him to prove himself another Sáenz Peña by restoring free suffrage and honest elections. Unfortunately, Ortiz suffered from diabetes and this forced him to turn over the administration to Vice-President Ramón S. Castillo during most of the highly critical period from July 1940 to June 1942, when Ortiz resigned.*

Castillo, a National Democrat, belonged to the ultra-conservative group of the oligarchy which seemed to have learned nothing and forgotten nothing since 1916; and besides, he was pro-Axis. To him the Japanese attack on Pearl Harbor was only a pretext for declaring a state of siege in Argentina so as to cripple the domestic opposition; and as the election scheduled for September 1943 drew near, he offended even his fellow-oligarchs by preparing to impose the choice of his own hand-picked successor, one Robustiano Patrón Costas. These things, together with the resentment of the Army over its own special grievances,† led to his overthrow by the coup of June 4, 1943.

The state of affairs that assured the success of this coup and the subsequent rise of Perón is illuminated by the sad history of the chief effort at concerted opposition that was made in the years just before the coup. This effort grew out of *Acción Argentina*, a nonpartisan, anti-Axis organization established in June 1940, with branches all over the country, and with support from such widely different groups as those represented by former Presidents Alvear and Justo, Justo's former cabinet ministers Saavedra Lamas and Pinedo, Radical deputy Emilio Ravignani and one of the founding fathers of Argentine Socialism, Alfredo L. Palacios. Originally, Acción Argentina concerned itself only with foreign affairs and was substantially the Argentine counterpart of the Committee to Defend America by Aiding Britain which was set up simultaneously in the United States. Gradually, however, the growing seriousness of the domestic threat from Axis sympathizers led some of the leaders of Acción Argentina to try to develop it into a coalition of all the anti-Axis parties and

* Ortiz died the following month.
† See below, p. 114.

groups in Argentina, under the name of *Unión Democrática,* for the defense of democracy in Argentina itself.

Ironically, one of the few lasting achievements of Acción Argentina was the adoption of a program of economic and social reform which was later taken over by the Perón regime — the very type of regime whose establishment Acción Argentina sought to prevent. It is indeed extraordinary how many of the leading features of Perón's program were anticipated by Acción Argentina — social justice, economic independence of foreign nations, industrialization, development of mineral resources, land reform, and many others. Even Perón's vaunted "Third Position" between capitalism and communism was only a slight variation on Acción Argentina's emphatic pronouncement in favor of an "intermediate" position between uncontrolled private enterprise and a regimented economy.

In the end the effort to form an anti-Axis coalition was defeated by the inability, which that country's democratic elements have so often demonstrated, to lay aside their party, factional, and personal rivalries even in the face of imminent danger. They well knew that great danger was imminent now, and yet nothing had been accomplished in the way of union when the blow fell on June 4, 1943. Some six weeks later — ironically, on July 14, Bastille Day — Acción Argentina was suppressed by order of the military dictatorship, on the pretext that it was infected with communism.

4. Cultural Development

It is at least as true of the cultural as of the other aspects of Argentine life that the roots of the present lie deep in the past; and these roots are still mainly Spanish and Catholic, as has always been the case. Nevertheless, since the colonial period the plant has been greatly altered by the soil from which its roots draw nourishment, by changes in the world climate, and by deliberate graftings from foreign plants.

1. DIVERSIFICATION

In the three colonial centuries, the area that was to become Argentina was not one of the chief cultural centers of Spanish America. It had only one of the two dozen colonial universities — the one in the north at Córdoba, which was noted mainly as a center of theological studies; there was no university in or near Buenos Aires until the nineteenth century. Colonial Argentina produced no great writers or scientists to compare with the Mexicans, Sor Juana Inés de la Cruz and Carlos de Sigüenza y Gongora, or the Peruvians, Pedro Peralta and Hipólito Unanue. It was hardly more productive of notable public buildings; most of these were built in the last colonial century, and few of them would be given more than one star in the most generous Baedeker.

Nevertheless, colonial Argentina developed in a high, if not the highest, degree the same general type of literary culture as most of the rest of Spanish America. Down to the eve of independence, this was almost exclusively Spanish-Catholic and preponderantly ecclesiastical, and it reached its fullest development in Córdoba and above all in that city's famous university, whose influence was predominant throughout most of the River Plate area. Founded in 1624 by Jesuits of that city and Bishop Trejo of Tucumán, in whose diocese the city lay, it was one of the major universities of the Spanish empire, both legally and intellectually. Sanctioned by both the king of Spain and the pope (and hence called "royal and pontifical"), it was modeled on the great Spanish universities of Salamanca and Alcalá and its degrees had equal validity. Conducted by the Jesuits until their expulsion from all the Spanish dominions in 1767, the University of Córdoba was essentially a theological school devoted to the study of scholastic theology and moral philosophy according to the doctrines of Thomas Aquinas, Suárez, and the founder of the Jesuit order, Ignatius Loyola. Broader instruction, however, was provided in the three-year preparatory training in the Faculty of Arts, which included the study of logic, physics, and metaphysics; and the range of studies conducted by members of the university community extended to such subjects as botany and astronomy. Whether academic or not, the culture of colonial Córdoba was Spanish to the core. For example, the city's first native poet, Luis de Tejeda, was a disciple of the outstanding Spanish poet of the seventeenth century, Luis de Góngora.

The persistence of Córdoba's influence far into the nineteenth century is attested by the fact that in nearly all the important Argentine constituent assemblies down to 1880, most of the members were graduates of its university. A century earlier, however, a rival center had begun to develop in Buenos Aires, whose secular, cosmopolitan spirit proved to be in closer accord with the trend of the times than Spanish, theocratic Córdoba; though there was a *tertium quid* in Argentina, a cultural growth of the soil, which was not at home in either city, or any city, and which found very tardy and only partial expression in the gaucho literature of the late nineteenth and twentieth centuries.

Traces of this native growth are found in the cultural history of Buenos Aires. Indian musicians, trained by the Jesuits, were favorites in the city's fiestas; one of the only two plays known to have been written in Buenos Aires during the colonial period,

El amor de la estanciera, had as its setting that thoroughly
Argentine institution, the estancia; and the first viceroy was
honored by a ballad purporting to be written in "the country
style" and sung by a gaucho. For the most part, however, the
culture of Buenos Aires was European and, until the late eighteenth century, Spanish. In architecture the baroque predomi-
nated. In style as well as subject matter (religious scenes and
portraits), Argentine paintings might as well have been done in
Spain. Also as in Spain, two kinds of plays were given, one
religious, the other secular; and among the latter, few were given
that were not Spanish classics.

The cultural development of Buenos Aires, slow at first, accelerated greatly after the early eighteenth century. The first
orchestra was established about 1714 in a Jesuit college, in 1742
the first printing press was introduced, in the same year the first
book written by a *porteño* anthor was published (not by this
press, however), and in 1757 the first theater was opened. The
number of "firsts" multiplied at the turn of the century and included a medical school in 1798, a school of drawing in 1799, a
school of painting in 1801, and a newspaper the same year, followed by another the following year. These journals bore names
well suited to this busy port: *El Telégrafo Mercantil* and
Semanario de Agricultura, Industria y Comercio. In 1771 there
were at least three foreigners (one French, two Portuguese) who
made a livelihood by teaching music and dancing, but the city's
most popular music teacher was an Indian who had taken a
Spanish name, Juan Antonio Ortiz, and who, though "master of
the clavichord," also gave lessons in voice, the violin, the spinet,
and the guitar. In the last half century of the colonial period
three painters of considerable talent (two Spaniards and an
Italian) made their homes in Buenos Aires. Foreign musicians
came in even larger numbers and one, a Frenchman, built an
organ in the cathedral that lasted nearly a century. One of the
city's several orchestras in the late colonial period was maintained
by the cathedral; the director of one of the others, Blas Parera,
was later the anthor of Argentina's national anthem.

Oddly enough, this thriving city and cultural center, which

after 1777 was also a viceregal capital, never had a university to
the end of the colonial period. This is odd because between
1750 and 1770 the city fathers made several efforts to bring about
the establishment of one, or to have the University of Córdoba
transferred to Buenos Aires, and because on three subsequent
occasions (1784, 1786, and 1798), the king of Spain ordered that
a university be established there and that the confiscated property of the Jesuits be used to finance it. Why the royal orders
were not carried out is an enigma, the best authorities tell us;
and there we shall have to leave the matter. At any rate, the
Spanish crown had done its part; and this fact is only one of
many proofs of the falsity of the fantastic but oft-repeated assertion that the Spanish government sought to keep its American
subjects in a state of ignorance.

The government did, of course, try to exclude the subversive
ideas that were rife in the Atlantic world in the late colonial
period, particularly those associated with the American Revolution of 1776 and the French Revolution of 1789. Needless to say,
the effort failed, and, as we have seen in an earlier chapter, these
subversive ideas combined with other factors to bring about
the disruption of Spain's empire in America between 1810 and
1825. In all the new states the political upheaval hastened the
disintegration of the traditional colonial culture.

2. REORIENTATION AND ENLIGHTENMENT

In Argentina the cultural reorientation was slow and unsteady
until the mid-nineteenth century, though it began early among
the intellectual leaders of the new nation. For example, according to a recent study, one of the first of them, Mariano Moreno,
was decisively influenced by Montesquieu and the French En-
cyclopedists. In the 1820's another, Bernardino Rivadavia, tried
to broaden the political break with Spain into a cultural revolution against Argentina's Spanish heritage, and to replace this
with a more liberal, progressive, dynamic culture modeled on
England, France, and the United States. According to the Argentine philosopher, Francisco Romero, one of the leading intellec-

tuals in Latin America today, Rivadavia ably represented the continuation of the Age of the Enlightenment in its practical as well as its Utopian aspects and set Argentine civilization on the course it was to follow in later years. In Rivadavia's own generation, however, little was accomplished. The struggle for independence made the martial spirit and political passion so all-pervasive that a sharp cultural decline set in. The University of Buenos Aires, founded with great fanfare in 1821, attracted so few students that by 1828 only one heroic professor still kept up his lectures.

Moreover, many Argentines reacted strongly in favor of the old cultural order, and they found a champion in the tyrant Juan Manuel de Rosas.* His tyranny (1829–1852) not only suffocated free inquiry among the majority who obeyed him but channeled into politics most of the activities of the intellectuals who opposed him. A striking example is the case of the poet Esteban Echeverría, pioneer of literary Romanticism in the Hispanic world, who in 1830 founded a literary society, only to have it forced underground and into politics and revolution by Rosas' persecution. Echeverría himself is best remembered not for his poetry, but for his essentially political book, *Socialist Dogma* (1838), which stated most of the themes that were to be developed by the next generation of Argentine leaders.

The new generation, headed by Domingo Sarmiento, Juan Bautista Alberdi, and Bartolomé Mitre, came to power with the overthrow of Rosas in 1852. They inaugurated a revolution which produced a new Argentina culturally as well as politically and economically, and brought the fusion of culture and politics to its highest point in both thought and action. Its fusion in their thought is shown by their major reason for making education the first plank in their revolutionary platform. This illustrates the pathetic fallacy of their age in equating literacy with liberalism: "An ignorant people will always vote for a Rosas."

All three men combined eminence as writers with eminence in politics. Sarmiento was journalist, editor, essayist, and polemist; Mitre, journalist, editor, general, and historian of the wars of

* See above, pp. 52–53.

independence in southern South America; and both became presidents of Argentina. Alberdi was more the closet philosopher and jurist, never held high political office, and spent most of his life outside of Argentina; nevertheless, he contributed greatly to shaping the Argentine Constitution of 1853 and coined the phrase that was to be the watchword of Argentine statesmen for three generations to come: "To govern is to populate."

Though they differed with one another profoundly on many points, these three were agreed that Argentina must undergo nothing less than a cultural revolution through reëducation with the aid of Europe and the United States. Alberdi explained his famous phrase by saying that

to populate is to educate, to improve, to enrich and make great . . . as has happened in the United States . . . To educate our America in liberty and industry it is necessary to populate it with people from Europe, which is farther advanced in liberty and industry, as is being done in the United States . . . The English language, the language of liberty, of industry, of order, must be made more obligatory than Latin . . .

Mitre, as president, accorded top priority to the promotion of a national system of education, gave it a modern and secular character by stressing the role in it of the natural and physical sciences, and called in European experts to help design it and make it work.

Sarmiento practiced what he preached about North American-ization. By this he did not mean slavish imitation — he was far too good a patriot for that — and he contemplated the reorienta-tion of Argentine life on a broad front, of which education was only one sector. Nevertheless, he regarded this as a key sector, and he did not hesitate to borrow directly from the United States for aid in developing it. The guiding ideas underlying his mani-fold contribution to the Argentine educational system — new national and provincial schools, special schools of mining, agronomy, telegraphy, night schools for adults, mobile schools for thinly populated areas — were strongly influenced by his Massachusetts friend Horace Mann. The normal schools at the core of the system were run by teachers brought from New

England, and a Bostonian, Benjamin Apthorp Gould, was made director of the new astronomical observatory at Córdoba, the first ever established in Argentina.

3. TOWARDS LATIN AMERICAN LEADERSHIP

Thanks to the stimulus and direction given by these three men and their worthy successors, Argentina achieved a cultural leadership in Latin America from the 1880's to the 1930's which matched her economic and political leadership in the same period. Only occasionally did an individual of another country, such as the Nicaraguan Rubén Darío and the Uruguayan José Enrique Rodó, overtop the best that Argentina could offer.

That Argentine leadership extended into the field of the fine arts will surprise most North Americans of the present day, who are accustomed to think of Latin American art as a Mexican monopoly, and of Argentina as the land of beef and wheat, of troublesome dictators and diplomats, and (if they remember *The Four Horsemen of the Apocalypse*) as the mother of Parisian playboys. In fact, however, the artistic tradition which was well established in Argentina by the end of the colonial period has been maintained with distinction ever since.

In the judgment of a leading authority, two of the three greatest Latin American painters of the hundred years from independence to the Mexican renaissance in the twentieth century were Argentines.* One, Prilidiano Pueyrredón, was Argentine by birth; the other, Juan Manuel Blanes, by adoption. Pueyrredón, son of the patrician statesman, studied painting in Spain; Blanes, a native of Uruguay, studied in Italy. Both men painted a variety of subjects — among their best works are the former's portrait of Rosas' daughter, Manuelita, and the latter's "Incident of the Yellow Fever" (in Buenos Aires) and his decorations in General Urquiza's private chapel in Entre Ríos. Both men, however, are well remembered for their scenes of gaucho life, and both, though more particularly Pueyrredón, helped to make the gaucho

* Lincoln Kirstein, *The Latin-American Collection of the Museum of Modern Art* (New York, 1943), p. 20.

a familiar figure in the world of art long before he achieved a literary vogue. Another *costumbrista* of note was, surprisingly enough, an immigrant who did not come to Argentina until he was nearly thirty. This was Charles Henri Pellegrini, of whose son's political career we have already spoken, and who was also a talented portraitist as well as an engineer.

Local themes continued to occupy later generations of Argentine painters, but the scenes, like the artists, tended to concentrate more and more in Buenos Aires and to follow the rapidly changing styles of European painters, especially those of France and Spain. Thus, Argentina's most famous painter in the present century, Benito Quinquela Martín, whose works were acquired by the Luxembourg in Paris and the Metropolitan in New York, specialized in waterfront scenes of the Limehouse of Buenos Aires, the Boca, which were done in a style reminiscent of the Spanish Sorolla.

Architecture and sculpture, too, continued to flourish, thanks mainly to the high standards maintained by the Superior School of Fine Arts, a government institution — even before Perón, Argentine art was largely official. An outstanding product of the last decade before his rise was José Fioravanti's arch to Bolívar, which our same authority (not an Argentine) describes as one of the handsomest monuments erected anywhere in America in that decade.

Modern Argentina was unexcelled in the number and quality of her intellectual élite and unmatched in the broad popular base of her culture. The combination of these two things alone would have made Argentina unique and outstanding among the nations of Latin America. Her culture was oriented towards Europe, not the United States, but that would not have bothered Sarmiento much, if at all, for the qualities most characteristic of Argentine culture in this period were those that he had in mind when he spoke of North Americanization — freedom, tolerance, diversity, courage, and a cosmopolitan receptivity combined with independence and originality. In the space at our disposal we can give only a few concrete illustrations of this development.

Between 1895 and 1936, the number of high school students

increased from 6395 to 100,449, and from 1.6 to 7.9 per 1000 inhabitants. The education of the Argentine masses is reflected in the steady reduction of the percentage of illiteracy. For the whole country, this was 78 at the time of the first national census in 1869, but it was brought down to 54 in 1895, 35 in 1914, and 16.6 in 1945. In the city of Buenos Aires, always more literate than the rest of the country, the rate of illiteracy had been cut from 67.7 in 1869 to 7.7 in 1945, the latter figure being only slightly higher than that for the United States as a whole in the same year.

In the field of higher education, Argentina pioneered the way for Latin America on two occasions. The University of La Plata, founded in 1909, broke with the tradition that the function of a university is either merely to preserve and transmit culture or to train young men for the professions. The founder and first rector of La Plata, the great Joaquín V. González, designed it to promote and extend knowledge by basic research, as well as to diffuse general culture. In his planning, González took as his guide "the new tendencies in higher education, the needs of Argentine culture, and the example of the best institutions of a similar type in Europe and America," and was profoundly influenced by Leo S. Rowe, then a professor of Political Science at the University of Pennsylvania and later Director General of the Pan American Union.

In 1918 and 1919, Argentina reformed her whole university system to insure the autonomy of the universities by making faculty appointments competitive, guaranteeing academic freedom, and giving the students a share in the administration. In 1919 the system was expanded by the establishment of the University of the Litoral, the four main divisions of which were in the next few years located in as many different cities: Santa Fe, Rosario, Paraná, and Corrientes. In the next two decades the Argentine university system was without a peer in the rest of Latin America. There was also a threefold increase between 1917 and 1944 in the proportion of university students to total population, the ratio rising from 1.1 per thousand in the former year to 3.4 per thousand in the latter.

In the meanwhile, Argentina had developed an intellectual élite whose voices were heard in nonacademic as well as academic circles at home, and sometimes reached throughout the Spanish-speaking world. It was characteristic of the new Argentina that this group were not only cosmopolitan in spirit but also represented many different national origins: the sociologist José Ingenieros, Italy; the philosopher Alejandro Korn, Germany; the litterateur-historian Paul Groussac, France; and the historian Mitre and the humanist González, Argentina herself. Ingenieros was the best known of these in his lifetime (he died in 1925). This many-sided man, who was biologist, psychologist, criminologist, and historian of ideas as well as sociologist, is said to have been "for a time the most widely read author of Spanish speech."

In Argentina, as in the rest of Latin America, positivism enjoyed an enormous vogue and provided the main theme of discussion in the generation before 1910, only to lose its hold shortly thereafter. In some important respects, however, the Argentine brand of positivism differed from that in the other countries. It drew its inspiration from Darwin, Huxley, and Spencer rather than from Auguste Comte; its significance was primarily philosophical and scientific rather than political; and insofar as it developed political implications, these were not identified with any single party or school of thought, but on the contrary served as grist to all the many different political mills in Argentina.

In this latter respect the contrast with Mexico is particularly striking and instructive. Mexican positivism did become identified with a single group — the *Científicos,* or "scientifics," a bourgeois oligarchy who made a good thing out of administering Mexico for the dictator Porfirio Díaz from the 1880's to his overthrow in 1911. In Argentina, the oligarchs likewise justified their works by positivist faith; but they had no monopoly of the faith, for some of its chief Argentine apostles were democrats, while perhaps the greatest of them all, Ingenieros, was for several years an active member of the Socialist party.

This may help to explain why the revolutions which took

place in both countries just after 1910 differed so profoundly from each other, Mexico's being violent, bloody, prolonged, and total, whereas Argentina's was peaceful, orderly, comparatively brief, and largely political. It certainly helps to explain why the decline of positivism was so much less abrupt in Argentina — Ingenieros continued to preach it, and to hold his audience, to the day of his death in 1925, whereas in Mexico it was thrown out with Díaz and the Científicos in 1911.

4. GENERATION OF 1910: NATIONALISM AND NOSTALGIA

Though the shift of interest and mood in Argentina was gradual and uneven, we may for convenience speak of "the generation of 1910," for the centenary of independence in that year greatly stimulated the nationalism strongly tinged with nostalgia which was a leading feature of Argentine thought in the next three decades. Despite the all-pervasive nationalism, this was a deeply divided generation. The divisions are illustrated by two of its outstanding representatives, Ricardo Rojas and Manuel Gálvez. Both men were born in 1882 and both reacted strongly against the cosmopolitanism of their elders, confined their reaction mainly to an attack on Anglo-Saxon materialism, and made an exception in favor of Hispanic and, more broadly, Latin culture.

Also, in typically Argentine fashion, both of these men of letters were deeply concerned with political and social problems; but their solutions of these problems differed widely. Rojas' ardent nationalism found expression in 1916 in a book *La Argentinidad* ("Argentinity"), which made a profound impression both at home and abroad. Contrary to his intentions, the book helped to build up the reactionary super-nationalism of the rising generation in Argentina and inspired similar elements in other Spanish-speaking countries to imitate his neologism — for example, in Spain, they coined *Hispanidad*, and in Peru, *Peruanidad*. To Rojas himself, *Argentinidad* meant loyalty to the country's democratic tradition as represented by Sarmiento;

his perceptive, discriminating biography of the schoolteacher-president is one of his best books. He was a regionalist because he regarded the provinces as the chief source both of this tradition and also of many of the best and most distinctive traits of the nation's "personality." Yet he also championed Spain and Hispanicism because he saw (as Sarmiento had failed to see) that Spain had a long and still vigorous liberal tradition.

Gálvez, on the other hand, expressed the anti-democratic reaction that was mounting in Argentina between the two world wars. His most notable biography is devoted not to Sarmiento, nor to anyone like him, but to the twentieth-century caudillo Irigoyen. In a book published in 1934, *What This People Needs* (*Este pueblo necesita*), Gálvez called upon his fellow-Argentines to scrap their made-in-U.S.A. Constitution of 1853, their corrupt political parties, and the whole rigmarole of democracy, and to profit by the example of the Italy of Mussolini and the Germany of Hitler in achieving order, hierarchy, and social justice under the leadership of a strong man. That seemed made to order for Perón; but he was more subtle about it.

Argentina has a leadership tradition of her own, represented by the tyrant Rosas. It lay submerged for many years after his overthrow while the new Argentina fashioned by his enemies grew rich and strong; but in the troubled interwar years it came to the surface again. By the 1930's a Rosas cult had taken shape. One of its high priests was the historian Carlos Ibarguren, who later became for a time a member of the government set up by the military coup of June 1943.

A favorable climate was created for the Rosas cult by the literary vogue of the romanticized gaucho in the generation after 1913. In that year a young intellectual named Leopoldo Lugones gave a series of lectures which started this vogue by establishing the forty-year-old gaucho poem *Martín Fierro* as a national epic. For many of its host of admirers, the poem had no political significance; it was simply escape literature which responded to the yearning of an increasingly urbanized society for the good old days of the open frontier. But the poem did have strong political implications. As Arturo Torres-Rioseco has well said:

"Martín is a gaucho persecuted by the Argentine authorities because his views of life do not agree with those of modern society . . . [He] fights this society that tries to displace the old order of things." The "modern society" that Martín Fierro fought was the kind of society that Rivadavia and Sarmiento and their kind had sought to build up in Argentina, and "the old order of things" that Martín defended was the one which many people associated with a romanticized Rosas. It is worth noting that Leopoldo Lugones, who did so much to popularize *Martín Fierro*, was in his later years (he died in 1938) a supporter of the anti-democratic reaction in Argentina.

The Rosas cult of the interwar period was Rosas with a difference. Since his time the concept of what constituted Argentina's national culture had been altered by the reconciliation with Spain, and by the 1920's Hispanicism had gained a strong foothold in Argentina, especially in the less democratic circles. While the two groups of Rosistas and Argentine Hispanicists were never identical, there was a good deal of overlapping. By the late 1930's their interaction had produced a more favorable atmosphere for *Hispanidad*, as the new Pan-Hispanism of Franco Spain was called, than would have been conceivable at any time in Argentine history before 1920. Conversely, while Hispanidad, like the original Pan-Hispanism of a generation earlier, was ostensibly cultural in its main objectives, it helped to create a more propitious climate for authoritarianism, whether under the Rosista or another label, than had existed in Argentina since the mid-nineteenth century.

Concurrently with the rise of Hispanicism, and partly as a result of it, there developed a vigorous anti-imperialist movement which was cultural as well as political — in Argentina, whose *pensadores* have frequently been preoccupied with politics, these two strands are exceptionally difficult to separate. The main targets of the attack were the "Anglo-Saxon" powers, Great Britain and the United States, particularly the latter and its Pan-American movement. The plan of attack was outlined by José Enrique Rodó in his *Ariel* (1900), which cast Latin America in the title role and the United States in the role of Caliban.

Rodó was an Uruguayan, but the idea of his book was eagerly caught up in Argentina and endlessly repeated and elaborated upon there in the next generation. As a result, the attitude of the Argentine intelligentsia towards the United States, which had been generally favorable from Sarmiento to Joaquín González, became generally unfavorable in the early decades of the twentieth century.

Even Ricardo Rojas, avowed continuator of Sarmiento, was not immune to the contagion. Here he parted company with his mentor. Sarmiento's classic, *Facundo*, had described the basic conflict in Argentina as one between that country's own barbarism and civilization. Rojas, on the other hand, held that there was an even more crucial conflict between native Argentine forces and the exotic forces which threatened to overwhelm them, and that chief among the latter were those represented by the United States.

5. PUBLISHERS' BOOM

Down to World War II there was a constant increase in the means of diffusing the products, great and small, of this Argentine culture among the increasingly literate people of that country. Newspapers abounded. Twenty-six were published in Buenos Aires alone in 1943 — nineteen in Spanish and seven in foreign languages (two each in English, Italian, and German, and one in French). Two of these, *La Nación*, founded by Bartolomé Mitre in January 1870, and its senior by one year, *La Prensa*, were among the oldest in Latin America and the best in the world.

The combined press of Buenos Aires and the provinces gave Argentina in 1943 a total newspaper circulation of 1,907,000. This was more than twice as large as the newspaper circulation in the second-ranking Latin American country, Brazil, and nearly three times as large as that in the third, Mexico, though both these countries greatly exceeded Argentina in population — Mexico by 50 per cent and Brazil by 300 per cent. In per capita newspaper circulation, Argentina stood second only to Uruguay, and that by the narrow margin of 1:7 as compared with Uruguay's 1:6. Most of the rest were far behind; for example, Chile's ratio was 1:15, Cuba's 1:18, Mexico's 1:30, and Brazil's 1:52.

Specialized groups were served by a host of periodicals. *Sur* ("South") and *Nosotros* ("We"), journals of literature and public affairs, had large followings in the 1930's among sophisticated readers not only in Argentina but wherever Spanish was spoken. Many professional groups had their own journals. The historians were particularly active in the interwar period and by the end of it they had placed Argentina in the forefront of the Latin American countries in this field, thanks partly to the leadership of two institutions in Buenos Aires: the new Institute of Historical Studies, and the older Academy of History, founded in 1893 by Bartolomé Mitre. For more casual or general readers, there were illustrated magazines that gave a broad panorama of the current scene, from religion, politics, and finance to fashions and horse-racing. In short, by the 1930's Buenos Aires was producing newspapers and periodicals for almost all tastes and in several different languages. They were also still imported in considerable volume, however, particularly from France, whose preëminence in letters and fashion remained unshaken on the banks of the Plata.

The book-publishing business in Buenos Aires grew from nothing in 1800 to first place in the Spanish-speaking world in 1940. A period of expansion began in the second half of the nineteenth century, when the city's growing wealth and population attracted more and better specialists in the book trade. One of these was a German, Wilhelm Kraft, of Brunswick, who after a long residence in Paris, emigrated to Argentina, became Guillermo Kraft, and in 1864 established a publishing house under that name. It soon won and still holds a leading position there, and its authors' list includes such distinguished names as Bartolomé Mitre in the late nineteenth century and Ricardo Rojas in the twentieth.

After 1914 both the volume and quality of production were greatly increased under the stimulus provided by a series of developments that started abroad: first, World War I and the depression after 1929, both of which made it more difficult for Argentine readers to obtain books and periodicals from rival publishers abroad; then the Spanish Civil War of 1936–1939, which crippled Spanish publishing and shifted part of it to Buenos Aires; and finally World War II. By 1943 Buenos Aires was producing 80 million books a year and exporting 10 million. Though a similar publishing boom had taken place in Mexico City in the past decade, Mexico was Argentina's best customer, taking one-third of the total exports. Next came Venezuela, Colombia, and Uruguay, which took over a million and a half books each, followed by Chile and Peru, with close to a million each.

6. ACHIEVEMENTS AND MISGIVINGS

On the eve of the Perón period, any Argentine looking back over the record of his country's cultural development in the past half century had many reasons for taking solid satisfaction in it. Argentina now had the best schools and universities in Latin America, the largest publishing center in the Spanish-speaking world, and two of the best newspapers in the world. At the national capital its culture, though still Spanish and Catholic at the core, had incorporated so much from France, England, Italy, Germany, and the United States that Buenos Aires boasted with some reason that it was one of the world's most cosmopolitan cities. It had certainly been given the appearance of one, and this combined urban features of both the Old World and the New. With its broad avenues, palm-tree-lined plazas, and far-spreading parks, its modern port facilities and a multitude of fine buildings, both public and private, its prevailingly low skyline punctured by a rare skyscraper, its mammoth opera house, dozens of theaters, scores of motion picture theaters, and thousands of blaring radios, and in and around all this its acres of slums — the city reminded one by turns, if not simultaneously, of Paris, Chicago, New York, and Madrid.

The benefits of Argentina's cultural advance had been widely diffused among its people and the means of diffusion were being steadily augmented. In its cultural relations with Europe, and probably also with the United States, Argentina still received a good deal more than it gave in the way of basic ideas and techniques, but its people showed so much vigor, skill, and independence in adapting and applying these to Argentine conditions that the relationship could not properly be described as one of cultural colonialism.

Nevertheless, culturally as well as in its economic, social, and political life, the Argentina of the period just before Perón revealed several serious pathological symptoms. One that greatly disturbed many enlightened patriots was the cultural conquest of the "true" Argentina of the interior by the polyglot and essentially alien national capital, whose orientation was overseas. As Ricardo Rojas put it, things had come to such a pass that the rest of the country aped Buenos Aires, while Buenos Aires aped Europe. Moreover, the Argentine culture that we have described rested increasingly upon the middle class, and, as pointed out in an earlier chapter, while that class increased rapidly in numbers during the decade after the Great Depression, it also suffered a deterioration in morale which did not cease with the end of the depression.

Finally, among the intellectual leaders of Argentina there was an increasingly deep disquietude over the cultural state of the world at large and of their own country and capital in particular. In 1937 this feeling was frankly expressed to the foreign delegates from many countries — among them Jules Romains, Georges Duhamel, and Jacques Maritain of France, José Ortega y Gasset of Spain, Alfonso Reyes of Mexico, Baldomero Sanín Cano of Colombia, and Emil Ludwig, representing a "Group of Germanic Writers" — attending the International Congress of P.E.N. Clubs in Buenos Aires. The address of welcome by the President of the P.E.N. Club of the host city, Carlos Ibarguren, stressed the existence of a "world crisis," which was the result of the "terrible collapse" of the culture built up in the nineteenth century on "the basis of individualism and materialistic philosophy," and which was characterized by a revolt of the masses, whose "violent drive sweeps intellect away and imposes the predominance of passions and instincts." Manuel Gálvez, another Argentine delegate, spoke more particularly of Buenos Aires, and while he remarked that "social unrest and economic problems are the same everywhere," it was mainly of the cultural immaturity and confusion of his own city that he complained.

> Its emotional worth is almost null [he said]. Buenos Aires . . . is the capital of a nation that has thought and suffered but little . . . Europeans can hardly imagine how tragic is our loneliness in the world . . . We Argentines, as well as other Latin Americans, are indebted to foreign cultures for our whole intellectual being . . . We do not possess, nor shall possess for a long time yet, a culture all our own. We are a cosmopolitan people, a modern Babel . . . built up with fragments of other peoples.

Yet even in this somber mood Gálvez did not fail to voice the typically Argentine belief that his country was destined to Latin American leadership. "Our [spiritual] message remains concealed, unknown even to us. But we are under the impression that it exists. And quite probably it will not be the message of this country only, but the message of all Latin America."

5. Relations with the United States

In the past half century there has been a revolutionary change in the importance of the relations between Argentina and the United States for both countries. It was normally slight for both of them until about 1900. Since that time it has increased greatly, first from the point of view of Argentina, as the weaker power, and then from that of the United States. In the case of the latter, the change not only began late but proceeded slowly. In 1953 a former American ambassador to Buenos Aires published a book whose keynote was the statement, made as a self-evident proposition, that, of all the twenty Latin American countries, Argentina was the most important to the United States. Most informed observers probably agreed with him; but few if any would have done so before about 1940. Up to that time, one or more of several other Latin American countries stood ahead of Argentina in this respect — usually Mexico, Cuba, and Brazil, frequently Venezuela and Colombia, and sometimes Peru and Chile.

As a result, until the very eve of Perón's rise to power, Argentina received little sustained attention in the United States, where the history of Argentine foreign policy was a closed book to all but the smallest handful of specialists. This may explain why an important fact about the Perón regime itself has been overlooked by almost all North Americans — the fact that some of the policies and attitudes of that regime which have been most unwelcome to the United States are deeply rooted in the Argentine past.

There has, in fact, been a remarkably high degree of continuity in Argentine foreign policy from the earliest days to the present, and it is all the more remarkable in view of the far-reaching economic, political, and social changes that have taken place in that country in the past seventy-five years. There is nothing essentially new even about the role Perón has played as chief Latin American gadfly to the United States. Before he came to power, and at a time when he was still only an unknown army colonel, Argentina's foreign policy was described by a leading North American historian as having exhibited for some time past "a deep-seated and inveterate resentment . . . at the Latin American policy of the United States." *

To round out the picture, it should be added that by this time there had likewise grown up in Washington a deep-seated and inveterate resentment against the Latin American and other policies of Argentina. On both sides, however, the antagonism was of comparatively recent origin, for until the close of the nineteenth century their attitudes towards each other had been usually indifferent, sometimes friendly, and rarely hostile. The present chapter will sketch the development of their relations from the beginning of Argentine independence to 1943 and will seek to explain the apparent contradiction contained in the fact that the growth of antagonism between the two countries in the twentieth century coincided with their growing importance to each other. The contradiction is all the more striking in view of the fact that, until the 1930's, the foreign policies of the two countries were very much alike in some respects and, indeed, they agreed on more points than they did with the foreign policy of any other American state.

1. POLICY TRENDS AND CONDITIONING FACTORS

First, let us take a bird's-eye view of the major policies of the two countries, and the conditions under which they were developed, in the 130-year period under consideration.

The high degree of continuity in Argentine foreign policy points to the fact that, in addition to the changing economic,

* S. F. Bemis, *The Latin American Policy of the United States* (New York, 1943), p. 261.

demographic, and political factors, the international role of that country has all along been powerfully influenced by other and more constant factors. Of these the most important seem to have been the geographical location of Argentina, her power position, her economic interests, and certain traditions, which will be discussed below.

Argentina's location far down in the Southern Hemisphere, remote from the great powers of the Northern Hemisphere and even from the majority of nations in the Latin American group, had a threefold effect. First, it tended to make the Argentine nation psychologically as well as physically peripheral to the great international currents, whether inter-American, European, or universal. Second, it reduced the effectiveness of Argentina's exceptionally strong economic and cultural ties with Europe and thus tended to keep the country politically peripheral to Europe as well as to the American system. Third, it made Argentina's power position during the century-long Pax Britannica depend largely upon her relations with her immediate neighbors in South America. All of these were weaker, except perhaps Brazil, and, for a time, Chile, neither of which offered a serious, sustained threat to Argentina. As a result, her power position was generally strong, which probably explains why Argentina consistently showed far less enthusiasm for international coöperation than did many other Latin American countries, including her next-door neighbor, small and precariously situated Uruguay.

While, politically, Argentina kept her distance from Europe, her strongest economic and cultural ties have always been European and their strength increased greatly as modern Argentina took shape in the late nineteenth and early twentieth centuries. That, as it happened, was the period when the United States was launching the Pan-American system. It was also the period when Great Britain's long-standing economic preponderance in Argentina became so great that the latter was regarded by many observers as, in effect, a British dominion.

The four most persistent traditions of Argentine foreign policy have been those of her hegemony in the River Plate area, her opposition to intervention, her special relationship to the other Latin American states, and her avoidance of multilateral alliances and other security arrangements. All four date from the beginning of independence. The first has still deeper roots, in the colonial Viceroyalty of the Río de Plata, and is therefore often referred to as the viceregal tradition. In the national period this manifested itself, first, in an effort to unite or reunite the other succession states of the former viceroyalty with Argentina, and after that failed, to convert them into satellites of Argentina. The other three traditions were established by the founding fathers of 1810. Somewhat contradictorily, in view of their own record in the River Plate area, the Argentines have always opposed intervention by any nation in the affairs of another. Their views on this question took shape early, in opposition to an effort to establish the reciprocal right of intervention among Latin American states which had strong support in other countries, and Argentine views on this subject have never changed except to be sharpened and fortified. Also, from the very start they asserted the existence of a special relationship among Argentina and the other new states of Spanish America, and accordingly gave military aid to the independence movement in neighboring states, notably Chile and Peru.

Yet likewise from the start, the founding fathers laid down the rule that Argentina must not enter into multilateral alliances with other states, not even with other members of the Spanish-American family. In accordance with this rule, Argentina took no part in the Latin American congresses held at Panama in 1826 and at Lima in 1847 and 1864 for the purpose of establishing an inter-American security system, and rejected the Continental Treaty of 1856 drawn up by Chile, Peru, and Ecuador with the same end in view. Even when Argentina subsequently developed a fifth tradition, that of her leadership of all Latin America, no effort was made to implement this through the establishment of a multilateral security system. Finally, another relatively late-comer is the tradition of peace: since the Paraguayan War (1865–1870) Argentina has never fought a foreign war.

Of the foreign policy of the United States we shall speak more briefly, and mainly in relation to Argentina. The first thing to be noted is that the policy of the United States towards Argentina has in the main been merely a specific application of its general Latin American policy. The second is that the latter apparently possessed a degree of continuity comparable to that of Argentina's own foreign policy, since its chief expression, the Monroe Doctrine of 1823, was still in effect in the 1930's. In fact, however, as every schoolboy knows, the interpretation of the Monroe Doctrine varied greatly from time to time. Moreover, whenever a crisis arose, policymakers in Washington seemed to doubt whether remote Argentina belonged fully within its scope. From 1838 to 1850, French and British violations of it by interventions in the River Plate area failed to evoke a protest from Washington. In 1845 President Polk's restatement of the doctrine seemed to exclude Argentina, along with most of the rest of South America, from its effective operation. In 1902 President Theodore Roosevelt seriously considered making a similar declaration; and in 1940, under another Roosevelt, there was strong support in Washington for reducing hemisphere defense to a quarter-sphere defense that would extend southward only to the bulge of Brazil — again, to the exclusion of Argentina and some of her neighbors.

Until the twentieth century, the United States found little of economic interest in Argentina to compensate for its remoteness. Non-complementary at first, their economies became competitive when the United States was soon followed by Argentina in the development of commercialized agriculture and large-scale exports of meat and cereals to Europe. The United States alone, however, also built up manufactures and investment capital on a large scale, and in the overseas economic expansion that followed, it acquired a substantial stake in underdeveloped Argentina. Again, however, as in the case of the Monroe Doctrine, the diplomatic record shows Argentina lying largely outside the scope of what was commonly regarded as the typical Latin American policy of the United States. The Dollar Diplomacy of the Taft administration reached Argentina only in the limited form of "battleship diplomacy" — the administration's effort to help shipyards in the United States sell warships; and Argentina never felt Roosevelt's Big Stick at all.

Pan-Americanism was another matter, and it provides one of the major clues to the development of relations between Argentina and the United States since 1890. Promoted mainly by the United States, the Pan-American movement was at first primarily designed to support its economic interests in Latin America. Beginning in 1936, however, the character of the movement was profoundly altered under Washington's leadership, in order to meet the rising threat from the Axis, by the addition of political and military functions which ultimately transformed it into a regional security system. Argentina, which had looked askance at the Pan-American movement from the start, but had not too grudgingly given it a kind of lip-service during the commercial phase, strongly resisted the transformation from its beginning in 1936. This is not surprising, for the change not only revolutionized the Inter-American System but also cut across all the traditional Argentine policies which we have outlined.

Argentina's resistance, which continued with only one brief interruption through 1943 and beyond, created a growing tension in her relations with the United States, which had already reached a state of crisis when Perón came to power. As will appear below, there were other fruitful sources of discord as well, particularly the growth of pro-Axis influence in Argentina, but the initial cause of the continuing crisis after 1936, and a major cause throughout its course, was the policy conflict over the Inter-American System.

2. NINETEENTH-CENTURY BEGINNINGS

The United States had already established commercial contact with Argentina a decade before the beginning of the latter's independence movement in 1810; shortly after it began, Buenos Aires was visited by one of the first official agents sent from Washington to any part of Latin America; and Argentina was one of the first four Latin American states to be accorded recognition by the United States. After the initial interest in Argentine independence wore off, however, the United States soon became indifferent, as had Argentina even earlier. Almost from the start the latter had exhibited that preference for Great Britain which was to characterize Argentine foreign policy with little interruption until 1940.

The nature of the early relations between the United States and Argentina, and the importance of Britain's role in connection with them, can be illustrated by three episodes: the reception of the Monroe Doctrine in Buenos Aires, the Falkland Islands controversy, and the establishment of Uruguayan independence.

The reception that the Monroe Doctrine met with in Buenos Aires is partly explained by the diplomatic background. Argentina declared her independence in 1816 and sent envoys to the United States to obtain recognition of it. This was not granted until 1823, partly in conformity with the general Latin American policy of the United States, which until 1822 was dictated by the fear that recognition of any of the new states by Washington would provoke countermeasures by the much stronger European powers composing the so-called Holy Alliance, and partly because the government at Buenos Aires did not seem sufficiently stable and effective to meet the tests of recognition. Despite the delay, the United States was the first established power to recognize the independence of Argentina, but the latter felt less gratitude on this account than irritation over the delay. When recognition was accorded, Argentina no longer had an envoy in Washington to receive it, though she did have one in London. Consequently, it was the United States that took the initiative in establishing diplomatic relations, and several years passed before Argentina reciprocated. Her first envoy to the United States after recognition, General Carlos de Alvear, made only a brief visit to that country late in 1824 in connection with a more important mission to Europe.

President Monroe's message to Congress containing his famous doctrine was published in Buenos Aires early in 1824. The representative of the United States there was pained by the coolness of its reception in governing circles. The few liberals, he reported, were loud in their praise of it, but those in power regarded it with "an unwelcome apathy," which proved to him that "all we have done for this people is poorly appreciated." The explanation, he was sure, lay in "the overweening partiality of the dominant party and the highest classes of Society here for the English." He may have been right, though the hypersensitive nationalism of the Argentines may also have had something to do with it. At any rate, although General Alvear, who discussed the message with Monroe during his brief visit to the United States, sent back a favorable report of the author's elucidation of it, another forty years was to pass before the first Argentine holding a responsible position, Domingo Sarmiento, had a really good word to say for the Monroe Doctrine.

Caught in the backwash of the Falkland Islands controversy between Argentina and Britain, the United States handled its side of the question in such a way as to displease Buenos Aires without delighting London and to reflect no great credit on the succession of statesmen in Washington who had it in charge. These bleak islands, lying far out in the Atlantic off the southern coast of Argentina, were used almost exclusively by whalers and occasional merchantmen, though their potential strategic value in relation to the route around Cape Horn or through the Strait of Magellan was not negligible. In the eighteenth century they were the subject of a dispute between Spain and Britain, which was settled in favor of the latter; but the British had not perfected their title by occupation when Argentina won its independence. The Argentines soon set up a claim to the islands based upon the revival of Spain's title through Britain's failure to perfect title and upon their own inheritance of Spain's title because of the former dependency of the islands upon the colonial government at Buenos Aires; and they proceeded to make the claim good by occupation. For Argentina, one result was a brush with North American* sailors who resisted Argentina's attempt to exercise authority over them in the islands. Another result was a more serious controversy with Britain,

---

* Here and in a few other places, "North American" refers to the United States.

which has continued to the present day, for Britain promptly retook the Falklands — this was the period when she was completing her round-the-world chain of bases — and has never relaxed her hold on them.

The chief connection of the United States with this controversy arose from Argentina's appeal to Washington for aid under the terms of the Monroe Doctrine. Though there is much to be said for the Argentine claim, the United States steadily resisted embroilment in the dispute; but its policy was inconsistent from the start and remained so for the next hundred years. On the one hand, Secretaries of State Webster and Bayard took the position that, so far as their government was concerned, the controversy was not settled; but on the other hand, a Supreme Court decision of 1839 and several subsequent presidential messages held that early executive pronouncements had denied the validity of Argentina's claim. Likewise, from 1851 to 1908 the consular practice of the United States accorded British jurisdiction at least implied recognition, and in 1902 the State Department listed the Falkland Islands among the possessions of Great Britain; but in 1938 the Department reverted to a noncommittal position, and there, so far as the United States is concerned, the matter still rests.

The case of Uruguayan independence was one in which the United States was conspicuous by its absence. In the context of that period, its absence would hardly call for comment but for the fact that it was rendered conspicuous by the presence of Great Britain. From 1825 to 1828 Argentina and Brazil fought a war for possession of the *Banda Oriental* or "Eastern Shore" of the River Plate, with its metropolis, Montevideo, as the chief prize. Neither side could win a decisive victory, and as the exhausting war dragged on, it threatened to do lasting injury to the whole region. Britain, which had extensive commercial interests throughout the region, at last stepped in and brought about a settlement under which neither side won the disputed territory. Instead, it became the independent state of Uruguay — a buffer state like Belgium, which was created shortly thereafter, also through British influence.

The whole vast area of eastern South America from the Amazon to Cape Horn now seemed in a fair way to become a British sphere of influence. British preponderance was already firmly established in Brazil and almost as firmly rooted in Argentina; and now a new state had been set up in the area which owed its very existence to British mediation. And the United States did nothing about it. Since the fiasco of the Panama Congress of 1826, the people of the United States had turned their backs on Latin America as well as on Europe, and when they looked beyond their own borders it was usually towards contiguous Canada or nearby Cuba, or, more and more frequently, towards Texas and the Pacific, where Manifest Destiny beckoned. With remote Argentina and her River Plate neighbors, they had little concern.

The first major check to Britain's growing dominance in this area was administered by the tyrant Rosas in the 1840's, but that did not result in a corresponding increase in the influence of the United States, for Rosas' fervid nationalism expressed itself in jealousy of any nation stronger than Argentina.

3. TWO SCHOOLS OF THOUGHT

In the generation after the overthrow of Rosas in 1852, most of Argentina's leaders were distinctly friendly towards the United States, from whose political and educational system they borrowed freely; but in the end the new Argentina that they helped to fashion was bound more closely than ever before to Great Britain. Among the Argentine leaders of this period who looked with favor on the northern republic were Presidents Bartolomé Mitre and Domingo Sarmiento — above all, the latter. Mitre, in an oft-quoted phrase, described his government's foreign policy as "American and good-neighborly"; but unlike many Argentines and other Latin Americans, to whom "America" meant only "our America," that is, Latin America, Mitre insisted that it meant the United States as well. The exclusion of the latter from the continental treaty of 1856 and the Lima Conference of 1864 was one of the main grounds on which Mitre and his Minister of

Foreign Affairs refused to support either of those essays in inter-Americanism.

At least among men of prominence and influence, Sarmiento was the warmest admirer the United States ever had in Argentina, or probably in any Latin American country. Argentine to the core, he was never an unconditional Yankeephile. Born in 1810 in Argentina's Far West, the province of San Juan, he was in many ways a typical product of the quintessentially Argentine interior in the generation of independence. But there was also a strong strain of cosmopolitanism in his make-up, which was fortified by his experiences as an exile from the tyranny of Rosas, particularly by his long residence in Chile, where an intellectual ferment was then at work, and by his visit to Europe and the United States in 1846 and 1847.

This visit marked a turning-point in his career and the beginning of his admiration for the United States, which was to last the rest of his life. He was one of those Argentines who felt that their country's political independence must be completed by striking off the shackles of the cultural and social heritage from decadent and reactionary Spain and by creating a new, dynamic, progressive nation with the aid of foreign models. France was his first model, but his visit to that country on the eve of its Revolution of 1848 ended in complete disillusionment. In this mood he made his first visit to the United States, in 1847. There he found the model he was looking for. He embraced it with an instant enthusiasm which lasted the rest of his life and which was only increased by a second visit, as Minister Plenipotentiary to Washington, from 1865 to 1867.

The North Americanization of Argentina now became his favorite theme. What he admired most about the United States was its political democracy, its social mobility, the free, enterprising spirit of its people, and its educational methods and institutions, especially as represented by the public school system built up in Massachusetts by Horace Mann.*

With regard to the Latin American policy of the United States, however, Sarmiento had many reservations. In this respect he was

* See above, Chapter 4.

most typically Argentine. He departed from the type to the extent of speaking well of the Monroe Doctrine in an address to the Rhode Island Historical Society, delivered while he was Minister to the United States; but even on this occasion he made it clear that he saw hegemonic implications in the doctrine and warned the United States, through his Rhode Island audience, that these must not be developed. What he praised as the Monroe Doctrine was a rather unorthodox conception — in modern parlance, a kind of Point Four system operated, not by the government, but by individuals. His encomiums were reserved for the North Americans, including some members of his audience, who as merchants, entrepreneurs, or otherwise, were helping to raise standards of living, technology, culture, and political behavior in Latin America, and who were also helping to make its problems better known and its people better understood in the United States.

Sarmiento did not revolutionize either the policy of Argentina or the attitude of its people towards the United States — to the end of his career, a great many of his fellow countrymen regarded his North Americanism as excessive, if not fundamentally wrong. He did, however, contribute greatly to the formation of one of the two rival schools of thought which emerged in Argentina in the closing decade of the century. One school was oriented towards the United States and American regionalism; the other, towards Europe and universalism.

The latter was given typical expression in a speech delivered in 1890 at the first Pan-American conference by Roque Sáenz Peña, who was later to become President of Argentina. Held in Washington and presided over by Secretary of State James G. Blaine, chief pioneer of Pan-Americanism, the conference had on its agenda a project for the creation of a Pan-American customs union which was inspired by the German Zollverein, sponsored by the United States, and based on the maxim, "America for the Americans." Strongly opposing the project, Sáenz Peña declared that, instead, the conference should follow the maxim, "America for humanity." What he really was thinking of, however, was not humanity at large, but Europe. "What I

lack is not love for America," he said, "but suspicion and in-
gratitude towards Europe. I cannot forget that in Europe are
Spain, our mother; Italy, our friend; and France, our elder sister."
In order to complete the picture, he should have added, "and
Great Britain, our financier, best customer, and night watchman."

The other school of thought is represented by the Drago
Doctrine of 1902. This was contained in a note to Washington
from the Argentine Minister of Foreign Affairs, Luis M. Drago,
in which he proposed the adoption of an inter-American policy
prohibiting armed intervention by any European power in any
American state for the collection of a public debt. The proposal
was designed to develop American regionalism as a defense
against the rising tide of European imperialism, which was being
illustrated at that very time by the tripartite armed intervention
of Germany, Britain, and Italy in Venezuela.

Drago himself described his doctrine as an economic corollary
to the Monroe Doctrine. This made it a wholly new departure in
Argentine foreign policy. There was nothing new about Drago's
attack on intervention. From the beginning of independence all
Argentine statesmen had opposed intervention, and since the
1860's a noted Argentine jurist, Carlos Calvo, who was strongly
influenced by a leading North American jurist, Henry Wheaton,
had sought to circumscribe intervention by an interpretation of
international law known as the Calvo Doctrine. Here lay the
difference between the two Argentine doctrines, for Drago
conceived his doctrine, not in the universal terms of international
law, but as an exclusively regional American policy, and he
stressed his doctrine's severance of the American system from the
European system by tying it to the Monroe Doctrine. This was
indeed a new departure in the foreign policy of a country which
had hitherto been cool towards both the Monroe Doctrine and
American regionalism.

If Drago's idea had been carried out, the whole history of
inter-American relations in the decades ahead might have been
different; but that was not to be. The United States first
rebuffed him and his own government then reversed him. After
replying noncommittally to his proposal early in 1903, the United

States came forward in 1904 with its own solution of the problem of European intervention, the Roosevelt Corollary. In 1906 the Argentine government (of which Drago was no longer a member) held that his endorsement of the Monroe Doctrine was in conflict with the country's settled foreign policy, and in 1907, in the Second International Peace Conference at The Hague, it joined with the majority in turning an emasculated version of his regional doctrine into the very thing he had all along insisted it should never be, a rule of international law. Appropriately enough, the Argentine spokesman on the latter occasion was the universalist Roque Sáenz Peña.

Yet down to World War I, relations with the United States were not in the least disturbed by this reversal of Drago's American regionalism, and in some ways they improved. The new "Yankee imperialism" operated mainly in the Caribbean and stopped far short of Argentina. The Pan-American customs union project, defeated in 1890, was not revived, and by 1906 the Pan-American movement had been rendered innocuous in Argentine eyes; as Secretary of State Elihu Root defined its purposes in a famous speech at the Rio de Janeiro Conference in the latter year, it had been reduced to little more than a series of periodic good-will gatherings. So coöperative had Argentina now become that the next Pan-American conference, in 1910, was held in Buenos Aires; but to the people of that country it was only a side show to the main attraction, the centenary celebration of Argentine independence.

About the same time the Taft administration took advantage of a naval arms race in South America to try to draw Argentina and her neighbors closer to the United States through battleship diplomacy. As a part of the effort, the American ministers in Buenos Aires and the neighboring capitals were instructed to assist United States firms in obtaining arms contracts. Contacts with the Argentine Navy were also cultivated from this time forth, and with such good results that within the next generation a particularly friendly attitude towards the United States had been built up in Argentine naval circles. On the other hand, from this same period dates the Germanization of the larger and politically more important Argentine Army; it began in 1912.

The naval race just mentioned wrecked a promising peace movement that Argentina and Chile had started in 1902 by their *Pactos de Mayo*, so-called because they were concluded in the month of May. Besides settling long-standing boundary disputes, one of the pacts, which provided for the limitation of naval armaments, was warmly praised by Secretary of State Stimson in 1930 as the first treaty of its kind in modern history.

In commemoration of the May Pacts and as an earnest of perpetual peace, the now famous statue of the Christ of the Andes was erected on the frontier between Argentina and Chile in 1904. Unfortunately, in this very same year, Brazil, imitating the great powers, started an ambitious program of naval construction. Argentina and Chile promptly canceled their naval limitation agreement of 1902 and the race was on.

Before too much harm was done, however, the statesmen of the three countries turned from rivalry to coöperation and formed the A.B.C. bloc. For Argentina, this involved no conflict with previous policies, since it rested not on a triple alliance but an entente cordiale, and was aimed at peace, not war. Appropriately, the best-remembered action of this bloc is its mediation between Mexico and the United States in Woodrow Wilson's first administration.* Nevertheless, other South American states saw in it a potential menace to themselves; Peru protested strongly against its exclusive character; and it soon lost its vitality under the tensions produced by the First World War.

4. IRIGOYEN AND WORLD WAR I

When that war divided most of Europe against itself and ended forever the century-old Pax Britannica that had been so advantageous to Argentina, the government at Buenos Aires showed that it loved peace more than it did Britain by remaining neutral throughout the conflict. It did so first under a Conserva-

---

* Through no fault of its own, the A.B.C. bloc's mediation was not very productive. See Howard Cline, *The United States and Mexico* (Cambridge, Mass., 1953), pp. 160–162.

tive government and then, after 1916, under the country's first Radical president, Hipólito Irigoyen.

Since all the other American republics likewise remained neutral until 1917, no serious question has been raised about Argentina's doing so. From that day to this, however, there has been sharp controversy about Irigoyen's resolute adherence to neutrality after the United States and half the Latin American states entered the war against Germany and several more Latin American states severed diplomatic relations with the latter. The three main points at issue may be summed up in the propositions that Irigoyen's policy was unpopular in Argentina, that it was pro-German and hostile to the United States, and that it was isolationist. The evidence does not sustain any of them, at least without extensive qualification; but they have been widely accepted and have continued to influence opinion and policy in both the United States and Argentina down to the present, and particularly during World War II.

That Irigoyen's neutrality policy was unpopular in Argentina is certainly not true, if this is taken to mean that the majority of Argentines wanted to enter the war against Germany. The most that any responsible political group demanded was the severance of diplomatic relations with Germany. Even on this issue Irigoyen, who opposed such a rupture, apparently had the majority on his side.

Evidence in support of the belief that Irigoyen was pro-German is lacking. There is much more evidence for the thesis, advanced thirty years ago by Percy Alvin Martin, that he was simply pro-Argentine. This of course raises the question of what "pro-Argentine" meant to Irigoyen. The answer is that it connoted two kinds of policy, one domestic, the other foreign. The domestic policy was uppermost in his mind. Though he never had a systematic program, he had come into office promising to put an end to the exploitation of the people by the oligarchy, and he feared that embroilment in the war would prevent his doing so. Moreover, Irigoyen was an anti-imperialist, and in his view the major imperialist threat to the Argentine nation came from Great Britain in unholy alliance with Argentina's own selfish and traitorous oligarchy. Accordingly, as the United States minister to Buenos Aires, F. J. Stimson, reported in 1918, one reason for Irigoyen's determined adherence to neutrality was his fear that the defeat of Germany would leave Argentina at the mercy of a British monopoly of her commerce and finance.

Irigoyen was not an isolationist, but his internationalism was of a kind which has had few admirers in the United States. He favored Argentina's coöperation regionally with other Latin American nations, and with the world at large in the right kind of League of Nations, but not in the Pan-American system or with the United States. His attitude towards the latter had in it something of antagonism towards a rising imperialist power, but much more of a determination not to let Argentina become a tail to Uncle Sam's Pan-American kite.

Accordingly, after the United States broke with Germany, Irigoyen twice tried in 1917 to hold Latin American conferences in Buenos Aires — one, a conference of neutrals, the other, a conference of both neutrals and belligerents, and both without the participation of the United States. Both failed, partly because the United States used its influence to defeat them. He had better success with the traditionally Argentine policy of bilateralism, for he established a close coöperation with Chile, which contributed, first, to defeating Woodrow Wilson's projected Pan-American Pact, and then to maintaining the neutrality of the two nations from 1917 to the end of the war. The spirit of their neutrality, however, does not appear to have been definitely either anti-United States or pro-German. Rather, as Dana G. Munro pointed out at that time, their chief motive was "their desire to compel recognition of their importance as world powers" and obtain the maximum advantage from their position as the strongest of the non-European neutrals.

When the war was over, Irigoyen put Argentina into the League of Nations as soon as that was established; but her active participation in it was terminated almost at once because certain amendments proposed in accordance with long-standing Argentine policies were not adopted. One of these would have opened membership in the League to all states, including Germany; but the one whose rejection probably rankled most was an amendment establishing the absolute equality of all member states by depriving the great powers of their privileged position in the League Council. Equal status for Argentina with the greatest powers was Irigoyen's *sine qua non*. Not until 1932, after he and his Radical Party had been ousted, did Argentina resume active participation in the League.

5. THE INTERWAR YEARS

From 1920, when the postwar world began to take definite shape, to the outbreak of another world war in 1939, relations between the United States and Argentina were characterized for the most part by themes that had become familiar by this time. Since most of the variations were introduced after 1929, as well as two new themes that sharpened the growing discord between the two countries, we shall discuss this second half of the interwar period more fully than the first. The focus of our discussion will be the so-called Inter-American System, which, though still far from systematic at the end of the period and though enjoying little more than nominal support from Argentina at any time, had nevertheless achieved sufficient importance by the 1930's to make it a touchstone of that country's relations with the United States.

During the 1920's their relations continued to present the familiar picture of similar policies and conflicting interests. Both followed a policy of modified isolationism. Their positions with regard to the League of Nations were much the same: the United States was not a member of the League, Argentina was a completely inactive member; and when at the end of the decade the United States moved towards a kind of coöperation with the League, Argentina soon resumed active membership in it. Likewise, their attitudes towards the Pan-American movement were much alike: both wished this to remain, as it had been before World War I, a narrowly circumscribed movement, completely nonmilitary and almost completely nonpolitical. Neither government sought to develop it into a regional security system.

The United States did not revive Woodrow Wilson's Pan-American Pact, and joined with Argentina in throwing cold water on a project for an American League of Nations first proposed by the President of Uruguay, Baltasar Brum, in 1920, and presented by the Uruguayan delegation to the Fifth Inter-American (or Pan-American) Conference at Santiago, Chile, in 1923.

Because of their conflicting interests, the applications of their similar policies did not often produce agreements such as this between Washington and Buenos Aires, and most of the major developments of the 1920's broadened the area of disagreement. As much the smaller and weaker power, Argentina was far more keenly aware of the importance of these developments. From her point of view, they added up to a rapidly growing threat of Yankee imperialism. The preponderance of power of the United States in the Western Hemisphere had already been sharply increased by the opening of the fortified Panama Canal in 1914 and by World War I, which weakened or for a time even eliminated some of the chief rivals of the United States in Latin America. The preponderance was further increased by the great-power naval agreements reached at the Washington Conference in 1922. These agreements formed "the concluding page of a revolutionary chapter in the annals of sea power and world politics," * for they ushered in a "new order of sea power," which replaced the old order of British world supremacy with a regional distribution of sea power. The region assigned to the United States was the Western Hemisphere.

The use that the United States made of its growing power in the 1920's — particularly its armed interventions in the Caribbean region — gave great offense to Latin Americans generally, and perhaps most of all to Argentina, long a leader of the anti-interventionist movement in that part of the world. Argentina herself was not threatened with intervention, but during this decade she felt the force of Yankee imperialism in a form that many of her people, and especially the Radicals who now controlled her government, regarded as no less dangerous — that of economic

* Harold and Margaret Sprout, *Toward a New Order of Sea Power* (Princeton, 1940), p. 278.

penetration. The investments of the United States in South America grew with vertiginous rapidity after 1920, and in 1929 they were larger in Argentina than in any other South American country, amounting to some $611,000,000, as compared with only $40,000,000 in 1913.* Moreover, the United States had forged ahead of Britain as the chief source of Argentine imports, but lagged far behind Britain as a buyer of Argentine exports, with the result that, to the great displeasure of the Argentines, their country had an "unfavorable" balance of more than $200,000,000 a year in its trade with the United States in the 1920's. To cap the climax, beginning in 1927, the United States excluded Argentina's beef on the ground of the existence of the hoof and mouth disease in that country. This sanitary measure, which was also protectionist in the economic sense, injured the pride of the Argentine nation at large as well as the pocketbooks of the country's beef barons, and has never ceased to be a sore spot in the relations between the two countries.

Early in the year following the imposition of this offensive measure, the Sixth Inter-American Conference was held at Havana. Mounting Latin American resentment against Yankee imperialism exploded at this conference, which is generally regarded as marking the nadir of the Pan-American movement. Argentina did not lag behind the rest in making things hot for the Colossus of the North. With a bilious eye on the hoof-and-mouth regulation, her chief delegate, Honorio Pueyrredón, demanded that the draft of a Pan-American charter then under consideration be amended to prohibit economic discrimination. The chief United States delegate, Charles Evans Hughes, replied that the introduction of issues of this kind into the Pan-American system would wreck it. Pueyrredón refused to sign and, though his government overruled him, it never ratified the charter.

On balance, the major developments during the Depression Decade that began in 1929 widened the gap between Washington and Buenos Aires. In both countries, as elsewhere, the depression

* Max Winkler, *Investments of United States Capital in Latin America* (Boston, 1928), pp. 275, 278. Other authorities give somewhat different figures.

stimulated political and economic nationalism, sharpened existing differences, and led to the adoption of measures — such as Argentina's Roca-Runciman agreement of 1933 with Britain — which created new grounds for disagreement. In Argentina, the restored Conservatives promptly revived the foreign policy of a universalism oriented towards Europe, without in the least relaxing the pretensions of the preceding Radical administration to Argentine leadership in South America; in both respects the policy was antagonistic to a vigorous Pan-Americanism. Yet almost at once the United States, under Franklin Roosevelt, launched a new Pan-Americanism, which was not only much more vigorous than the old one, but also of much broader scope.* At first this produced a result which was highly pleasing to Argentina — the triumph of absolute nonintervention; but the United States thereupon began to press hard for the development of the loose-jointed inter-American association into a regional security system.

Save for Woodrow Wilson's brief, abortive experiment with a Pan-American Pact, this was a new departure in the foreign policy of the United States; it was also one of the two new themes of Argentine–North American disagreement introduced during this decade. The other theme was the rise of the Axis threat, which to many Argentines was not a threat, but a promise. By the end of 1940, irritation had grown into a profound antagonism, which was to last for a dozen years; and during this time Argentina remained the Number One problem of the United States in Latin America, until at last, in 1953, it was displaced by the rise of a communist-controlled regime in Guatemala.

The first Inter-American Conference of the Depression Decade was held at Montevideo in 1933. It reflected some of the great changes that had taken place in the five years since the unhappy Havana Conference of 1928. Now the United States itself, through its chief delegate, Secretary of State Cordell Hull, intro-

*This is not to deny the well-known fact that in some important respects the Good Neighbor policy had been anticipated in the Hoover administration and even earlier.

duced a Pan-American declaration in favor of lowering trade barriers, and signed another one against intervention.

Argentina welcomed this shift, but she too had recently changed her position by resuming active membership in the League of Nations and tightening her economic bonds with Britain. Her policies, shaped mainly by the beef-baron conservatives and allied professional groups, were prosecuted with vigor and skill in the next six years by Foreign Minister Carlos Saavedra Lamas, a son-in-law of Roque Sáenz Peña and, in the opinion of Sumner Welles, "one of the ablest statesmen produced in the Western Hemisphere in our generation." Since these policies were pro-British and universalist when they were not aimed at Argentine hegemony in Latin America, they necessarily conflicted with the new Pan-Americanism now sponsored by Washington. Ambassador Robert Woods Bliss reported to Washington in February 1933 that Saavedra Lamas regarded the United States as "the principal obstacle" to his plan for a Latin American union under Argentine leadership. "While I do not think he is, *per se*, anti-American in sentiment," continued Bliss, "he follows the line of others in endeavoring to counteract what he considers the preponderant influence of the United States throughout America" and in opposing the Pan-American projects of the United States "as the most effective way of guiding Argentina to the fore."

At the Montevideo Conference the divergence between Washington and Buenos Aires was hidden by a horse trade. In return for Hull's partial abandonment of intervention and his support of a universalist Peace Pact fathered by Saavedra Lamas, the latter supported the declaration in favor of lowering trade barriers proposed by Hull. As a result, in sharp contrast to Havana, Montevideo turned into a love-feast, with Hull and Saavedra Lamas playing Damon and Pythias.

Outside the conference, however, the rivalry of their governments continued. Among other things, it contributed to delaying the termination of the Chaco War then in progress between Argentina's neighbors, Paraguay and Bolivia. Both the United

States and Argentina sought to restore peace, but in different ways, the former favoring at the outset Pan-American procedures, and the latter those of the League of Nations. Ultimately these two would-be peacemakers got together with four other American governments, nominally under League of Nations auspices, and arranged an armistice in June 1935. Another three years elapsed before the final peace treaty was arranged by a Peace Commission representing the same six neutral powers; by that time Saavedra Lamas was out of office. The Commission sat at Buenos Aires, and the head of the United States delegation was Spruille Braden, who was to return to the Argentine capital in 1945 on another diplomatic mission, but under very different circumstances.

At the next Inter-American conference, which met at Buenos Aires in 1936, the divergence between Washington and Buenos Aires was brought out into the open and widened. Saavedra Lamas, who had just served as President of the League of Nations Assembly and had just been awarded the Nobel Peace Prize, was more sure of himself than ever before and more than ever the universalist. On the other hand, the United States, alarmed by the mounting threat of totalitarian aggression, sought to strengthen the defenses of the New World by giving the Inter-American System political and military functions. Its specific proposals were tinged with hemispheric isolationism. As made by Secretary Hull, who again headed its delegation, these included a binding commitment of reciprocal assistance in case of an attack by a non-American power, new Inter-American machinery to implement this pledge, and the Pan-Americanization of neutrality legislation just adopted by the United States with a view to keeping it out of the approaching war in Europe.

Though the concession begun at Montevideo in 1933 was now completed at Buenos Aires by the United States' acceptance of an absolute ban on intervention, Hull found Saavedra Lamas not coöperative, as at Montevideo, but hostile. He could hardly have been otherwise, for Hull's first two proposals ran counter to Argentine foreign policies, current and past, and his third proposal, an isolationist neutrality, would have exposed Argentina to greater economic losses than any other American nation in case of war in Europe, for Argentina was dependent in an exceptionally high degree upon her trade with Europe. The Argentines were all for neutrality and they adhered to it, as did the United States, throughout the Spanish Civil War, which broke out six months before the opening of the Buenos Aires conference and lasted until 1939. What they objected to at Buenos Aires was the kind of neutrality proposed by the United States.

National interest aside, most readers will probably agree that Saavedra Lamas was right in opposing Hull on this point. The neutrality legislation in question was an expression of the isolationism then rampant in the United States. Few, if any, now believe isolation to have been a sound policy, whether on a national or a Pan-American scale, and the United States itself was to abandon it only four years later.

In the end, the Buenos Aires conference rejected Hull's neutrality policy and adopted a watered-down version of his first two proposals, in the form of a provision for inter-American consultation in case of an attack on any American nation by a non-American nation. With enormous exaggeration, commentators in the United States hailed this as Pan-Americanizing the Monroe Doctrine, through the creation of a hemisphere defense system. Argentines knew that it had done nothing of the sort and that their government, like all the rest, had committed itself to do nothing more than consult. Sumner Welles, a member of the delegation, appraised the action more coolly, but still hopefully, as providing a starting-point for the creation of a hemisphere defense system.

Hull, however, took a gloomy view of the results of the conference, which fell far below his expectations. Apparently unable to understand either his easy success at Montevideo or his inability to repeat it now, he came away from Buenos Aires feeling that Saavedra Lamas had failed him, and henceforth he looked on all Argentine governments with a jaundiced eye. His views, communicated to some of his associates and to many others in the

United States, were to be an important factor in the growing discord between Washington and Buenos Aires in the next decade.

So also were the very different, if not opposite, views disseminated by Pan-American optimists during and shortly after the conference. As a result, opinion in the United States tended to polarize about two answers, both wrong, to what was coming to be commonly referred to as the Argentine problem. One view was that the Argentine government's recalcitrance towards Pan-Americanism did not represent Argentine public opinion, which, given time, would force it to become a good neighbor. Time proved this view wrong. The other was that the Argentine government was responding to a new and sinister force, Nazi-Fascism. Documents subsequently published show that this response did not actually begin until 1940. In the meanwhile, the Buenos Aires government was simply following a traditionally Argentine policy, for Argentine reasons; and it appears to have done so with the approval of the majority of the Argentine people.

This policy was reminiscent of Rivadavia's when in 1825 he reluctantly agreed to take part in the Panama Congress. On both occasions the government's decision was dictated by a desire to avoid an open rift with the majority of the Latin American states, who were supporting the development of a regional security system; but also on both occasions the government was determined not to let lip-service lead to unwelcome commitments. Accordingly, Argentina continued after 1936 to take part in the conferences that strengthened inter-American ties; but by 1943 she had ratified only four of the fifty-six treaties and conventions adopted up to that time, thus making herself, in S. F. Bemis' phrase, "easily the greatest non-ratifier of all time."

6. PRUDENT NEUTRALITY, 1939–1943

In the two years preceding the fall of France in June 1940, there was a slight improvement in the relations between the United States and Argentina, for the Argentine presidency was now held by the relatively liberal Roberto Ortiz, who was friendly to the United States. Indeed, though even specialists are unaware of the fact, an Argentine proposal, communicated to the United States in October 1938, was responsible for one of the chief measures taken at the Inter-American Conference held at Lima, Peru, the following December. This was the authorization of meetings of American foreign ministers as a new form of consultation to deal with emergencies. The measure was in line with a proposal made by Hull at Buenos Aires in 1936, but the Argentines got no credit in the United States for their concession. They themselves were partly to blame. At Lima they talked as if the Axis menace were a mare's nest and opposed taking further steps to meet it. Their delegation was pointedly made up of second-rate figures, the Foreign Minister did not deign to head it, and after putting in a brief appearance at the beginning of the conference, went off on a vacation. When impatient Pan-Americanists in the United States, disappointed by the results obtained at Lima, unjustly called the conference a failure, they also unjustly laid the blame for the failure on Argentina.

Relations between the two governments took a turn for the better at the first of the new meetings of foreign ministers, which was held at Panama in September and October 1939, just after the beginning of World War II. Though the United States, represented by Sumner Welles, still maintained its leadership, Argentina was pleased by the results. That, however, was mainly because the meeting in effect made neutrality a Pan-American policy on terms which, unlike those proposed in 1936, would not automatically cut off Argentina's foreign trade, and because the United States promised extensive aid to Latin American countries whose economies were upset by the war.

The old antagonism broke out afresh when, after the fall of France, the United States unilaterally abandoned the neutrality affirmed at Panama and became the "arsenal of democracy" which supplied arms through Lend-Lease to the enemies of the Axis. But Washington's policy revolution was gradual and at first unavowed, and it had not taken visible shape when, to deal with the new emergency, the second Meeting of American Foreign Ministers was held at Havana in July 1940. Here the emphasis was still on keeping America out of the war and the war out of America; and that suited Argentina perfectly.

Two major measures were adopted at the Havana meeting: (1) The transfer of the American possessions of European powers (France, Netherlands, Britain) to any other power was prohibited and provision was made for inter-American administration of such possessions in case of need. Argentina took this occasion to reassert her claim to the Falkland Islands and made it clear that if Britain fell, these islands would pass into Argentine, not inter-American, control. (2) Inter-American security arrangements were strengthened by a convention stipulating that the signatories (one of whom was Argentina) would regard an attack on one American nation as an attack on all. This went far beyond the previous stipulation for mere consultation, and yet it fell short of constituting a treaty of alliance because, among other things, it did not define the obligations of the parties to it. It therefore left open a wide area of interpretation about which honest men could disagree.

In the year and a half from the Havana meeting to the Japanese attack on Pearl Harbor, disagreement between Argentina and the United States became acute as the latter developed an unneutral policy of aid to the enemies of the Axis which many Argentines regarded as inviting the attack that would bring the Havana convention into force. Even Argentines who hoped for the defeat of the Axis were unwilling, as Irigoyen had been, to have their country dragged into the war as a tail to the Washington kite. Two prudential considerations reinforced this feeling. For one thing, it was widely believed that Hitler was likely to win the war (the period of his greatest power coincided precisely with this transition period from July 1940 to December 1941) and that if he won, he would inflict severe reprisals on the nations that had opposed him; whereas no such reprisals were feared from the anti-Axis powers in case they should win. In the second place, it was well known in Argentina that high authorities in the United States were so doubtful of their country's ability to defend the whole Western Hemisphere that they were advocating a "quarter-sphere" system of defense which would stop at the hump or bulge of Brazil, thus leaving Argentina to defend herself unaided.

In addition to all this, the long illness of pro-democratic President Ortiz (who finally resigned in June 1942) placed the direction of Argentine foreign policy in this critical period in the hands of Acting President Ramón Castillo. Pro-Axis himself, Castillo had in his key cabinet post, the Ministry of War, the even more strongly pro-Axis General Pedro Ramírez; and both men were deeply impressed by the propaganda which Hitler's agents in Madrid poured out of Franco Spain under the Hispanidad label. Both believed that Argentina's national interests would be best served by a policy of prudent neutrality, since this would give her, a minor power, the maximum degree of security in the world-wide conflict of giants and would enable her to extract the maximum advantage from it for her economy, which was based to an exceptionally high degree upon international trade. Finally, this issue of foreign policy had become deeply involved in party politics. The opposition parties, Radical and Socialist, who had control of the lower house of Congress, were using it to pillory Castillo's neutrality policy, so that his abandonment of it would be a political victory for them.

Castillo was firmly set on this course when the Japanese attack on Pearl Harbor on December 7, 1941, and the German declaration of war two days later, brought the United States fully into the conflict as a belligerent. Except to draw secretly closer to the Axis, Castillo did not materially alter his course in the remaining year and a half of his administration.

His first response to the Pearl Harbor attack contrasted sharply with the quick expressions of solidarity with the United States that came from the majority of the Latin American states. These ranged all the way from the freezing of Axis funds, through the severance of diplomatic relations, to declarations of war by nine of them before the end of the month. Castillo, on the other hand, merely accorded the United States the status of nonbelligerency (December 13), which carried with it certain practical advantages, such as greater freedom in the use of Argentine ports than

belligerent status would have permitted; but by the same decree
he reaffirmed Argentina's neutrality. Three days later he proclaimed a state of siege, thereby suspending constitutional guarantees, for the declared purpose of enabling the government to
"fulfill its international obligations" and suppress "tendentious
propaganda." Where Castillo's sympathies lay was indicated by
the fact that his first action under this decree, taken the very next
day, was to cancel a mass meeting which had been called "to pay
tribute to President Roosevelt and reaffirm the devotion of the
Argentine people to the democratic cause."

While the Argentine government was in the minority in Latin
America, it did not stand alone. This was made clear when a
showdown came at the third emergency Meeting of American
Foreign Ministers, called just after Pearl Harbor and held at Rio
de Janeiro in the second half of January 1942. When it assembled,
several countries besides Argentina had not severed relations with
the Axis powers. The United States, represented by Under Secretary of State Sumner Welles, pressed hard for a resolution making
the severance obligatory. Strenuous opposition was offered by
the Argentine representative, Foreign Minister Enrique Ruiz
Guiñazú, and after a hard fight he succeeded in getting the
resolution made merely recommendatory.

Welles committed the United States to the resolution in this
form, and the scene of battle was thereupon shifted to the State
Department. Secretary Hull, who had not been consulted and
was highly displeased, called Welles by telephone from the
White House, with President Roosevelt listening in, and a
spirited colloquy ensued. Hull accused the Under Secretary of
violating his instructions and making a weak-kneed surrender to
Argentina. The latter countered with a vigorous defense, the
essence of which was that insistence on an obligatory resolution
would have split the conference wide open, since Argentina
would not have been alone in rejecting it, but would have been
joined by several other Latin American governments, including
two of the most important, Brazil and Chile. President Roosevelt,
after vainly essaying the role of peacemaker, finally terminated

the conversation with the remark that no useful purpose would
be served by continuing it.

This episode has been recorded here because it had an important bearing on the future development of relations between
the United States and Argentina. It contributed to widening the
gap between Hull and Welles, and so to the resignation of the
latter, which came in 1943 just after the overthrow of Castillo's
government had opened a still more critical phase of the controversy between the two governments. The episode also sharpened the dichotomy between the two different approaches to the
Argentine problem represented by these two men—Welles, who
believed that in the long run the best results would be obtained
by patience, persuasion, and, when unavoidable, by concession
and compromise in the interest of unanimity; and Hull, whose
opinion of the fractiousness of Argentine governments was
strengthened by this episode and who regarded the compromise
resolution as an escape clause which would facilitate Argentina's
evasion of her inter-American obligations.

From the end of the Rio de Janeiro meeting of foreign ministers on January 28, 1942, to the overthrow of Castillo on June 4,
1943, the latter adhered tenaciously to his policy of "prudent
neutrality." His neutrality was now only nominal; it had become
in fact definitely pro-Axis. Castillo tried secretly to obtain arms
from Germany, mainly on the ground that Argentina's refusal to
join in the war effort against Germany had put her in danger of
attack from other American countries, particularly Brazil. Only
one other Latin American country, Chile, remained neutral, and
Chile was more genuinely so than Argentina. At the end of the
year even the British Foreign Office, whose handling of the
Argentine problem as a rule was gingerly through these years,
issued a statement deploring Argentina's continuance of relations
with "the enemies of humanity," whereupon the publication of
the statement in that country was prohibited.

Aside from tightening its bonds with Franco Spain, the Castillo
government's foreign policy was otherwise chiefly notable for its
rivalry with Brazil for influence in the border countries of Para-

guay and Bolivia. Castillo did not, however, bestir himself sufficiently in regard to the balance of power with Brazil to suit the
nation's impatient armed forces. As far back as 1937 Argentine
sensitiveness on this subject had been expressed in Foreign
Minister Saavedra Lamas' vociferous public protest against a
projected transfer of six over-age destroyers from the United
States to Brazil, on the ground that this would upset the South
American balance of power. Now the war lords of Buenos Aires
fumed as Lend-Lease military aid from the United States poured
into Brazil, but was of course withheld from uncoöperative
Argentina which likewise failed to obtain arms from Germany
because the German General Staff advised that they could not
be spared. The Army's anger over this situation, together with the
catastrophic decline of Argentine political morale described in an
earlier chapter, led to the coup that overthrew Castillo on June 4,
1943.

6. How Perón Came to Power

As an actor in the tragedy has said, President Castillo encouraged the propagation of German Nazism, Italian Fascism, Spanish Falangism, and Argentina's own Rosas cult; this mélange produced the military dictatorship of 1943; and the dictatorship's first victim was Castillo himself.

Colonel Juan Perón was a member of the conspiratorial band of nineteen Army officers calling itself the G.O.U.,* whose revolt on June 4, 1943 overthrew Castillo, established the dictatorship, and thus ushered in the regime that bears Perón's name. During the first two years there was a bitter struggle for power within the regime, as well as between it and its many enemies at home and abroad. Though Perón emerged at the top, it is a moot question whether he was there from the start or whether, at first, he was only a minor member of the G.O.U. The present writer takes the latter view, if only because Perón was outranked by several members of this rank-conscious group of German-trained officers.

However that may be, Perón finally won this battle royal by revolutionizing the revolution of 1943 and giving it a social content that won him the passionate devotion of the Argentine

* G.O.U. stood both for *Grupo de Oficiales Unidos* (Group of United Officers) and the group's slogan, *Gobierno, Orden, Unión* (Government, Order, Union).

underdogs. On the now-famous October 17, 1945, their support enabled him to snatch victory from defeat in one of the most amazing political recoveries of modern times. Towards midnight on this spring day — in Argentina, October is the season of renewal — an immense crowd in the Plaza de Mayo cheered themselves hoarse as the President of the Argentine nation, General Edelmiro Farrell, appeared on the balcony of the Casa Rosada with Perón in a ceremony that symbolized the advent to power of their hero miraculously brought back from the underworld. From this time forth, Perón was the master of Argentina.

There is a mythical quality about this man's story. In his case the myth owed its power to the fact that it responded to an imperious need in the hearts of the Argentine underdogs — a fact which his cynical manipulation of their loyalty cannot obscure. They had long felt the need of a leader, a redeemer, and a generation earlier they thought they had found one in Irigoyen; but in his old age Irigoyen failed them, and with the fickleness of mobs they turned against him — only to be scourged for their inconstancy with another dozen years of domination by the hated oligarchy. Now Perón promised them a second chance, and this time they would not let it slip. How Perón gained their loyalty and thereby won the struggle for power is the subject of the present chapter.

1. YOUNG PERÓN

As Daniel Webster said that his whole life had been a preparation for his famous "reply to Hayne," so Perón and his admirers would have us believe that Perón's whole life had been a preparation for his harangue to the underdogs on the crucial October 17, 1945, which sealed his victory and theirs. The truth of this proposition is more obvious in relation to his family background and his training for command than to his program of social revolution. Since his family was far from prominent, some of the facts regarding his background and early life are easier to argue about than to ascertain. The following sketch is drawn from the canonical version.

Born on October 8, 1895, in the town of Lobos, Province of Buenos Aires, and christened Juan Domingo a week later, Perón came of a family which belonged to the highly unstable Argentine middle class and which in its multi-national origins was typically Argentine, except that none of his forebears was a recent immigrant. The first Perón to settle in Argentina was his great-grandfather, an Italian. His mother's family was of Spanish origin; one line had been settled in Argentina for two generations, another since colonial times. There were also French Basques and Scots in the family tree.

The middle-class character of the family is shown by the fact that Juan's grandfather Perón was a physician, his father a justice of the peace, farmer, and sheep-raiser, and his first cousin a schoolteacher. But it was middle class with a difference. Juan's birthplace, Lobos, lies in a region made famous by the exploits of one of the last of the lawless gauchos, Juan Moreira, who was frequently befriended by Perón's grandparents before he was seized by the law. Afterwards, the boy Juan used to play games with Moreira's skull. Ultimately, what was left of it was donated to the famous historical museum at Luján, not far from Buenos Aires.

For several years after 1900 Juan's father tried his fortune — without much success — in the new sheep-raising country of Patagonia; but in 1904 the family returned to Buenos Aires and the boy was educated there, first in parochial schools and then in the International Polytechnic School.

In March 1911, at the age of fifteen, he embarked on his military career by entering the Colegio Militar, a kind of Argentine West Point, established by the schoolteacher-president Domingo Sarmiento. The choice was a natural one, for one of his uncles was an army officer and a cousin was instructor in the Army School of Gymnastics and Fencing. Robust, intelligent, and hardworking, Perón proved admirably adapted for a career that was being Germanized just as he entered it. The training of the Argentine Army by German officers began in 1911.

2. PREFACE TO POLITICS

Promotion was slow for Perón, as it was for everyone else, for Argentina had not fought a war since 1870, none was in prospect, and the Army was not expanding rapidly. Fifteen years after graduation, he was still only a captain at the time of General Uriburu's revolution in 1930, and although he was on the winning side,* his promotion to major did not come until the end of the next year. Five years later he moved up to lieutenant-colonel. From 1930 to 1935 he held the chair of military history in the Army War College and part of the time he was also aide to the Army Chief of Staff and the Minister of War. He next served two years (1936–1938) in Chile as military and air attaché. Ousted for espionage, he returned to Argentina and was given another teaching assignment, this time in the Naval War College. He was now forty-two and still only a lieutenant-colonel. Up to this point his career had been good but hardly brilliant.

Then came his great opportunity. In February 1939 he was sent to Italy to "perfect his studies" — military, of course. He was gone almost two years, remaining in Italy most of the time until December 1940, though he also visited Germany, France, Hungary, and Albania, and returned by way of Spain and Portugal to Argentina, where he arrived in January 1941.

Perón was an eyewitness of the great ovation given Mussolini in the Piazza Venezia when the Italian declaration of war was announced in June 1940. Though refused permission to visit the front, he trained extensively behind the lines with Italian Alpine troops. Some of his time was spent with his fellow Argentine officers who were in Italy in large numbers at this time; two of them, Generals Sosa Molina and Pistarini, were to play an important part in bringing into being the G.O.U. and the New Argentina of 1943 and after.

An admiring biographer tells us that while in Italy Perón found time for discussions of "art, literature, science and life" — his

* See above, p. 60.

command of Italian, French, and English, as well as Spanish, facilitated these. He also found time to study the fascist system and took extension courses on economics, sociology, and politics at the Universities of Bologna and Turin. He was a careful student, and more than that, he was an assiduous writer on military history and strategy, having published three books on these subjects before his trip to Europe.* In the 1920's he had studied history under one of the leading Argentine historians, Ricardo Levene. In 1937 he contributed an article on San Martín's famous crossing of the Andes in 1817 to the International Congress of the History of America, which met in Buenos Aires under the chairmanship of Levene. Shortly thereafter the latter engaged Perón to contribute several chapters to the monumental and scholarly *History of the Argentine Nation* (1936–1942) which Levene was then editing. Perón accepted, but his trip to Europe diverted his attention to other matters.

What lesson did he learn from his two years in Europe? His own answer was, "I learned what not to do." Common report had him add to his intimates, "I will do what Mussolini has done, without his mistakes." By the time Perón and the rest of the G.O.U. came to power in June 1943, it was clear that Mussolini's worst mistake had been his entry into the World War, for this had already brought him to the verge of ruin; within another three months he had been overthrown and Italy had surrendered.

What Spain taught Perón to avoid was civil war. On his brief visit to that country, the ravages of the recent Spanish civil war made the deepest impression upon him. After a week in dismal Madrid and a visit to the ruins of its University City and the pockmarked battlefields around it, he exclaimed, "God alone knows what anyone gained here!" During his rise to power in 1944–45 he threatened more than once to lead a mass revolt; but both then and later he always stopped his successive "turns of the screw" (his own phrase) just short of provoking civil strife.

---

* *El frente oriental de la guerra mundial de 1914. Estudios estratégicos* (1928); *Apuntes de historia militar* (1932–1933, 4 vols.); *Las operaciones en 1870* (1939).

In fact, it was not so much to the battle-scarred Franco regime as to the more peaceful Spanish dictatorship of Primo de Rivera in the 1920's that he was to look for guidance in and after 1943.

Finally, the unpopularity of the Germans in Italy had warned him to play down any Nazi elements in his own system. Like his fellow army officers for thirty years past, he took Germany as his military model, but his chief civilian foreign sources were Spain and Italy, the mother countries of the great majority of the Argentine people. He may also have been influenced by the example of the authoritarian regime of Getulio Vargas in neighboring Brazil.

We must be careful, however, not to exaggerate the extent of Perón's borrowings from abroad. These were heavy in matters of technique and organization, particularly in the fields of propaganda and control of labor; but he used them to strengthen a system deeply rooted in his understanding of the history of his own country and in his own observations of the successive regimes of Irigoyen, Uriburu, and the Conservative Restoration. He found in Rosas his slogan of discipline and order, and the strong-arm squads of the Mazorca to support it; in Rosas and Irigoyen a fervent nationalism spiced with anti-imperialism; in Irigoyen the popularity of attacks on the oligarchy; in Uriburu the Army's mission of national regeneration; and in the Conservative Restoration the demoralization of the chief political parties and the abandonment of laissez faire in favor of economic controls.

He also "learned what not to do" from Argentine as well as European experience. Failing to organize their civilian support, the tyrant Rosas and the democratic Irigoyen alike had been overthrown when the Army turned against them. The same failure had likewise wrecked the military dictatorship which ousted Irigoyen. Its chief, General Uriburu, was wedded to the idea of government by an élite, which understandably had a limited popular appeal, and the Army's regenerating mission soon ended in the transfer of power to the civilian neo-oligarchy.

After his return from Europe early in 1941, Perón had to wait nearly two and a half years before putting into practice the system he had assembled from Argentine and foreign sources. Promoted colonel at the end of 1941, he spent most of this interval with Argentine mountain troops in the Andes, far away from the nation's political capital; but as it turned out, the time was well spent politically, for among his closest associates in this period were Generals Edelmiro Farrell and José Humberto Sosa Molina. Like Perón, both generals had served in the Italy of Mussolini and they were leading members of the G.O.U.

3. THE 1943 COUP

Threatened with the perpetuation of the intolerable Castillo regime through the farce of an election scheduled for September,* the G.O.U. struck at dawn on June 4, 1943, with all the Army units of the big Campo de Mayo garrison behind them and also the Navy. In form as well as substance an exclusively military coup, this revolt was less popular than Uriburu's in 1930, but it was better organized among the armed forces. One of the conspirators was Castillo's own Minister of War, General Pedro Pablo Ramírez, who had served as a lieutenant in the German Army from 1911 to 1913. Though few civilians were enthusiastic about the coup, many of them acquiesced in it readily since they felt that almost anything would be better than a continuation of the Castillo regime. As the Socialist leader Enrique Dickmann later admitted, this view was taken even by a considerable fraction of his own party, which had suffered less from the current demoralization than the other parties.

The coup met with only sporadic resistance, which was quickly overcome. President Castillo resigned on June 5; and in the next two days the G.O.U. proceeded to consolidate its position by declaring martial law, setting up a Provisional government, dissolving Congress, and obtaining the Supreme Court's recognition of the Provisional Government as a *de facto* government in the same terms that this court had used in recognizing Uriburu's revolutionary regime in 1930.

Widely different statements of the objectives of the revolt were

* See above, p. 64.

contained in two manifestoes, one circulated secretly among Army officers three weeks in advance (May 13, 1943) and the other published to the world at large on the day of the coup. Leading features of the former were the redeeming mission of the Army at home, Argentine hegemony in South America, and admiration for the Hitlerian techniques that combined armed might with thought control. On the other hand, the public manifesto of June 4 represented the armed forces to be mere agents of the restoration of civic virtue, constitutional guarantees, and loyal inter-American coöperation.

Critics of the new regime have treated the manifesto of May 13 as a true exposition and that of June 4 as mere camouflage. Actually, both manifestoes must be taken into account in assessing the aims of the revolutionists. If the result is confusion, this only underlines one of the most important facts about the coup, which is that there actually was confusion among its leaders arising out of the deep disagreements among them over its objectives.

On one thing only were they all agreed: that the armed forces must be built up speedily. As measured by the national budget, this was done to perfection in the next two years. Figures published in 1946 by the State Department in Washington showed that from 1941 to 1945 Argentine military expenditures were multiplied more than fourfold and increased their share of the total national expenditures from 22 per cent to 50 per cent.

Otherwise, almost none of these military men seems to have known just what to do with their control of the government, or how to do it. Perón was an outstanding exception and the internecine conflict within the G.O.U. opened his way to power by eliminating some of the early leaders who stood in his path. It also created an unstable equilibrium between opposing forces in the Army and Navy which Perón upset in his own favor by building up an outside force of his own — his civilian "army" of workingmen.

The struggle within the regime involved both personalities and policies, domestic as well as foreign. The first outward sign of discord was the forced resignation of the first provisional president, General Arturo Rawson, within forty-eight hours of the coup and before he had even had time to take the oath of office. He was replaced by Castillo's ex-minister of war, General Ramírez, who held on for eight months and then was ousted in favor of Perón's friend, General Farrell.

There also soon occurred an apparent change of heart in the G.O.U. about the length of its tenure of power. Its revolutionary manifesto of June 4 portrayed the armed forces as the restorers of the rights and liberties of the Argentine people, and on June 7 Provisional President Ramírez took an oath of office which committed him to "the re-establishment of the Constitution in full force" and "the strengthening of the republican institutions" of Argentina.

Eight days later, however, Ramírez, quoting St. Thomas Aquinas and Pope Pius XII on the duty of living together in peace and order, declared that what the Argentine people wanted was justice, not elections, and accordingly announced that, although there would be elections in due course, it was too early to talk about them yet. After another three days he issued two decrees that implemented this idea: one removed the word "provisional" from the title of the Provisional Government; the other suspended indefinitely the presidential elections scheduled for September 5, 1943. The Provisional Government began to look like the man who came to dinner.

The new government, no longer provisional, was made up almost exclusively of military men. Its only civilian member of cabinet rank was the minister of finance, Jorge Santamarina, a well-known banker. The hypersensitive ministry of war was held by General Farrell, who made Perón the head of the ministry's secretariat.

There was a shift in foreign as well as domestic policy. In the manifesto of June 4 the new regime had pledged itself to "give effect to an absolute, true, and loyal American union and collaboration" and to comply with Argentina's international obligations. That may have been said with tongue in cheek and only for the purpose of facilitating recognition by foreign governments. At any rate, after this was promptly accorded (by Bolivia, Brazil, Chile, and Ecuador on June 9, and by Great Britain, the United States, and most of the remaining American governments on June

11), strong opposition to effective fulfillment of the promise developed within the regime. The first stage of the internecine conflict over this point ended with an exchange of notes between the foreign minister, Admiral Segundo Storni, and Secretary of State Cordell Hull. Storni dispatched an extraordinary note to Washington, in which he said in effect that his government would after all keep this promise only on condition that the United States extend to Argentina the Lend-Lease aid which had hitherto been withheld from it but given to Brazil, thereby, Storni complained, upsetting the balance of power in South America. Hull replied in a scathing note that the United States took no part in balance of power politics in South America and would consider the question of military and other aid to Argentina after the new regime had fulfilled its overdue obligations to aid in the war effort against the Axis.

The two notes were published in both Buenos Aires and Washington on September 6, 1943, and in the former capital the reaction to the rebuff administered by Hull produced far-reaching consequences. Foreign Minister Storni, who had laid his government open to it, was forced out of office; the elements in the regime who were opposed to inter-American coöperation gained the upper hand; and the civilian nationalists who had flocked to the support of the military dictatorship had a field day. Anti-Semitism flourished, religious (that is, Catholic) instruction was made compulsory in the schools, the political parties were dissolved, and the restrictions on freedom of speech and assembly were tightened up. It began to look like a repetition of Uriburu — a government by an élite, a regimented society, open hostility to democratic institutions and processes, including the Sáenz Peña Law of 1912, with the addition of Nazi motifs developed since 1931, such as racism and systematic thought control.

4. PERÓN, LABOR, AND SOCIAL REVOLUTION

In the following month, however, occurred another event, which, though little noticed at the time, was to prove far more important than any of these and was to give a very different development to the revolution from that planned by the civilian nationalists. This was the appointment of Perón as head of the Department of Labor and Social Security (October 27, 1943). The post was an apparently minor one, and did not even carry cabinet rank, for the Department was merely a subdivision of the Ministry of Interior.

Without surrendering his place in the Ministry of War, Perón immediately began to increase the importance of his new post. On December 1 he got his department raised to an independent secretariat, which gave him cabinet rank. What is even more to the point, he had already begun to make vigorous use of his powers with a view to regimenting Argentine labor in support of the regime. Resistance on the part of the established labor unions was discouraged by the arrest on October 28 of forty-eight of their leaders; new unions were set up to take care of the hitherto unorganized workers, who constituted the great majority of the labor force; and lavish promises of higher wages, social security, and other benefits were made to the coöperative members of both groups.

Thus by December 1943 Perón had formulated and begun to carry out the policy of social and economic revolution in the interest of the Argentine underdogs that was to become one of the most characteristic features of his regime. This was apparently some months before he first met Eva Duarte,* whom he was to marry shortly after he triumphed with her aid on the fateful October 17, 1945, and who was later to make the cause of the Argentine underdogs peculiarly her own.

Perón's program of social revolution provided one of the major themes of the struggle for power that went on remorselessly in Argentina until it gave him the victory in October 1945. The lower-class bias of his program provoked strong resistance from supporters of the regime as well as from the opposition — from many of the Army and Navy officers, as well as from the leaders

* According to some reports they first met during the crisis of September 1943, but the weight of opinion favors the latter half of January 1944, when they are said to have met during a fund-raising campaign for the victims of the earthquake of January 15 which destroyed the city of San Juan in western Argentina.

of the chief political parties, almost all of whom came from either the middle 'class or the upper class. Even the pro-labor Socialist party was acutely unhappy over Perón's program for the very good reason that it had long been the party of Argentina's labor leaders, and now it saw him weaning or wrenching the labor movement away from it.

The other two themes of the struggle for power both related to foreign policy. One was the new regime's effort to promote Argentina's hegemony in South America, as secretly promised in the manifesto of May 13, 1943 to the officers. The other was its resistance to pressure from the United States in favor of effective Argentine coöperation in the war effort, which had been promised three weeks later to the nation at large by the manifesto of June 4.

5. PERÓN MOVES UP

In the next two years first one and then another of these three themes were dominant, but they were at all times so closely inter-related that no effort will be made to trace their separate development in the following sketch of the main stages of this remorseless and complex struggle for power.

The first stage lasted until the forced retirement of President Ramírez on February 24, 1944. This period was distinguished by the climax both of the new regime's intrigues with Nazi Germany and also of its bid for power in the River Plate area. In both respects it suffered from exposures and checks that contributed to the fall of Ramírez. In July 1943 he had renewed the effort, begun under Castillo, to obtain arms from Germany on the plea that Argentina's refusal to break with the Axis threatened to involve her in war with her American neighbors and that she could not hope to defeat "much better armed Brazil" without help from Germany. In order to promote a deal with the Nazis, one Alberto Hellmuth was sent to Spain disguised as an Argentine consular official. In January 1944 Hellmuth was intercepted by the British authorities at Trinidad and the plot was exposed. Though the Argentine government of course denied complicity, no one was deceived; but only after the end of the war was it revealed, through captured German documents, that the Hellmuth mission had been arranged by Perón.

Actually, any threat of war in the River Plate area came from the military dictatorship at Buenos Aires itself, and the most likely target was Uruguay, where Argentine refugees were carrying on a vigorous campaign against the Ramírez regime. The analogy with the Rosas period was striking, and it was widely feared that it would now be completed by another Argentine assault on Uruguay. So tense did the situation become that a warning demonstration was made by a United States naval force in the form of a friendly call at Montevideo. This apparently had the desired effect at Buenos Aires, and the tension eased.

The Ramírez regime's designs on Uruguay accorded with the major objective of its foreign policy, which was to build up an anti-United States bloc in South America. To the same end it sought to promote revolutions in neighboring countries. The effort failed in Chile, but it succeeded in Bolivia, where in late December 1943 a "friendly" regime was brought to power by a revolution plotted in Buenos Aires with financial and other support from officials of the Argentine and German governments.

Ramírez' success in Bolivia proved his undoing in Buenos Aires, for it provoked the United States to countermeasures that forced him into a concession which in turn cost him the support of key members of his regime. Of the two major countermeasures, the first was the adoption by almost all the American governments of the so-called Guani Doctrine, which stipulated that before recognizing any new American government set up by force the other American governments would consult with one another to determine whether it was pro-Axis. The second and more effective measure was Washington's threat that unless Argentina immediately broke with the Axis, it would publish the evidence it had assembled of the pro-Axis activities of the Ramírez regime in Bolivia and elsewhere.

The threat worked. On January 26, 1944, President Ramírez severed relations with the Axis powers, and on the following day he suppressed the notoriously pro-Axis newspaper *El Pampero* for criticizing the severance. Almost immediately, however, the reaction against his new policy began to take effect in Argentina. On February 8 *El Pampero* resumed publication under a new name, *El Federal* (a tribute to the cult of the Federalist Rosas), but with same old pro-Axis editorial policy. On February 15 a group of army officers headed by Perón seized the Ministry of Foreign Affairs and forced the resignation of the minister. On February 24 Ramírez himself retired. In order to preserve the continuity of the regime and thus prevent the issue of recognition from being raised, he was dragooned into representing his retirement as voluntary and as constituting not a resignation but merely a delegation of the executive power to Vice-President Farrell. On March 9, however, he went the rest of the way and resigned in favor of Farrell, who formally assumed the presidency the following day.

The second stage extended from Farrell's assumption of the presidency to Argentina's last-minute declaration of war on Germany and Japan a year later (March 27, 1945). This period was characterized by the emergence of Perón as the key member of the regime; by the intensification of his appeal to the masses through his program of social justice; and by a long duel between Buenos Aires and Washington which ended in a capitulation by Buenos Aires on terms that gave it most of the fruits of victory.

Again Perón followed Farrell up the ladder, becoming Minister of War on February 26 and Vice-President on July 7. He continued to occupy both these positions, as well as the Secretaryship of Labor and Social Security, until October 1945. The combination of these three offices enabled him to build up the twin supports of army and labor upon which his regime has since rested.

His hold over the army officers was strengthened by a change in the character of their extracurricular organization. The G.O.U., which was dominated by the generals and in which Perón, still only a colonel, therefore played a subordinate part, was dissolved on March 14. Its place was taken by the informal "Colonels' Clique" headed by Perón himself. Sharp rivalry developed between the two officer groups, senior and junior, but the latter won ut. On March 22 the generals protested to President Farrell gainst the colonels' political preponderance; their answer was 1e packing of the high command with Perón's friends among the olonels, seventeen of whom were promoted to general on April with the president's approval. Perón still needed Farrell's sup- ort to keep him in power, but by the time he was promoted to ice-president in July it was obvious that the decisions as to how ower was to be used were made by Perón rather than by his ominal chief.

Increasingly, Perón used power to build up his following mong the masses, particularly through the mushrooming and egimented labor movement. An exceptionally effective public peaker, he made the conquest of social justice a favorite theme f his public addresses. Thus, he told a huge labor rally on May)ay 1944 how badly the Argentine workers had been treated efore 1943, how much had been done for them by the "revolu- on," especially in the six months since the creation of his Secre- iriat of Labor and Social Security, and how much still remained) be, and would be, done. The conquest of social justice, he romised, would be completed, no matter what the obstacles or 1e cost. When he was promoted to vice-president in July, his rincipal address was delivered to a labor audience; he gave the orkers the credit for his promotion and interpreted this as proof 1at President Farrell (who was not present on this occasion, ecause, explained Perón, he had "completely lost his voice") tood squarely behind the program of social reform. This pro- ram was not neglected even in his sensational address of June 0, though this was primarily concerned with the national organ- ation and international role of Argentina.

. HULL CRACKS DOWN

What Perón had to say on the latter subjects made his address f June 10 the starting-point of the most critical phase in the /hole history of Argentine–United States relations; by the time 1e crisis was over, eight months later, one side or the other had mployed almost every expression of mutual ill-will except a

declaration of war. Speaking four days after the Allies bega
their invasion of Europe across the Normandy beaches, Perón de
clared that it was not a matter of great moment to Argentin
whether the Allies or the Axis won the war and that in eithe
case the legitimate national aspirations of Argentina could b
realized only through a combination of vigorous diplomacy
military might, and "total" organization.

To Secretary of State Hull in Washington this seemed a cha
lenge that could not be ignored. Hitherto, the United States ha
done little more than withhold recognition from the uncoöpera
tive Farrell regime. Now that non-coöperation had becom
defiance, Hull decided to apply the heaviest pressure possible
always in the name of inter-American solidarity and the Unite
Nations war effort. In the following weeks he employed a num
ber of diplomatic, economic, and moral sanctions. When thes
had no noticeable effect, he invoked the enormous authority
President Roosevelt, who responded with a statement on Sep
tember 29 pillorying the Buenos Aires regime as the citadel
Nazi-Fascist influence in America; but even this trumpet bla
failed to bring down the walls of the South American Jericho.

The trouble was that the only enforcement measure whic
might have succeeded was drastic economic sanctions, includin
the closing of the British market to Argentine products, and th
was never tried, for the simple reason that Britain would n
coöperate. With beef already in short supply, and no substitut
offered but pork from the United States, even the liberal *Man
chester Guardian* was unwilling to cut off imports from Arge
tina. "We like the Argentine brand of Fascism as little as do
Mr. Cordell Hull," said the *Guardian,* "but we also prefe
Argentine beef to American pork." Why Hull went ahead withou
first obtaining an iron-clad guarantee of British coöperation ha
never been satisfactorily explained. At any rate, ignoring Winsto
Churchill's urgent admonition to "look before you leap," Hu
leaped first.

The result was a stalemate which was broken only after Hull
resignation on November 27, 1944. By this time both sides wer
ready to make concessions. Contrary to Argentine expectatio

June, the Normandy invasion had succeeded and Germany was
ing; in October the Great Powers had completed and pub-
1ed the Dumbarton Oaks Proposals for a new international
ganization which was to be established at a full United Nations
nference in 1945, and Argentina did not wish to be left out.
1 its part, the United States had been greatly embarrassed by
gentina's request in October for an inter-American conference
discuss its case, and by rapidly multiplying evidences that
veral other Latin American governments were, if not in sym-
thy with Argentina, at any rate weary of the stalemate. The
aracter of the new State Department "team" facilitated an
1icable settlement. Secretary of State Edward R. Stettinius had
en Lend-Lease Administrator, and in that capacity had not had
deal with Argentina and hence had no settled antagonism
wards the Buenos Aires authorities. His Assistant Secretary of
1te for Latin American affairs, Nelson Rockefeller, had been
ordinator of Inter-American Affairs, and as such his chief
nction had been to promote coöperation and good will.

Accordingly, a setttlement was arrived at early in 1945. Nomi-
lly this took place in two stages, both public: first, in the adop-
n of terms for Argentina's readmission to inter-American good
1nding by the Inter-American Conference on Problems of War
d Peace, held at Chapultepec (Mexico City) in February and
arch 1945, from which Argentina was excluded; and second, in
gentina's subsequent consideration and acceptance of these
rms. Actually, as we now know, the settlement had been
cretly arranged beforehand, and the public process was mainly
signed to save faces, particularly in Washington.

The strength of the face-saving motive is understandable, for
gentina gained a great deal more than she gave up. Under the
rms of the settlement she was bound to declare war on the
maining Axis powers and to take vigorous measures against
is nationals and interests in Argentina as stipulated in the
greements reached by the Chapultepec Conference. On the
her hand, she was permitted to sign those agreements, thus
llifying her exclusion from the conference, and was restored to
rmal relations with the other American states, though her

government was the same one that President Roosevelt had on
a few months since denounced as the citadel of Nazi-Fascism
America. Finally — and, as it then seemed, most important of :
— she was promised the support of the other American gover
ments for admission to a seat in the impending United Natio
Conference in San Francisco, which would give her charter mer
bership in the new international organization. On balance, t
Farrell-Perón regime had won a notable victory in a crucia.
important test.

7. "BRADEN OR PERÓN": FIRST PHASE

The third, final, and most dramatic stage in Perón's rise exten
from the declaration of war on Germany and Japan on Mar
27, 1945 to his definitive victory over his domestic rivals
October 17 of that year. This period was marked both by
recrudescence of the controversy with the United States and a
by the development, from several sources and in maximu
strength, of the opposition in Argentina to Perón. The domes
and foreign strands of the story are closely interrelated, and th
was fortunate for Perón, since it enabled him to make a plausil
identification of his cause with the defense of national indeper
ence and the welfare of the masses against an unholy allian
of the Argentine oligarchy with the predatory imperialism of t
United States and Great Britain.

Actually, the opponents of Perón included many Argentin
such as the great majority of the university professors a
students, who had no connection with either the oligarchy
imperialism and who disliked these quite as much as did Per
but fortunately for him, several of his most prominent oppone:
did have such a connection. Thus, the campaign against Per
reached its height shortly after the arrival in May 1945 of the n
United States Ambassador, Spruille Braden, who openly took
leading part in it; the first major assault of this phase of t
campaign took the form of an anti-Perón manifesto of June
signed by such quintessentially oligarchical elements as t
Argentine Chamber of Commerce and the Buenos Aires Sto

:change; and though the manifesto attacked many features of
e Farrell-Perón administration, including the expensive arma-
ents program, its fire was concentrated mainly on Perón's own
cretariat of Labor and Social Security, which the manifesto
arged with sowing economic heresies and class hatred among
e masses.

Perón, warning that he now had a labor "army" of four million
en to support him, unhesitatingly accepted the challenge to
;ht it out on the issue as thus defined by his enemies. Well he
ight, for it was a godsend to him. It gave an appearance of
uth to his chosen role of champion of the hitherto neglected
asses in their impending conflict. It also enabled him to appear
the custodian of two of the most popular Argentine traditions
- hatred of the oligarchy and resistance to Yankee imperialism.
erhaps the most useful single element in the whole situation
as the fact that Ambassador Braden seemed to be the main-
ring of the opposition to him. Though Braden returned to
'ashington in August, two months before the crisis was resolved,
e did so only to become Assistant Secretary of State in charge
f Latin American relations, and in his new post he obligingly
ntinued his attacks on Perón until after the latter was so
rmly entrenched in power that he no longer needed the help
iven him by Braden's opposition.

Yielding to the clamor for a return to constitutional govern-
ent, President Farrell announced at the annual dinner of the
rmy, Navy, and Air Force officers on July 7 that this would be
rought about through elections to be held before the end of
ie year, and that the elections would be free and honest, with
o effort made to impose an official ticket. Apprehensions on
ie latter point were promptly aroused by the cry "Perón for
resident" set up by his captive labor unions and other hench-
nen. The pot boiled over when on August 6 Farrell lifted the
tate of siege for the first time since December 1941. Taking full
dvantage of their newly recovered liberties, Perón's enemies
taged a dizzying series of meetings, strikes, and demonstrations.
'he culmination came on September 19 with a mammoth "March
f the Constitution and Liberty" which was so successful —

250,000 persons of various political persuasions joined in it — th
it was taken as marking the beginning of the end for Perón.
week later the state of siege was reimposed.

8. DESCENT TO THE UNDERWORLD — AND RETUR

The chief reliance of Perón's opponents, however, was
driving a wedge between him and the Army, just as he soug
to split them, mainly by bringing Radicals into the governme
In the end his strategy prevailed, but his opponents came close
victory, for so many of the officers in all three services — Arm
Navy, Air Force — had been alienated by his program of soc
revolution that as early as July 7 President Farrell had f
called upon to deny publicly that there was a schism in t
armed forces. On September 14 Perón published in the *Bolet
Militar* a warning against the "desperate effort" his enemi
were making to bring about such a schism. Eleven days lat
Farrell's denial was given the lie and Perón's warning w
justified by an uprising led by General Rawson, the 48-hour ch
of the revolution of June 4, 1943.

Rawson's uprising was suppressed, but on October 9 anoth
group of officers in the key Campo de Mayo garrison, led
General Eduardo Avalos, struck with better success. Perón w
forced to resign all three of his offices, and a few days later
was "detained" and sent on a naval vessel to Martín Garc
Island in the River Plate. In a "farewell" address to the worke
on October 10, Perón told them he had just drafted an order f
a general wage increase, and hoped they would get it.

The extraordinary course of events in the week followir
Perón's ouster provided striking proof of the great strength
had built up, and of his opponents' almost incredible weakne
and ineptitude. They were unable to form a government or ev
to agree upon the procedure for forming one, some demandir
that the Supreme Court take over (thus ousting Farrell as w
as Perón), and others that a conservative cabinet be formed und
Farrell.

While they fiddled, their Rome burned. As day after day passe

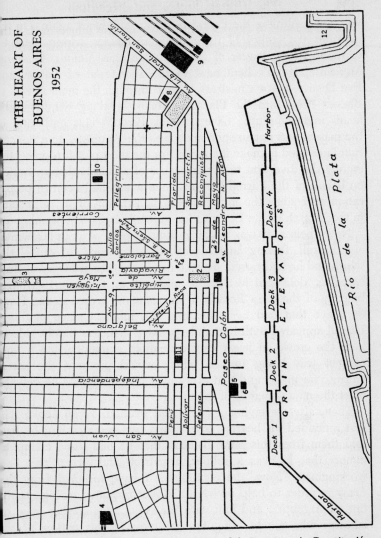

THE HEART OF
BUENOS AIRES
1952

1. Casa Rosada 2. Plaza de Mayo 3. Plaza del Congreso 4. Constitución Railway Station 5. Eva Perón Foundation 6. C.G.T. (Labor) Building 7. Plaza San Martín 8. Ministry of Foreign Relations 9. President Perón Railway Station 10. Teatro Colón 11. National Library 12. New Port

without a solution, the Peronista forces took heart again. On th
morning of October 17 the proletarian masses, whipped up b
Cipriano Reyes, leader of the slaughter-house unions, Doming
Mercante, Perón's lieutenant in the Secretariat of Labor, an
Eva Duarte, Perón's mistress, poured through the main streets (
Buenos Aires into the Plaza de Mayo, breaking windows an
heads and shouting: "Give us back Perón!" This gathering (
the masses was not so spontaneous as the Peronista *Acta Sanct(
rum* later tried to make it appear. For the most part it represente
merely the diversion to Perón's cause of a counterdemonstratio
on behalf of the Farrell-Perón regime which had been in prepa
ration ever since the impressive demonstration of its opponent
in the "March of the Constitution and Liberty" on September 2!

Nevertheless, it was a hair-raising display of popular wrath
and Farrell, fearing anarchy, called Perón back to control th
whirlwind he had raised. This he did in another of his irresistibl
speeches, delivered just before midnight on October 17 from
balcony of the Casa Rosada to the immense crowd in the Plaz
de Mayo that had been awaiting this moment since mornin
Farrell appeared with him and, speaking first, was barely able t
hold the crowd in leash long enough to announce that a ne
cabinet was being formed which would preserve the socia
gains so far made, and that everything possible would be done t
meet the new demands of labor.

Then, after receiving a prolonged ovation, Perón spoke. H
first reminded his hearers how, nearly two years earlier, he hac
told them from this same balcony that he had three claims t
honor: that he was a soldier, a patriot, and Argentina's firs
workingman. "Now," he continued, "I have resigned from th
Army in order to help revive the almost forgotten civilian tradi
tion of Argentina and join with the sweating, suffering mass o
laborers who are building the greatness of this nation." Mos
of the rest of his short speech (as reported, it could not have
taken fifteen minutes to deliver) was devoted to urging the
crowd to disperse in orderly fashion and get back to work —
though first taking a day off for rest and jubilation over thei

triumph, as he himself was going to take a much-needed vacation before returning to lead them on to new victories.

The upshot of all this was that Perón confirmed his resignation of all three of his government posts. One might therefore be tempted to regard the whole nine-day crisis as an elaborately contrived hoax; but in fact it was a genuinely critical period and a turning-point for Argentina as well as for Perón. He had first resigned in defeat; he now adhered to his triple resignation because he was so sure of his control over the government that he no longer needed to hold office in it pending his election as president. The government had been revamped and packed with his friends — including his associates in the Italian mission of 1939–40, Generals Sosa Molina and Pistarini — and had accepted his program of social reform. As a result, by standing aside from it during the presidential campaign he would lose nothing and, on the contrary, would strengthen the fiction that he was not an official candidate.

Moreover, this crisis had enabled him to bring the armed forces to heel. They had first turned him out and then, overruled by the civilian underdogs, had taken him back. Faced with the alternative of civil war or compromise, the military had chosen the latter. They had not surrendered — in fact, Perón consulted them both just before and again just after his dramatic reappearance at the Casa Rosada on the night of October 17, and they held all the chief posts in the revamped government not assigned to Radicals. They did, however, concede the major point at issue by backing down from their original demand that Perón and his social program must go. This meant that they agreed henceforth to share control of the government with labor, thus completing the process by which Perón had revolutionized the revolution of 1943. The fact was now underlined by his fourth resignation, that of his colonel's commission in the Army; though after the election was safely won, he got back his commission and was promoted brigadier general.

The October crisis also fixed the name *descamisados*, "shirtless ones" or "ragamuffins," upon Perón's mass following. First em-

ployed in a spirit of disdain by people of the better sort, the
epithet was promptly adopted by its plebeian targets, for these
sockless Jerry Simpsons of Argentina, resenting the aristocratic
pretensions of the oligarchy, wanted the world to believe that
they were proud of their rags.

Finally, the crisis led to Perón's marriage (his second) to the
twenty-six-year-old Eva Duarte, who, inverting the mythical
roles and with better success than her prototype, had just played
Orpheus to his Eurydice when he was sent down to the nether
world of Martín García Island. His "detention" there might have
been the end of his power but for the fury with which she
whipped up the masses for the decisive demonstration so cannily
organized by Reyes and Mercante on October 17.

Evita's origin was obscure, her recent past shady, and hitherto
most of her life had been hard and disappointing. By turns
burlesque girl and actress on stage, screen, and radio, her vaulting
ambition had never been crowned with more than mediocre
success in any of these roles. But she had glamour, and the new
role she was about to take up — that of the descamisados' idol —
fitted her like a glove, for frustration had embittered her against
the existing social order, and above all against its capstone, the
oligarchy, and she possessed a toughness of fiber and language
that the descamisados recognized as their own.

On October 21, four days after Perón's political resurrection
with Evita's aid, the two were secretly married in a civil ceremony which regularized a tie formed some time since. Six weeks
later, a church wedding publicly sealed their union.

7. How Perón Consolidated His Power

Perón has been the master of Argentina ever since the crucial October 17, 1945. For the first eight months he was out of the government, but his friends controlled it while he was elected president for a six-year term. Inaugurated on June 4, 1946, he still holds that post, having been reëlected for a like term in November 1951. His party has from the beginning dominated both houses of Congress, and in 1947 he captured the remaining power, the judicial, by impeaching most of the Supreme Court justices. With all these powers in his hands, he has carried out a large part of his promised program of social revolution and economic nationalism.

All along, he has been faced by a strong opposition, and at the outset this included almost all the leaders in the political, cultural, economic, and social life of Argentina before 1943, embraced elements ranging from the Chamber of Commerce to the Communist Party, and had on its side all the principal newspapers and almost all the university people, faculty and students alike. The present chapter will show how he overcame this opposition, not by one smashing blow but by successive turns of the screw, and not by blood purges but by harassment and intimidation liberally seasoned with arbitrary arrest and torture, but also frequently sugar-coated with legalism and always adorned with appeals to the higher law of social justice and to national honor.

To the system built up in this way his critics have applied names, such as Nazi-Fascist, neo-Fascist, totalitarian, and military dictatorship, most of which suggest parallels with regimes in other countries. His own tag for it is "democracy" and he claims

to have given Argentina genuine democracy (or, to use his neologism, "justicialist" * democracy) in contrast to the "pluto-de-
mocracy" of the United States. But whatever the label one
chooses to give it, Perón's system is *sui generis,* and its main
roots lie in Argentina.

Far from being a dictatorship in the usual sense, it is apparently supported by the majority of the Argentine people. In
this respect it differs greatly from the regimes in most of the
other underdeveloped countries of the world in which economic
nationalism is rampant today. In these, control still rests with
elements corresponding to the oligarchy that once ruled Argentina, whereas Perón rose on the ruins of the oligarchy and was
supported not only by the Army but by the "shirtless" masses,
the descamisados, who caught the contagion of that champion
rabble-rouser, the late Eva Perón, with her fanatical devotion to
her husband.

Yet at the same time Perón has turned the rule of law into the
rule of force and has systematically violated those personal
rights — freedom of speech, press, and assembly, freedom from
arbitrary arrest and imprisonment — which have been generally
regarded as essential to a democratic system. Consequently, the
Perón regime can best be defined as the tyranny of a majority
over a minority under democratic forms.

1. SOURCES OF PERONISTA STRENGTH

Before we trace the steps by which Perón consolidated his
regime, let us first take a bird's-eye view of the chief sources
of his support in the period since 1945.

All observers agree that the descamisados, the labor unions,
and the armed forces have all along been major sources of Perón's
strength; many add the Church, and some add industry, meaning
the new industrial leaders, as other major sources. Since the bulk
of the descamisados were almost from the start regimented in

* Perón appears to have adopted "Justicialism" as the label for his
program at the suggestion of an international philosophical congress held in
Argentina in 1947 under the auspices of his government.

government-controlled labor unions, we shall for the sake of brevity treat the two as forming a single sector and refer to it as labor.

The view taken here is that labor and the armed forces have been by all odds the most important sources of his strength, the two legs on which his regime has stood at all times down to the present writing; that it is inaccurate and misleading to say that Perón ever had the support of the Church and industry; and that such support as he received from clergymen and individual industrialists came to him at the beginning of his regime, was not a major source of strength to him even then, and was in most cases converted into opposition as the true character of his regime emerged in 1946–1948.

A strong labor element has always been the feature that has distinguished Perón's regime most sharply from the military dictatorships so familiar in Latin American history. While the armed forces have likewise been indispensable to him, labor seems to have played a somewhat more dynamic role on crucial occasions. It was decisive in forcing the Army leaders to take him back after ousting him in October 1945; it subsequently deterred most of them from trying to repeat the ouster, by making it clear that this would precipitate a civil war, for which they had no stomach; and the social revolution effected in labor's interest led, by a kind of osmosis, to the Peronization of the lower ranks of the armed forces themselves. Perón claims that this social content is what differentiates his revolution from all previous revolutions in Argentina since independence and that it explains why his has succeeded while all the others failed; and if we accept his definition of success, he is right.

His major means of winning and keeping the indispensable support of labor has been his social revolution. In addition to the normal complement of wage increases and favorable social and labor legislation, he has courted popularity through the wealthy Social Aid Foundation, which Eva Perón headed until her death in 1952. She never made any accounting for the huge sums she acquired for it from various sources, which included periodic levies on all wages and salaries in Argentina; and a large part of the fund is said to have gone into graft. Nevertheless, enough still remained to finance manifold activities on behalf of the descamisados, which ranged from personal charity to schools and low-cost housing. Perón has used the club as well as the carrot, however, imprisoning and beating up recalcitrant labor leaders (who were numerous at first), firing and blacklisting the lesser fry, and denying the labor unions the right to strike.

The armed forces have long been an important factor in the political life of Argentina, as in nearly all the other Latin American countries — a fact concealed most of the time from the mid-1890's to General Uriburu's coup in 1930, but not altered by concealment. They have been a better instrument than in most other Latin American countries, because of their better *esprit de corps*, especially since German training began in 1911. Whether they are good soldiers or not, it is hard to say, since Argentina has not fought a foreign war in over eighty years. At any rate, the quality of their leadership has been good, though it has been impugned — witness the popular story about the Argentine mother who, having three sons, one a genius, the second average, and the third a dolt, decided to make them respectively a judge, the manager of the family estate, and an army officer. Actually, the Army has had a long line of intelligent and able leaders, from San Martín through Mitre and Roca to Perón himself.

For this reason, and because of the increasing mechanization of warfare, the weight of the Argentine armed forces in the national scale had been increasing until Perón created the labor counterpoise. But he made labor only a counterpoise, not a replacement. For a time in the critical period 1944–45 he also built up a military counterpoise in the shape of a large national police force. Once his position was secure, however, he lavished funds upon the regular armed forces, including the common soldiers, and gave political preferment to the officers, who were given posts in the cabinet, as interventors in the provinces, and as managers in government-controlled enterprises in industry and mining. From the start he made it clear that so long as the military supported him, he would take care of them and share the conduct of public affairs, civil as well as military, with them. The Perón regime has been essentially a coalition of labor and the armed forces under the supreme command of Juan Perón.

Any discussion of the role of the Church (meaning, of course, the Roman Catholic Church) in relation to Perón's regime should begin with a definition of terms. Properly speaking, the Church consists of the clergy and the laity; and if Perón had had the support of the Church in this sense, there would never have been any opposition to him worth mentioning, since the people of Argentina are overwhelmingly Catholic. The fact is that at the outset (notably in his first election, in 1946) he had the support of almost all the clergy. Even then, however, a group of the most prominent laymen banded together *as Catholics* in public opposition to him; and one of his most outspoken critics from his first emergence to the present writing has been Monseñor Miguel de Andrea, titular Bishop of Temnos and leader of the Catholic labor movement in Argentina.

Even if by "the Church" one means only the Catholic hierarchy, there is nothing in Argentine history to sustain the belief that the support of the Church was worth anything like as much to him as that of labor and the armed forces. The historic role of the Church in Argentina denied it the political influence and experience necessary for that purpose. James Bryce gave a good description of its role as he saw it on a visit to Argentina in 1911:

[Argentina] is, of all the Spanish-American republics, that in which the church has least to do with politics. Though Roman Catholicism is declared by the constitution to be supported by the state . . . that freedom of religious worship which is guaranteed by law is fully carried out in practice . . . Still more noteworthy is it that there seems to be little or no effort on the part of the church to influence public affairs. No political party is allied with the clergy, no clerical influence is felt in elections.

The situation as Bryce described it continued substantially unaltered down to the coup of 1943. Then, to be sure, the internecine struggle within the military dictatorship brought to power for a few months at the end of the year an ultra-Catholic group; but this group was soon ousted by the rise of Perón.

This checked the new clerical trend, but did not at once reverse it, and for a time all went well between Perón and the hierarchy. By 1950, however, a rift had opened between them, for Perón's regime contained strong anticlerical and neo-pagan as well as Catholic elements, and the result of these opposing thrusts was the government's support of measures unacceptable to the hierarchy, such as the legalization of divorce and prostitution, and a shift of the emphasis in education from Catholicism to Peronismo. Significantly, the clergy did not again support Perón in the election of 1951; and in his long May Day message to Congress the following year, he made several references to God and Christianity, but not one to the Catholic Church.

The thesis that industry supported Perón need not detain us long. It probably reflects the propensity of some observers to interpret his rise in Hitlerian terms. The trouble with this interpretation is that no one can point out Perón's Thyssen — the Austrian émigré Fritz Mandl will not do, for he was the creature, not the creator, of Perón — and from the start the pro-labor measures and demagogic harangues that formed the very core of Peronismo were poison to the industrialists. The most one can say is that in the confusion of his early rise some individual industrialists conceived the quaint idea that what his regime meant for them was emancipation from the rule of the old agrarian oligarchy; and that when they soon discovered that they had only exchanged that Scylla for a worse Charybdis, they resigned themselves to making the most of the tidy profits Perón permitted them to reap pending their infallibly decreed expropriation. The developments of 1953, which will be discussed below, put the matter in a new light and suggested that the Perón regime might end up in an alliance with industry; but it had not begun, nor, in its first six years, had it developed in that way.

Communism and a youth movement are sometimes described as other sources of Perón's strength; but it is doubtful whether either has counted for much at any time in his regime. The Communist Party in Argentina was, in fact, both his enemy and his victim at the outset. Later, after it had split, one wing supported him and was used by him; but at all times it was a splinter group, small in influence as well as numbers. As for a youth movement, Perón, like most modern revolutionaries, did try hard to build up one, both through the schools and otherwise — one of the songs most sedulously played at Peronista rallies is "The Peronista Boys" (*Los Muchachos Peronistas*). The effort has met with success to the extent that there are many youthful supporters of the movement, but so are there many youthful opponents of it, and the division between them generally follows much the same political and social lines that divide their elders. The Argentine youth, as youth, have not flocked into the movement. The age of its leaders has not encouraged them to do so. Perón himself was nearly forty-eight when he began his rise to power in 1943, and fifty-one when he first became president. The man who has emerged as his second-in-command, Alberto Teisaire, is four years older then Perón. The youngest of the top flight leaders who have survived to the present, Angel Borlenghi, was born in 1906. And so it goes.

Our brief discussion of Perón's support should not conclude without emphasizing the fact that, until he had had time to consolidate his position, one of the chief elements of his strength lay in the weakness of his opponents. One main source of their weakness lay in their inability to unite among themselves. Another was the failure of many of them, including political liberals as well as industrialists, to perceive the trend of Perón's regime until too late. One of the first to felicitate Perón on the fateful October 17, 1945 was the grand old man of Argentine Socialism, Alfredo Palacios.

2. "BRADEN OR PERÓN": SECOND PHASE

Though the crucially important national election of February 1946 and the campaign preceding it were conducted under a military dictatorship devoted to Perón's candidacy, they were featured on the part of the government by a sustained effort to give them the appearance of a free expression of public opinion. On the part of the opposition, they were featured by disunity and poor judgment in the early stages and by overconfidence at the end.

On October 30, 1945, the government rescinded a decree of December 1943 dissolving all political parties, and it also suspended the enforcement of a recently adopted Organic Statute for Political Parties which might have handicapped the old-line parties by the novelty of its provisions. These parties, all of which were opposed to Perón, were accordingly permitted to reorganize themselves along familiar lines. They were then given a considerable measure of freedom in conducting their campaigns through the mails and public meetings as well as by press and radio. For the first and last time in Argentine history, provision was made for the equal treatment of all parties by the radio broadcasting stations. To be sure, law was one thing and enforcement another, and on January 31, 1946 the opposition parties published a manifesto denouncing "the climate of intimidation and violence" which the Peronistas had given the campaign.

There was a remarkably long delay in the nomination of the presidential candidates, Perón's being made on December 14 and that of the opposition standard-bearer, José Tamborini, two weeks later. In Perón's case the delay was not significant, since his candidacy was a foregone conclusion and the announcement of it a mere formality. In the end, he was supported by three parties, all new. Two of these were labor parties and the third a Radical splinter group. The last-named contributed his running mate, J. Hortensio Quijano, lawyer, banker, and Minister of Interior in 1945, and its support enabled Perón to keep the opposition from monopolizing the mantle of Irigoyen.

In Tamborini's case the delay was significant. He was the candidate of a coalition of most of the opposition parties — Radical, Socialist, Progressive Democratic, and Communist — formed in November 1945 under the name of Democratic Union. So sharp were the traditional rivalries among these parties, however, that they found it difficult to coalesce even in the face of the threat from their common enemy, Perón. Even after the coalition was formed they lost a precious six weeks in haggling over the candidate and the platform. At the end of that time they came up with a worthy but colorless candidate and a negative platform. Tamborini was a sixty-year-old physician who had been deputy and senator at various times, and a member of Alvear's cabinet in the 1920's. Nothing in his record or personality could approach Perón's popular appeal. His coalition's platform was no help, for it amounted to a demand for a return to normality, which the Argentine masses did not want.

They did want a social revolution, and that was what Perón promised to give them. In point of personality, too, he had an enormous advantage over Tamborini. Some idea of Perón's magnetic appeal to those who did not detest him for his policies can be obtained from the following description of him by a hostile correspondent of the *New York Times* in July 1945, when his fate still hung in the balance:

Colonel Perón is a strong, vigorous man of medium height, dark-haired, clean-shaven, with an aquiline nose and ruddy complexion. He is close to 50, but considerably younger in appearance, and looks very smart and handsome in his uniform. He is endowed with great personal charm and speaks well and convincingly, both in private conversation and in public. His energy is unbounded and one can see at a glance that he is one of those men who know what they want and are ready to fight to obtain it. All these things fit him admirably for the task he has set himself of having himself elected the next President of Argentina . . .

Yet for some strange reason the leaders of the Democratic Union seem to have been confident of victory, provided the government and the Army kept their promise of a free and honest election. In the very same manifesto of January 31 in which they complained of the "climate of intimidation and violence" created by the Peronistas, the leaders of the Democratic Union attributed this to their opponents' realization that they faced "the certainty of a crushing defeat." "In a fair election," continued the manifesto, "the rout of the Nazi candidate [Perón] will be crushing, definitive." On the eve of the election the Democratic Union leaders still held this optimistic view, and on February 7 one of them, Julio A. Noble (a leader of the democratic *Acción Argentina* group in 1940–1943), charged that the Peronistas were planning to seize the government by force because they knew that they were doomed to defeat in the election.

These confident prognostications turned out to be badly in error, and yet they were made by veterans in Argentine political life. Had the democratic leaders lost touch with the Argentine voters? Or could it be that they were right until the eleventh-hour headlining of the issue of Yankee imperialism enabled Perón to turn an incipient rout into victory?

Perón's exploitation of this issue was facilitated by the diplomatic campaign conducted against him from Washington, to which former Ambassador Spruille Braden had returned to become Assistant Secretary of State. Two weeks before the Argentine election, the campaign reached its climax with the publication of the State Department's "Blue Book on Argentina." * This 131-page booklet was the work of Assistant Secretary of State Braden and his staff. It gave what it called "incontrovertible evidence" (much of it drawn from recently captured German documents) that "the present Argentine Government and many of its high officials were so seriously compromised with the [Nazi-Fascist] enemy that trust and confidence could not be reposed in that government." Perón himself was prominent among the Argentines against whom such evidence was presented. Consequently the Blue Book's publication on the eve of the Argentine election stamped it as an obvious effort to defeat Perón.

Though we have no sure means of measuring its effect on Argentine public opinion, the evidence indicates that the Blue Book gained Perón more votes than it cost him, for it was a fresh and flagrant example of that Yankee intervention in Latin America which Argentines had long taken the lead in opposing. Also, Braden's responsibility for it gave it the air of another shot in the feud he had begun with Perón the preceding year. The latter was now able to make more telling use than ever before of a line of propaganda that he had been following since the beginning of the campaign, which was that the choice before the

---

* Popularly so called. The actual title was *Consultation among the American Republics with Respect to the Argentine Situation. Memorandum of the United States Government.*

Argentine voters was not "Tamborini or Perón" but "Braden or Perón."

Above all, however, Perón's popular appeal was aided by what he called his struggle for social justice, though his opponents called it reckless demagoguery. The government came to his aid by decreeing, on December 20, 1945, the general pay increase which he had initiated just before he was forced out in October. The increase was a substantial one; ranging from 13 to 33 per cent, it applied to all workers and white-collar employees. And of course Perón, though no longer in office, received the credit for it. The main employer group, the Argentine Industrial Union, voted to ignore the decree; but the government's threats of heavy penalties soon brought compliance. In the end, the employers' resistance only increased the average descamisado's conviction that he would never be able to better his lot without Perón to protect him.

When the election was held on February 24, 1946, under Army supervision, the popular vote was close enough to give it the air of a real contest — a free and honest one; but Perón's majority was large enough to make the victory clear-cut. Of the 2,734,386 votes cast, he received 1,527,231, or 56 per cent of the total, to 1,207,155, or 44 per cent, for Tamborini. This made Perón's margin of victory larger than that in most presidential elections in the United States since the Civil War. As often happens in the United States, whose Electoral College had been closely copied by the framers of Argentina's Constitution, the electoral vote was much more one-sided: Perón 304, Tamborini 72. Perón carried all but four provinces (Córdoba and Corrientes in the north, San Juan and San Luis in the west). In Congress, his supporters won two-thirds of the seats in the Chamber of Deputies and an even larger proportion in the Senate.

From all the evidence, the election appears to have been free and honest, as the government had promised. Just after the polls closed, the opposition leaders themselves, including Tamborini, described it as a model of democratic rectitude and the best election ever held in the history of Argentina; and, at that time, they did not complain that their preëlection campaign had been seriously hampered by the harassment to which they had been subjected. To be sure, that was before the votes were counted, and when they still believed their preëlection forecasts of a crushing defeat for Perón. After the votes had been counted and, contrary to all their expectations, Perón had won, they changed to complaint, but the change was too long delayed, too great, and too obviously not disinterested to carry conviction.

As for the representative character of the election, the number of voters in proportion to total population was much the largest in the history of the country; it was about 50 per cent larger than the average in the most democratic of the previous elections (those of 1916, 1922, and 1928), and the margin was of course even greater than in the case of all other previous elections.

Consequently, there seems to be no blinking the fact that Perón was the choice of a substantial majority of the Argentine people in 1946. Also, we should note that this was a personal triumph for him. He did not owe it to a party; there was no united Peronista party, but only three splinter parties, all new, which received more help from him than they gave in return. And he was not imposed by the Army, for it discharged its obligation as nonpartisan guarantor of the purity of the election of 1946 with a zeal for that task which may have been related to the lack of zeal of many of the officers for the demagogic Perón.

3. PURGING THE SUPREME COURT
AND THE UNIVERSITIES

Inaugurated on June 4, 1946 — the third anniversary of the military coup — Perón promptly set about completing his conquest of the Government by reducing the last opposition stronghold, the Supreme Court of Justice, whose members held life tenure, and which had used the power of judicial review to nullify some of the measures adopted by the new regime since 1943. Though the attack was made for partisan purposes, it was given a cloak of legality by employing the constitutional process of impeachment.

Perón himself publicly incited the attack on the Supreme Court, and in doing so he at times hardly rendered even lip-service to legality. As early as April 1945 he had created a national sensation by charging, in an address to a meeting of labor leaders, that the court was undermining the government's program of social justice, and by declaring that if the moment came when the workers had to fight in order to defend the justice they had so laboriously gained, he would be on their side. He returned to the charge in his inaugural address of June 4, 1946:

> For my part [he said], I put the spirit of justice above the judicial power . . . Justice must be not only independent but efficacious, and it cannot be efficacious unless its ideas and concepts keep pace with the march of public sentiment . . . [It] must be dynamic, not static. Otherwise, worthy popular aspirations will be frustrated and social development checked, to the grave injury of the working classes. The latter . . . when they see lawful roads closed to them, have no other recourse than violence.

A month later, a Peronista deputy dutifully introduced a bill calling for the impeachment of the Supreme Court justices, and Perón again helped the attack by saying to a meeting of the Peronista deputies: "If the government is to function successfully, the three powers [executive, legislative, judicial] must work in harmony with each other . . . At present, the judicial power, with the exception of some magistrates, does not speak the same language as the other two powers."

The impeachment of four of the five justices and the attorney general was duly voted by the Chamber of Deputies and tried by the solidly Peronista Senate. One of the four resigned, and the fifth was let alone because he yielded to the Peronistas. Most of the fifteen counts in the impeachment were as farcical as the trial itself. The height of absurdity was reached in a count which charged that the Supreme Court had "set itself above the Constitution" in granting *de facto* recognition to the military dictatorship set up by the coup of June 4, 1943.

Despite the absurdity of the charges and the skill and courage with which the defense was conducted by such men as Alfredo Palacios, pioneer of Argentine labor legislation, and Mariano Drago, son of the author of the Drago Doctrine, conviction was a foregone conclusion. If there had ever been any doubt about this, it would have been removed by a statement made on May

22, 1946, at the beginning of this nominally judicial proceeding, by Diego Luis Molinari, who had been a prominent member of Irigoyen's second administration and who was now one of the most influential Peronista members of the Senate, which was to sit as a court of impeachment. "The revolution must reach everywhere!" thundered Molinari. "The executive and legislative powers — national, provincial, and municipal — have been completely renovated, as required by the program of the revolution. But the judicial power, the universities, and the bureaucracy have so far escaped it, and these too it must reach."

In April 1947 the Senate voted overwhelmingly for the conviction of all three judges and the attorney general, as expected. Their places, together with the one vacated by resignation, were filled with reliable Peronistas. Henceforth the Supreme Court gave no more trouble. The inferior courts were completely purged two years later under a "transitory article" adopted by the Constitutional Convention of 1949, which made all existing judicial appointments subject to reconfirmation by the Senate.

Peronista Senator Molinari had demanded in his speech of May 1946 that the universities as well as the Supreme Court be revolutionized. The process had in fact already begun when he spoke, though it was not completed until January 1, 1948. As the Argentine universities, now six in number, had developed into the best in Latin America since the comparatively recent reform of 1918, one may wonder why it was felt necessary to purge them now. Surprise is likely to be all the greater when one reads that most of the faculty members took no part in politics and did not even belong to a political party. In fact, however, after 1943 they, and the students as well, took a very active part in politics by opposing first the military dictatorship and then Perón. In many other Latin American countries of Europe and America the universities had done likewise, but never with less success, for Argentina now had a new kind of dictatorship.

Action against the universities was sporadic at first, but systematic and thorough in the final phase. It began in October 1943 with the dismissal of many professors who had signed a manifesto calling on the dictatorship to support "effective democracy and American solidarity," and the dissolution of the 40,000-member student federation which had supported the manifesto. Early in 1945 the professors were reinstated, for at that time the Argentine government was trying to get back into the good graces of the democratic powers which, contrary to its expectations, were winning the war. That accomplished, it moved against the universities again. Its first move was to imprison all their rectors and deans as a warning to the rest of their personnel.

Only after Perón had safely won the election of February 1946 did the systematic purge begin. On the following May 2, a month before his inauguration, all six universities were "intervened" — that is, placed under administrators appointed by the government; this was the first time in the history of Argentina that all of them had been "intervened" at once. Then came a wholesale purge of their faculties: in the last three months of 1946, 1250 of their members (70 per cent of the total number) were dismissed, prematurely "retired," or eliminated in some other way. In 1947, a new University Law, replacing the existing one, which dated from 1889, was adopted for the avowed purpose of making it impossible for the universities ever again to "oppose the will of the Argentine people," that is, the Peronistas. This destroyed academic freedom and the autonomy and administrative democracy of the universities, and made them the creatures of the government.

The University Law took effect on January 1, 1948. Regarding it, Perón piously remarked that nothing worse could happen to a university than to become involved in politics. Actually, the law contained nominal safeguards against that danger, but they were ineffective from the start. The purge continued, until by 1953 90 per cent of the faculty personnel of 1945 had been ousted. And, as we shall see, that was not all.

4. PERONIZING THE CONSTITUTION

Perón's next step, made easy by his sweeping victory in the congressional elections of March 1948, was to revamp the

Constitution. It may seem surprising that he bothered to do this since he now had control of the Supreme Court, and it is as true in Argentina as in the United States that the Constitution is what the Supreme Court says it is. But if as true, it is no truer, and the existing Constitution contained some features which Perón did not like but which could not be altered by judicial interpretation and which even he did not dare to alter by executive fiat, such as the explicit prohibition against the immediate reëlection of a president. He also wanted additional powers in the economic field and the modernization of certain features of the Constitution of 1853 which, as he said, repeating a well-known phrase, belonged to the horse-and-buggy age. Finally, the amending process could have great propaganda value for him, since it would enable him to record in the basic law of Argentina his solicitude for the "suffering, sweating masses."

A specially elected convention was accordingly held at Buenos Aires from January 24 to March 11, 1949. Its chairman was Domingo Mercante, one of Perón's chief lieutenants from the early days of his rise to power. Originally, it was made up of 48 Radicals as well as 109 Peronistas, but the latter used steamroller tactics so shamelessly and effectively that the Radicals soon withdrew.

The most important changes made in the constitution were as follows: (1) The prohibition against immediate reëlection was scrapped, so that henceforth a president could succeed himself indefinitely. Perón had deprecated this change, but no one was foolish enough to believe him. (2) The Electoral College was abolished and provision made for the direct election of president and vice-president. (3) The government's economic powers, already extensive and increasingly employed since 1930, were further expanded at the expense of private property and private enterprise, for example, by placing foreign trade in the hands of the state, by declaring all minerals and almost all natural sources of energy to be the property of the nation, and by providing for state ownership of all "public services" (a term which it did not define). (4) Perón's social program was written into the Constitution along with enumerations of "The Rights of the Worker" (which did not include the right to strike), "The Rights of the Aged," and similar homiletic articles. There were also many other detailed changes, such as those strengthening the president *vis-à-vis* congress and bringing the Constitution up to date, for example, by increasing from 30,000 to 100,000 the minimum size of a deputy's constituency.

Yet, with all these changes, what the convention produced was not a new constitution, but an amendment of the existing Constitution of 1853, as already amended in 1860. Only if this is understood may one properly follow the common usage of calling it the Constitution of 1949. The fact is that it preserved most of the earlier basic law intact, including the latter's description of the government as federal, republican, and representative, its distribution of powers between the national government and the provinces, its threefold separation of powers (executive, legislative, judicial), and its attribution of these powers to, respectively, a president, a bicameral congress, and a federal judicial system headed by a Supreme Court of Justice.

This question of terminology is not important in itself, but it is important that the term "Constitution of 1949" should not be permitted to obscure the fact that constitutionally, and therefore institutionally, there is a high degree of continuity between the Perón regime since 1949 and its predecessors in Argentina since 1853. His regime operates very differently from its predecessors, but that fact only reflects the often-forgotten truth that the ideal of a government of laws, not of men, is seldom realized in practice.

On March 16, 1949, five days after the convention adjourned, Perón proclaimed the reformed constitution.

5. TOWARDS A SINGLE PARTY UNDER A SINGLE CHIEF

Perón then proceeded to his next task, that of reorganizing his political following. He had started out with a prejudice against all political parties, which he probably shared with most of his fellow army officers and certainly inherited from his chief in the

revolt of 1930, General Uriburu. For several years after 1943 he
clung to the idea that he was the leader not of just another party
but of a national "movement." Even as late as the presidential
campaign of 1946 he represented himself as the candidate of
this broader movement rather than of the three splinter parties
that had formally nominated him. The bickering among these
parties, however, brought home to him at once a lesson he
would have had to learn sooner or later, that is, that the ingrained political habits of the Argentine people made the formation of a political party of his own unavoidable if he was going
to continue to pose as the chief custodian of Argentina's democratic tradition — as he certainly planned to do, and did.

Accordingly, immediately after the election of February 1946,
he set about merging the splinter groups into a single party,
which took the name *Partido Unico de la Revolución,* or Single
(Only) Party of the Revolution. The merger was bitterly opposed
by labor leader Cipriano Reyes, who had done so much to bring
about the miracle of Perón's comeback the preceding October 17,
but who now feared that *laborismo* would be swallowed up by
Peronismo and Reyes by Perón. That is just what happened.
Reyes was first broken politically and then (1949) imprisoned;
at the present writing he is reported to be still in jail.

The Single Party of the Revolution functioned well enough
and, indeed, won a sweeping victory in the election of March
1948. Its name proved a poor choice, however, and was soon
dropped. This was done not so much because "single party" had
embarrassing associations with the late regimes of Hitler and
Mussolini as because, to Argentine ears, *Partido Unico* was un-
pleasantly reminiscent of *Unicato,* the name popularly applied
to one of the most unpopular phases of the oligarchy's rule in
Argentina in the late nineteenth century.

Unsatisfactory though the name was, that was only a very
minor reason for the reorganization of the party under a new
name in July 1949. The main reason was that, having been made
eligible for reëlection by the constitutional reform completed the
preceding March, Perón now wished to bring his party to
maximum efficiency in order to insure his victory in the coming

election. That was still nearly three years off; but much time was needed to carry out the sweeping reorganization he had in mind and to train his political army for the campaign.

The new party was founded at a mass meeting of delegates in Buenos Aires on July 25, 1949. The delegates dutifully adopted the new name, *Partido Peronista,* and the intricate plan of organization carefully prepared in advance by their leaders. Though intricate, the plan has one feature that gives unity and simplicity to the whole: Perón dominates the party from top to bottom. He is assisted by a Superior Executive Council of twenty-four members elected for an indeterminate period by the Peronista councils of the city of Buenos Aires and the provinces and territories. The chairmanship of this important body was given to Rear Admiral (R) Alberto Teisaire, majority leader in the Senate, who had stood by Perón in the dark days just before October 17, 1945.

Other national organs of the party are its General Congress, which resembles the national party conventions in the United States (except that Perón may annul the election of any delegate), a Bureau of Party Information, which conducts the party's propaganda under the direction of Perón, and a Tribunal of Party Discipline, which consists of five members appointed by the Superior Executive Council, communicates the party line, and enforces it — when necessary — by expulsion, which has the effect of a medieval excommunication. Membership in the party is a precious privilege; although the "exact number of party members is a carefully guarded secret," it "probably ranges between 250,000 and 300,000, or about 2 per cent of the total population of Argentina." * But while a privilege for all, it is also an obligation for some: though the law does not require it, in practice all public employees have to be members of the Party.

Besides the national organs, there are others which form a complete and nation-wide network reaching down through the provinces to the local precincts. As former Ambassador James Bruce has said, although the Argentines do not as a rule take to community organizations, the Peronista Party has seen to it

* George I. Blanksten, *Perón's Argentina* (Chicago, 1953), pp. 335–342.

that one of its branches is established in every community in Argentina.

Since by this time increasing persecution had hamstrung the opposition parties, Argentina's ostensibly multi-party system had become for all practical purposes a one-party system; and now, by the reorganization of 1949, Perón formalized and reinforced his position as the single party's sole chief.

6. THE CAPTIVE PRESS: "LA PRENSA"

The next step was to complete Perón's conquest of the press by the seizure on March 20, 1951 of *La Prensa,* Argentina's best newspaper, and the only one in the country that still dared to criticize the regime. There still remained the semi-independent *La Nación,* which had also been one of the country's and the world's best until Perón blighted it; but it had become more discreet.

Perón's gradual conquest of the press completed a process that had gone on almost unbrokenly since 1930. Up to that time the Argentine press had been remarkably free from federal control. Then, under Uriburu's dictatorship, freedom of the press was sharply curtailed; under Justo the Supreme Court, reversing its previous position, sanctioned a measure of federal control over it; Castillo, taking advantage of the new rule and the state of siege, anticipated most of the repressive measures later developed by Perón; and the chiefs of the military dictatorship who preceded Perón between June 4, 1943 and October 17, 1945 followed Castillo's example in this matter. For a long time *La Prensa* and *La Nación* enjoyed a high degree of immunity from the new controls because of their great prestige both at home and abroad. Thus, in 1930, when dictator Uriburu threatened to close down the critical *La Prensa,* its owners countered with the threat to resume publication in Paris and carry a streamer on the first page of every issue telling the world why it was no longer being published in Buenos Aires; and Uriburu backed down. By 1944, however, times had changed, and *La Prensa,* which had never missed a day's publication in the seventy-five years of its life, was now closed down for five days by dictator Farrell. This, as it proved, was the beginning of the end; but the end was long delayed.

Perón conquered the Argentine press piecemeal. In most cases he acted with his characteristic caution and indirection. Instead of trying to crush with a single blow, he applied successive turns of the screw and resorted to open seizures only after other measures had failed. First, a pattern to which all were expected to conform was set by the regime's own papers. Chief among these was *Democracia,* which was owned by the Eva Perón Foundation and had a circulation of about 200,000. One of its features was a column signed "Descartes," which was generally believed to be the pen name of Perón himself, though he never avowed it publicly. When conformity was not forthcoming and pressure had to be applied, he used various combinations of measures, which included harassment by government inspectors, reduction of supplies of newsprint (a government monopoly), inspired attacks by Peronista mobs and strikes by Peronista employees, subsidies to persons willing to be corrupted, and purchase of a controlling interest by his associates. And when seizure did become necessary — as in the case of *La Prensa* — it was given a cloak of legality.

During Perón's first presidential campaign a considerable degree of freedom was permitted the principal newspapers, and in the first six months of his administration he actually relaxed the controls still further. This proved to be only the calm before the storm, however, and beginning early in 1947 he carried on a systematic campaign against the free press. In October 1949 the campaign was facilitated by an amendment to the penal code which tightened up the law relating to *desacato* (disrespect) by making it a penal offense to "offend in any way the dignity of a public officer"; if the author of the offending item could not be found, the editor of the publication in which it appeared would be sent to jail. Another provision made it a penal offense to "disturb the friendly relations of the Argentine government with a foreign government." Then in January 1950 the recently established congressional Committee on Anti-Argentine Activities brought about the suspension of more than sixty newspapers in various parts of the country on the ground that their failure to display the Peronista device identifying 1950 as the "year of the Liberator General San Martín" was an anti-Argentine act. Later in the year many of these papers, and some of those which had been closed earlier, were permitted to resume publication, but some of the most prominent, including the famous *La Vanguardia*, remained closed.

La Prensa was the next target; but Perón found it a hard one to hit. It did not incite to violence or subversion, and it balanced attacks on some of Perón's measures with praise of others. Its comments on foreign affairs were equally discriminating and on occasion it castigated the imperialist powers, including the United States, with a severity matching that of Perón himself — which did not prevent him from making *La Prensa's* supposed subservience to the Anglo-Saxon imperialists and their international news services, particularly United Press, one of his chief talking points against it. Yet despite all his harassments and his efforts to discredit it with the public, *La Prensa* still retained its large circulation and therefore its influence. As late as October 1950 it was still selling 460,000 copies on weekdays and 570,000 on Sundays — a circulation which, in proportion to population, was larger than that of any newspaper in the United States. Moreover, its independence still rested on a firm financial basis: the bulk of its income was derived from its very large personal want-ad section, so that it could not be reached by putting pressure on a few big advertisers.

But Perón had other ways of reaching it. Beginning in October 1950 he gave the screw a final series of turns. *La Prensa's* newsprint supply was drastically reduced; a captive union of newsvendors struck and picketed the plant with police support; when the principal owner and editor, Alberto Gainza Paz, attempted to continue publication, he was indicted for "crimes against the safety of the state," and in March a special session of Congress voted the seizure of the paper.

Protests against this flagrant violation of the freedom of the press poured in from all parts of the non-communist world, but to no avail. Eight months later (November 19) *La Prensa* resumed publication under the same name, but as an organ of the captive General Confederation of Labor. Its management was vested in a board composed of union leaders and headed by the Confederation's General Secretary and Eva Perón's protégé, José G. Espejo.

7. TROUBLE FOR PERÓN AND EVA

Just before the denatured *La Prensa* resumed publication, the national election of November 1951 took place. As it approached, there were so many signs of increasing unrest that one might have thought the Perón team was losing its grip. Rising prices, shortages of consumer items, including food, and a general economic recession sharpened by the droughts of the last two years combined to provoke unrest even in labor circles. At the end of July something almost unheard-of occurred, a labor union went on strike. This was the railway union, *La Fraternidad*, which was one of the oldest labor organizations in Argentina, once the strongest, and since 1945 the least amenable to government control. Accompanied by dynamiting and other acts of sabotage, which the Peronista press promptly attributed to foreign (meaning both North American and communist) instigation, the strike was crushed by the proclamation of martial law and wholesale arrests of the railway workers.

Then in August occurred another unheard-of event: Evita herself suffered a humiliating political reverse when, after having in her grasp the nomination as vice-president, and therefore as her husband's running mate, in the November election, she was forced to renounce it. She described the decision as one that "I have taken by myself," but the truth seems to be that it was forced upon her, partly by civilian party leaders but still more by a large group of army officers headed by General Juan Pistarini, Perón's close associate since the time of their Italian mission of 1939–40, and now Minister of Public Works. The army officers objected because of Evita's shady past and their own dim future under a vice-president so closely identified with their chief rival for influence in the regime, the labor group, and also because, as vice-president, she might succeed to the presidency and thus become their commander-in-chief.

Even the withdrawal of Evita's candidacy failed to appease all of the army officers. Just a month later (September 28, 1951) a group of them staged a revolt which, though it was quickly suppressed, was fairly convincing evidence that there was substantial opposition to the regime among the officers of the armed services as well as in the other main pillar, organized labor. Originally, the uprising had been planned on a much larger scale, with formidable civilian as well as military support, but that plan was wrecked by quarrels over leadership and objective — as usual, Perón's opponents were unable to unite against him. Nevertheless, some of the officers decided to go ahead with a rump revolt, hoping that the others would follow their lead.

Two main reasons have been assigned for the failure of the revolt. The first was rivalry among the rebel leaders; their bickering over which of them was to lead the march on Buenos Aires and get credit for the expected victory gave just the time needed for Perón's quick countermeasures to rout them. The second was the refusal of many of the noncommissioned officers and other enlisted men to obey their officers' orders to revolt. Their refusal indicates that Perón's program of social revolution was paying him dividends in mass support. His program met with indifference or hostility among the officers, who were mainly of middle-class origin; but it enabled him to Peronize a large part of the enlisted ranks, who were drawn mainly from the descamisado masses and whose first loyalty was now to Perón, and not, as in times past, to their officers.

Perón took advantage of the fiasco to tighten his hold over the armed forces by getting his compliant Congress to give him the extraordinary power to promote, demote, or retire any officer at will. So confident was he after this easy victory that he not only avoided bloodshed in punishing the rebel officers (many were imprisoned, but none shot), but also put the purged and chastened Army in charge of the November elections.

For a time, strong encouragement was given to the opposition by the size and enthusiasm of the audiences that turned out to hear the Radical candidates for president and vice-president, Ricardo Balbín and Arturo Frondizi. Their last rally in Buenos Aires before the election drew a crowd estimated at 100,000. Despite all the obstacles placed in their way by the government, their drawing power often proved better than that of the leading Peronista speakers. Also, if Perón had been following the right vote-getting line in his nationalist, anti-imperialist campaign, they could expect to fare even better, for they were outdoing him on both issues.

He himself was unable to take the stump against them. On October 31 he was given a leave of absence by Congress for that purpose, but was held in Buenos Aires for the brief remainder of the campaign by the illness of his wife, who underwent an operation on November 5.

8. SIX MORE YEARS OF PERÓN

The opposition parties, however, were given little opportunity to present the issues to the people. Their situation in this respect was much worse than in 1946, for now they had no access to the radio and no newspaper on their side, and even the billboards were monopolized by Perón. Also in contrast to 1946, a coalition of the opposition parties was now prohibited by a recent act of Congress. As the only way of getting around this act, the Conservative Party made no nominations and instructed its members to vote the Radical ticket. The communists had a candidate, but he was shot and severely wounded by the police at a rally on October 31.

On the other hand, in addition to his monopoly of press, radio, billboards, and police protection for his campaign and harassment of the opposition's, Perón had an important new factor on his side. This was woman suffrage, which became effective in this national election for the first time in Argentine history. Here again, as in so many other cases, Perón gained an advantage by carrying through a measure which had been under discussion for a long time past but on which his opponents had failed to act. Even after woman suffrage was established, the opposition parties nominated almost no women candidates, whereas the Peronistas nominated scores of them and established a separate Peronista Women's Party, with Evita as its head.

Consequently, despite hard times, tension within the regime, and national unrest, Perón's victory seemed a foregone conclusion — another contrast with 1946. On November 11, the day of the election, a *New York Herald Tribune* expert explained that Perón would win because: "He has rigged the election; he has captured the decisive labor vote with years of 'handouts'; he has all but extinguished civil liberties, thereby stifling his opposition; he has created a neo-Nazi or neo-Fascist state whose jails are bulging with an estimated 3,000 to 4,000 dissenters, the incommunicado victims of a creeping terror." Most of this was correct as far as it went, though Perón did not rig the election in the sense of stuffing the ballot boxes or falsifying the returns. Again, as in 1946, the Army was in charge of the election, and again this seems to have been generally free and honest as far as the casting and counting of the votes was concerned; but this time the campaign itself was shamelessly rigged, for Perón allowed the opposition only the irreducible freedom necessary to enable him to say that an election had been held. He still felt it necessary to pay this much respect to Argentina's democratic tradition, but he had now reduced the democratic process to the merest ritual exercise.

Perón and his party naturally won easily. This time his percentage of the popular vote (there was no longer an electoral vote) rose to 65, as compared with 55 in 1946; and his party captured every seat in the Senate and all but 14 seats in the Chamber of Deputies. The new feminine representation in Congress (six senators, 23 deputies) was solidly Peronista.

The performance of the opposition at the polls could be interpreted in two quite different ways. On the one hand, the only important party, the Radicals, had garnered some 2,500,000 votes, or one-third of the total, for their Balbín-Frondizi ticket. This was a remarkably good showing in view of the fact that they had been forced to campaign in a strait jacket, and it was encouraging to know that there were still so many Argentines who would record their protest against the Perón regime.

On the other hand, even in the old Radical-Socialist stronghold of Buenos Aires, Perón had won by the ample margin of 829,955 votes to 618,725 for the opposition. To be sure his tactics of the handout, of "spend and spend and elect and elect," had reached its peak in Buenos Aires, and he had supported it by fomenting the immigration of thousands of back-country descamisados to the capital. But it was cold comfort for the opposition to reflect that their defeat in this important sector had not been turned into an utter rout. Another disturbing feature of the election was that in almost every electoral district Perón received an even larger majority of the new women's vote than of the men's vote. If this meant that new voters in general were going to line up behind Perón, the long-range outlook for the opposition was not bright.

On the whole, the results of the plebiscite tended to confirm the gloomy prognostication of the *Herald Tribune* expert on election day before the votes were counted. As he saw it, not only was Perón sure to win this election, but there were only two future developments which could "whip" him, and neither of these was likely in the immediate future. One was "a revolution backed fully by the Argentine armed forces and enjoying broad popular support." The correspondent's other hope lay in the "sudden failure of Perón's schizophrenic economic policy to surmount a growing crisis in Argentina's domestic and foreign commerce." The implication here was apparently that such a crisis would bring about the near-miracle required to precipitate the simultaneous revolt of the military and the citizenry against Perón, for economic crises alone, however severe, do not overthrow governments. It takes people to do that. Since it was unlikely that either of these conditions would be fulfilled, it required great optimism to hope that the two would occur simultaneously.

That such an economic cataclysm would occur and would lead to revolt was in fact the only real hope of Perón's opponents at home and abroad after his sweeping victory at the polls in November 1951; but up to the end of 1953 (at which our narrative stops) the hope had not been fulfilled, nor, so far as an outsider could see, had it come anywhere near fulfillment. Though the economic storm already in progress in 1951 became a hurricane the following year, Perón somehow weathered it and by the end of 1953 the sky was clearing for him again.*

9. DEATH AND TRANSFIGURATION OF EVITA

The severest shock to the regime in these two years came from a totally different direction and one which until late in 1951 was quite unforeseen. This was the death of Eva Perón from cancer on July 26, 1952, at the age of thirty-three. Again, however, Perón came through the crisis unscathed. Indeed, with luck and good management he seems to have emerged from it stronger than before. He had not lost the Midas-touch which, in October 1945, enabled him to turn the most unlikely materials into political gold.

Evita made almost her last public appearance at a descamisado mass meeting in the Plaza de Mayo on May Day, 1952. First the band played and the huge crowd sang the national anthem and two descamisado favorites, "Aurora" and "The Peronista Boys." Then the ailing Evita found strength enough to deliver an address which, though brief, was highly inflammatory. Her opening words were the now familiar salutation, "My dear descamisados," and her theme, "Be on your guard. The enemy are preparing an ambush for us. Stand by Perón, who stands by you, and then we can never be defeated, for we are the real Argentina." She left no doubt as to who the enemy were or what would happen to them if they dared attack Perón. "We will never again let ourselves be kicked around by the traitorous and corrupt oligarchy and their foreign masters. Woe be to them the day they lift a hand against Perón! For that day, my General [turning to Perón, who stood at her side], I will go out into the streets with the workingmen, with the women of the people, with the descamisados, and we will not leave one stone upon another that is not Peronista!"

In sharp contrast to Evita's harangue was the 100-page message on the state of the union that her husband read to the patient members of Congress the same day. It was a fighting speech, but

* For details, see below, Chapter 8.

not, like Evita's, inflammatory. He called it an accounting to the representatives of the nation, and a large part of it was devoted to a sober survey of the record of his first administration, though he also discussed party doctrine at length, and gave a preview of his plans for the future.

Certain passages were invested with special interest by the crisis through which his regime was passing. Inflation was wiping out many of the vaunted material benefits which he had conferred on the descamisados in his first years, but he disposed of complaint on this score by declaring that excessive preoccupation with material welfare has frequently been the cause of "great misfortunes and the fatal decadence" of nations, and that the "supreme objective" of his program of social justice was to "dignify the workers" by bringing about "a just distribution of spiritual and moral benefits." It is worth noting that although he talked at considerable length about spiritual values, he never mentioned the Catholic Church, with which his relations had cooled in recent years.

His exposition of his Third Position and Justicialism involved, of course, a discussion of capital and labor, and on this subject his address was ambivalent. Justicialism he defined as an application of the Third Position idea to the domestic affairs of Argentina. As to the meaning of the Third Position itself, he complained that this had been misrepresented by his critics as a foreign policy which committed Argentina to a systematic, rigid neutrality, whereas in fact it was a philosophy designed to free Argentina from capitalism without delivering it into the "oppressive clutches" of "collectivism," that is, communism. "International capitalism" then came in for the usual excoriation, which provided him with an occasion for exulting once more in his victory over Spruille Braden. The latter was described as "the symbol of a routed capitalist domination," whose disappearance "marks the beginning of that economic independence which is the basis of our definitive political liberty." As if this were not enough, he roundly declared: "Let no one deceive himself: the capitalist economy has nothing to do in our country. Its remaining redoubts will be the objects of our implacable destruction."

And yet, later on in his address, after asserting categorically that the only class which ought to exist in Argentina was the laboring class, he went on to note with approval that now at last the Argentine capitalist class was beginning to coöperate with the government and labor. "When the forces that represent capital," he continued, "shall have achieved the organization already attained by labor, our high ideal of an organized community . . . will have been realized." In order to resolve the apparent contradiction, he added that "by a natural evolution of our economic system, the workers will progressively acquire direct ownership of the capital goods of production, commerce and industry" — but the evolutionary process would be slow and piecemeal. Here was something for everybody: for labor, ultimate total victory; for capital, indefinite postponement of total defeat. His address ended with a glowing tribute, which also had the air of a threnody, to his wife, who "has sacrificed everything on the altar of our ideals" and worn herself out as the tireless champion of labor and "the humble people" of Argentina.

When Evita died less than two months later (July 26), her many Argentine enemies rejoiced; but public policy combined with the genuine grief of her henchmen and her host of descamisados to produce such an orgy of public and publicized mourning as the world has seldom seen. For a week the public life of the nation ceased, except to do honor to the departed. She was promptly proclaimed a saint by the Peronistas — "Saint Eva of America" was the title proposed by the powerful head of the General Confederation of Labor, José Espejo, who owed his power to Evita. Her mortal remains were not to be buried but, like Lenin's, kept perpetually on view. For this purpose a $30,000 coffin with a glass lid an inch thick was purchased from a firm in the United States — the country which Evita, an implacable hater, detested more than any other. Subsequently, it was decided to house her remains permanently in a monumental building especially constructed for the purpose, adorned with statues symbolizing the ideals of the Perón regime, and surmounted by the gigantic figure of a descamisado. Two items stressed in the official announcement of the plans would have been particularly pleasing to Evita: one, that the architect was ideologically sound, a thoroughgoing Peronista; the other, that this monument would overtop the Statue of Liberty.

With a rather gruesome efficiency, preparations for Evita's death had been begun long before it occurred. None of these was more striking, or probably more important, than the publication late in 1951 of a quasi-autobiographical book, *La razón de mi vida* (The Meaning of My Life), purporting to have been written by her. Actually, the book was ghost-written and it told very little about her life. On the other hand, it told a great deal in a supercharged emotional style about her three loves: for Argentina, for the descamisados, and for Perón.

The manifest purpose of the book was to make certain that on her death Perón would inherit the whole legacy of the descamisados' devotion to her. This should not be too difficult, for the policy of a social revolution in favor of the Argentine underdogs was his invention, not hers, and he had given it top billing in his program before he ever met Evita; but *La razón de mi vida* would help the good work along. Accordingly, it was made a required text in all the schools and universities of Argentina.

Just before her death the book had caused an international incident. Commercial publishers in the United States, who might have snapped up a genuine, frank autobiography by the notorious Evita, refused to handle an English translation of this sentimental and ideological effusion. Their refusal was publicly blamed by leading Peronistas on "censorship" by the State Department, a mass meeting of protest was held, and the United States Information Center in Buenos Aires was bombed twice in late June and early July 1952.

10. THERMIDORIAN REACTION FROM WITHIN?

The passing of this remarkable woman was an event of great significance for the future development of Argentina in both domestic affairs and foreign relations. By the end of 1953 it seemed possible to discern the major results, though, as usual where Perón was concerned, one could not be sure how lasting they would be, and in some respects the outlines were not yet entirely clear. The international significance of her death, particularly in opening the way to better relations with the United States, will be discussed in the next chapter.

At home, Evita's death unleashed a struggle for power and place. Perón promptly settled the first round in his own favor by taking upon himself the most important of her former roles. He succeeded her as head of the gigantic Social Aid Foundation and the Peronista Women's Party, and even replaced her in the weekly meetings with labor leaders and the semiweekly meetings at the Ministry of Labor where she had given personal interviews and handouts to all comers from among the descamisados. He trusted no one as he had Evita.

Next, it became clear that he was not going to permit anything like an Evita Perón machine to perpetuate itself. Accordingly, her chief henchmen were soon eliminated. One conspicuous example was José Espejo, head of the powerful General Confederation of Labor and its six million members. In this case Perón followed his favorite course of indirection. All of a sudden Espejo's appearance at a labor meeting became the signal for catcalls and heckling; this proved that he had lost the workers' confidence, which of course ended his usefulness; whereupon he was supplanted as head of the Confederation by a nobody who was obviously Perón's puppet. Another conspicuous example was Evita's own brother, Juan Duarte, who was Perón's private secretary and was said to have amassed a fortune while in his service. In this case the method of elimination was different. One fine day Duarte was found dead, with a bullet through his head, a revolver in his hand, and a suicide note beside his body. The note expressed repentance and boundless gratitude and devotion to Perón. Suicide was the official verdict, but the public's verdict found expression in the popular quip, "Yes, we know Duarte committed suicide, but we haven't been able to find out yet who killed him."

Behind all this lay two conflicts: one, a conflict for power between the two main pillars of the regime, army and labor; the other, a conflict over the whole orientation of government policy. Under Espejo, what Perón had called his "army of labor" during the critical days of his rise to power was being developed into a literal army, with a trained militia of its own, equipped with machine guns and anti-tank guns. This obvious labor bid for a monopoly of power was defeated by the ousting of Espejo. Perón had no intention of becoming dependent upon labor alone, for the balance between army and labor, which enabled him to play off one against the other, was the very foundation of his regime.

Stated in broad terms, the policy conflict was one between the leftward, proletarian swing represented by the late Evita, and a more moderate course which can be described as "somewhat left of center," provided this phrase is not understood to mean the same thing in the context of Perón's Argentina that the same phrase of Franklin Roosevelt's had when applied to the United States. Perón was both more radical and more conservative than Roosevelt — more radical in that he advocated the complete elimination of the capitalist system in Argentina; more conservative in that after Evita's death his renewed effort to make converts from the opposition had as a major target elements in the oligarchy itself. The effort met with some success; a conspicuous convert late in 1953 was Federico Pinedo, twice Minister of Finance during the Conservative Restoration.

Repentant sinners were welcomed from other quarters, too. One over whom there was great rejoicing in the Peronista heaven at this time was Enrique Dickmann, former Socialist deputy and editor of the now suppressed *La Vanguardia*. None of note came from among the Radicals. Indeed, the Radicals, under the new leadership of Balbín and Frondizi, were now living up to their party label and had become more radical than Perón himself.

His chief problem now was to put the national economy back on a sound footing and promote its further development. In doing so, he ran the risk of offending the descamisados, for he would have to put a stop to the increases in social benefits and wages to which they had become accustomed but which, he and his advisers now felt, the national economy could no longer support. Apparently convinced that, though the descamisados might grumble, they would remain loyal to him, he shifted the emphasis from social justice to sound business. So far and so fast did

he move along the line indicated by these considerations that, as
we shall see in the next chapter, before the end of 1953 he was
giving even the once-hated foreign capitalists promises of a
cordial welcome and good treatment in Argentina. The Peronista
revolution seemed to be entering upon a stage of Thermidorian
reaction under the leadership of Perón himself, though it was still
too early to say whether the change was one of policy or only of
tactics.

11. DESCAMISADO REFRAIN

If one could believe some of its leading spokesmen, Peronismo
had not changed at all. In April 1953 they applauded one of the
most sensational acts of descamisado violence that had yet
occurred — the burning of that citadel of the oligarchy, the
grandiose Jockey Club of Buenos Aires. On the same night the
mob burned the headquarters of the Conservative, Radical, and
Socialist parties, but left the Communist Party's headquarters
untouched.

In December of that year, Angel Borlenghi, Minister of Interior, representing the Government in an important debate on an
amnesty bill, rang all the familiar changes on the descamisado
theme. According to him, the famous October 17 was still the day
when the working class broke its chains, defied capitalism and
imperialism, brushed aside the contemptuous aristocracy and
hack politicians, and chose Perón to defend the dignity of labor;
"Comrade Evita" was still the guide pointing out the luminous
path for all to follow; and the government of Argentina was still
"the government of the working class." "We shall continue to
fight," he declared in his peroration, "against the oligarchy,
against oppression, against class privilege. We shall continue to
champion the cultural, social, and economic betterment of the
workers. We shall continue to carry forward our social program,
which is the heart of Peronismo."

In one respect at least, Perón himself had certainly not
changed, for he continued to tighten his grip on an increasingly

centralized administration. A perfect example was provided in December 1953 by the government's project for a new University Law, which his compliant congress was sure to pass. Not content with having "intervened" all the universities, purged their personnel in 1947, and brought these once autonomous institutions under strict government control by the University Law of 1948, he now prepared to take the reins openly into his own hands. The new law gave him unlimited power to appoint and dismiss the university deans as well as rectors; the latter were to appoint and dismiss all other administrative officers; Perón was given a free hand in his choice of rectors by the abolition of the previous requirement that a rector must have held a higher degree for ten years; and the previous prohibition against political activities in the universities was repealed.

Now the whole Argentine educational system, with Eva Perón's *La razón de mi vida* the only text required in all parts of it, was geared to the propagation of Peronismo. That was its avowed purpose, and the purpose was defended with what its champions took to be irresistible logic. As one of them put it in the December debate: "The schools of Argentina have always inculcated patriotism. Peronismo is the most perfect expression of patriotism. Therefore, in teaching Peronismo the schools of today are only carrying on the oldest and best tradition of Argentine education."

Similarly and at the same time the administration put through an amnesty act which was designed ostensibly to restore political tranquillity at home but actually to conciliate opinion in the United States. The amnesty left in full force the "state of internal war" established by congress at the time of the military uprising in September 1951. This was a species of martial law, unauthorized by the constitution, which conferred far more sweeping powers and established far heavier penalties than the two precautionary measures that had constitutional sanction — the old "state of siege" and the new "state of alarm" created by the constitutional convention of 1949. The "state of internal war" so completely nullified constitutional guarantees that a political prisoner released under the amnesty one day might be rearrested the next and held in jail at the government's discretion, without any possibility that a court of law would even give him a hearing through *habeas corpus* proceedings.

When the handful of Radical deputies protested, they were told that it was their own "combative" attitude which made the continuance of the "state of internal war" necessary. "We cannot," said the Peronista sponsor of the measure, "leave the democratic Justicialist state defenseless in the presence of its enemies."

In short, opposition to Peronismo had become a subversive activity, and the suspension of constitutional guarantees had accordingly been made a fixed feature of the new political normality in Argentina and would so continue until there no longer remained a minority that needed the protection of constitutional guarantees.

8. How the Argentine Economy Fared, 1946–1953

The preceding chapter showed how Argentina has been blighted culturally as well as politically by the Perón regime. The present chapter is addressed to the questions: How has the nation's economy fared? and What has this meant to its people and its international economic position? These questions will be examined at length, as their importance deserves. They involve two of the three major objectives announced by the regime: social justice and national economic independence, both of which have been made the subject of some of its most highly publicized pronouncements, including a formal Declaration of Economic Independence (July 9, 1947) and two Five-year Plans (1947 and 1953).

1. PANORAMA

The economic history of Argentina's first seven years under Perón could be summed up in three words: "Boom and crash." The temptation to adopt this simple text is strong, especially if one dislikes Perón's regime, for it can be (and has been) used to show that his regime is not only politically iniquitous but also economically incompetent.

Some of the most obvious facts support this view. The boom, which lasted only two years, was due mainly to two factors for which Perón deserves no credit, whereas he unquestionably helped to precipitate the crash. The two boom factors were the large wartime gold and foreign exchange balance ($1600 million) built up by Argentina before Perón came to power, and the premium prices commanded by Argentine foodstuffs just after the war because of the world-wide food shortage. After these fortuitous advantages were exhausted in 1948 the national economy slipped inexorably into the deep depression of 1951–52. Now, Argentina, so recently one of the world's greatest exporters of beef and wheat, had to ration beef, import wheat, and go on a black-bread diet. Fuel, too, was rationed, so that there was a general slowdown of transportation and industry; replacements of machinery for farm and factory became unobtainable; even labor in this "workingmen's republic" had to go on part time, and remorseless inflation wiped out successive wage increases decreed by the paternalistic government. Since Perón and his lieutenants had assumed full control over the Argentine economy, they must, the argument runs, be held responsible for the crash.

The problem is not quite so simple as that. For one thing, the crash as well as the boom was due in part to circumstances beyond Perón's control. Thus, the argricultural-pastoral depression had begun before 1943 and was deepened after 1949 by a series of droughts; and the fuel shortage was greatly aggravated by the Anglo-Iranian oil dispute. Again, by no means all the items in the balance sheet of these seven years are on the debit side. Considerable advances were made in industry, mining, and transportation, and even in certain branches of agriculture; and though the evidence is not complete, it seems likely that the workers were better off in 1953 than in 1943, if one considers not only wages but also fringe benefits, security, and their own estimate of their situation. Again, the decline in Argentine exports, which was a major cause of the economic crisis, was due in part to the reduction of the exportable surplus of foodstuffs (for example, beef) by increasing domestic consumption; so that what was a loss from the point of view of international economics was a gain from the point of view of the standard of living in Argentina.

However one may apportion blame and praise, this period was studded with so many new developments of great and probably lasting significance that it seemed likely to prove one of the major turning points in the economic and social history of Argentina. The most obvious of these developments were the great extension of government control over the nation's economy and the establishment of a far-reaching system of social welfare; but there were many more besides. For the first time in history, Argentine ships carried a larger share of the nation's foreign trade than the ships of any other country. Though the ambitious plans for industrialization had worked out badly in some respects, yet a considerable impulse had been given to industries, both old and new; one of the most important, potentially, was the steel industry. Also for the first time in history, the United States forged ahead of Great Britain as the largest investor in Argentina and as Argentina's best customer; it had already gained first place in Argentine imports before the war. A perhaps related development was the government's adoption in 1952 of a scientific, long-range plan for the reorganization of Argentina's agriculture.

Finally, it should be noted that both the Perón regime and the country's economy weathered the crisis without apparent lasting damage; that consumption remained at a moderately high level through the worst of it, so that for the whole period 1946–1952 the rate of consumption showed a substantial increase of 3.5 per cent per annum; that even in 1952 Argentina still accounted for 22 per cent of the total gross product of Latin America; and that 1953 was marked by a recovery that promised to continue.

2. ECONOMIC CONTROLS

Government intervention in the economic life of Argentina was not new when Perón came to power in 1946. As we have noted earlier, a few precedents had been set by the Radical presidents, Irigoyen and Alvear, and many were added by the Conservative Justo in dealing with the depression of the 1930's. Still further additions were made under the guise of war measures by Castillo and the military dictatorship that overthrew him in 1943. Taken all together, their range extended over exchange controls, the control of banking and credit, regulation of the production and marketing of agricultural products, meat, and oil, and the fixing of wages.

What Perón did was to extend these measures still further, systematize them, erect the system into a doctrine, and give the system and the doctrine the highest legal sanction and the greatest possible permanence by incorporating them in the reformed Constitution of 1949. The key provisions, contained in Articles 38 and 40, are as follows:

Private property has a social function and, as a consequence, it shall be subject to the obligations which the law may establish for the common good . . . By means of a law, the state may intervene in the economy and monopolize any given activity to safeguard the general interest . . . Importing and exporting . . . shall be in the hands of the state . . . [Otherwise] all economic activity shall be organized in accordance with free private enterprise, provided that it does not . . . aim to dominate Argentine markets, eliminate competition, or increase profits usuriously. Minerals, waterfalls, deposits of petroleum, coal and gas, and other natural sources of energy . . . are the imprescriptible and inalienable property of the nation . . . Public services belong *ab initio* to the state, and in no event may they be alienated or ceded for their operation. Those which are in private possession shall be transferred to the state, by means of purchase or expropriation with prior indemnity, when such is determined by a national law.

These provisions established Perón's Third Position between capitalism and communism. Together with other provisions aimed directly at the welfare of the workers, they summed up Justicialism and embodied the Peronista prescription for realizing the ideal of an Argentina which would be, in the words of the Constitution, "economically free, socially just, and politically sovereign."

The Argentine government has employed two methods of participating in the national economy as provided for by these articles. One is the creation of monopolies operated by the government itself; the other, the establishment, in conjunction with private capital, of semi-governmental "mixed companies." The most striking example of the former was the monopolistic

Argentine Trade Promotion Institute, commonly called IAPI from the initials of its official name, *Instituto Argentino de Promoción del Intercambio*. Created by executive decree in 1946, IAPI was confirmed by an act of Congress in 1947 — an example of Perón's proclivity for obtaining rubber-stamp legalization of his measures. It was given the sole right to purchase all major crops from the Argentine producers at its own price and sell them abroad at the best price it could get, and to purchase foreign goods for its own use and for other government agencies. For a time it also monopolized the purchase of agricultural machinery. Using these absolute powers, IAPI's first head and the economic czar of Argentina, Miguel Miranda, made barter deals with foreign purchasers which resulted in Argentina's obtaining farm machinery that might not otherwise have been obtainable in the early postwar years, when such items were still in short supply throughout the world. On the other hand, he forced Argentine farmers (prominent among whom were those leaders of the hated oligarchy, the great landowners) to accept ruinously low prices. Stated mildly, this reduced incentive; and it thereby accelerated the decline in agricultural production which was one of the major causes of the subsequent economic crash.

"Mixed companies" were authorized by law for the very broad purpose of promoting the general welfare and "initiating, encouraging, or developing economic activities." The ratio of private and government capital was to be fixed by agreement in each case. Whatever its share, the government was assured of control by being given the power to appoint the president, who was to have the right to veto any decision of the board of directors or the stockholders; and the government was also to appoint at least one-third of the directors. Examples of mixed companies are those formed by the Directorate General of Military Manufactures to explore for and exploit "copper, iron, manganese, wolfram, aluminum, beryllium, and other materials necessary for war purposes." By 1950 mixed companies thus established were engaging in "every phase of the mining and metallurgical industry from prospecting to ultimate industrial production of the tool product or refined chemical."

Government intervention was carried forward vigorously in other ways as well. An important illustration, but only one of many, was the nationalization (1946) of the Central Bank, which was made the depository for all accounts of other banks and given a veto over all loan operations based upon them. The powers of the government were, in fact, so comprehensive and detailed that there was not a nook or cranny of the Argentine economy into which they did not, or at any rate could not, extend. If private enterprise was nominally protected by the constitution, its actual operation depended upon government sufferance. Even the explicit provision that there must be no expropriation save with prior compensation and by act of Congress was no guarantee, since Congress always proved itself the willing instrument of Perón.

3. AGRICULTURE AND LIVESTOCK

Despite the substantial growth of industry in Argentina since the First World War, the economy of that country still rests on an agricultural and pastoral foundation. As pointed out in a recent study prepared by the Economic Commission for Latin America,* "the fundamental problem of economic development in Argentina, as in other Latin American countries . . . centers about utilizing primary exports in such a way as to gradually reduce the countries' dependence upon them."

The emphasis here should be on the word "gradually," and one of Perón's gravest mistakes was in trying to make the reduction too quickly. As noted above, Argentine agriculture had lost some of its vigor even before Perón came to power. It might have recovered in the postwar period when prices for cereals were high; but in his haste to industrialize and rearm, Perón not only denied it the opportunity to recover, but inflicted fresh injury upon it. Since the basic exports of Argentina are agricultural and pastoral products, Perón thereby came close to defeating his own objectives and wrecking his regime. Already by 1948 he had

* A commission set up by the United Nations Social and Economic Council.

begun to see the error of his ways and was trying, though rather half-heartedly, to mend them; but almost at once he was beset by a series of droughts and other misfortunes.

Whether he was responsible or not, the agricultural-pastoral economy suffered in a great variety of ways in this period. Government controls, mainly through IAPI, diverted a large part of the income from this sector of the national economy to other channels, such as armaments and public works. The large-scale migration of rural workers to urban centers brought on an acute labor shortage. The shortage might have been made good to a considerable extent by increased use of farm machinery, but the supplies of such machinery were not even maintained at the previous level. Whereas in 1950 it was estimated that 27,500 tractors would have to be imported the following year to meet essential needs, less than one-fourth of that number (about 6000) were actually imported in 1951. Incentives in this field were still further reduced by fuel shortages, a rise in minimum wages, and a decline in the purchasing power of the products. In the case of cereals, purchasing power had dropped by 1952 to 64 per cent of the 1948 level. As a result, a large sector of the agricultural-pastoral economy continued to deteriorate through 1952, and it was not until the following year that, thanks to the breaking of the drought and more vigorous government aid, the first substantial recovery was made.

The results were extremely serious for the whole Argentine economy; but this was because of the dominant position of foodstuffs in the export trade. They held no such preponderance in national production as a whole. As shown by the accompanying figures for Argentina's total gross product (that is, the value of all goods and services) from 1945 to 1952, even in their relatively prosperous years from 1945 to 1948 agricultural and pastoral activities accounted for only about one-fourth of the total in any year and for a much smaller fraction of the 50 per cent increase in the total from 1945 to 1948; they were first equaled and then exceeded by manufacturing alone; and by 1952 they accounted for less than one-eighth of the gross national product and for less than half as much of it as manufacturing.

GROSS PRODUCT, ARGENTINA, 1945–1952

(In thousands of millions of pesos at 1950 prices)

Year	All Activities	Agricultural-Pastoral	Manufacturing	Other Activities
1945	41.2	9.5	9.0	22.7
1946	47.6	12.3	10.8	24.5
1947	55.8	12.1	12.7	31.0
1948	62.3	12.3	14.0	36.0
1949	60.9	11.0	14.2	35.7
1950	53.6	9.7	12.6	31.3
1951	54.0	8.2	13.0	32.8
1952	49.3	6.0	12.5	**30.8**

On the other hand, Argentina's exports were still made up almost wholly of agricultural and pastoral products. Even in the depression year 1951, 92 per cent of the total value of Argentine exports were agricultural and pastoral products. This figure was divided almost equally between agricultural products (mainly cereals) and livestock products (mainly meat, wool, and hides), which accounted respectively for 45 and 47 per cent. It was with these exports that Argentina paid for the imports of machinery, raw materials, and fuels which were still necessary — in some respects increasingly necessary — for the very maintenance of her domestic economy, not to mention its further development.

The disastrous effect of Argentina's agricultural-pastoral decline on her ability to purchase the essential foreign goods is reflected in the export figures for 1945–1952. Measured in thousands of millions of pesos at 1950 prices, these rose from 6.4 in 1945 to 11.5 in the peak year 1947, and then dropped with occasional fluctuations to 3.9 in 1952. In the latter year things had come to such a pass that, despite a rigorous curtailment of imports, there was still an "unfavorable" balance (excess of imports over exports) which was almost two-thirds as large as the total value of exports. This was an impossible situation, particularly for a government whose chief was so dedicated to achieving Argentina's economic independence that he had sworn he would cut off his right hand before he would accept a foreign loan.

The decline did not affect all branches of the agricultural-pastoral economy equally; in fact, in some branches there was a distinct improvement. The decline was greatest in cereals, which were the chief sufferers from the almost unbroken drought of 1949–1952, and linseed, which lost its former market in the United States.

Realizing at last that halfway measures would not do, the government in 1952 bestirred itself vigorously on behalf of agriculture. For the first time since 1946 substantial price increases were granted the producers by IAPI: these ranged from about 50 to 100 per cent on such crops as wheat, flax, corn, and oats. The increases were made a part of the second Five-Year Plan (1953–1957), which shifted the emphasis from industrialization, the target of the first Five-Year Plan, to agriculture.

The new Five-Year Plan aimed at a 40 per cent increase in the area sown. It greatly increased tractor imports, granted a preferential rate of exchange for all imported farm machinery and replacements, established mechanized teams available on a rental basis to farmers who could not afford to buy their own equipment, provided subsidies for migrant farm labor and the transportation of cattle to fattening pastures, and liberalized agricultural credit facilities. In the latter connection it adopted an ambitious "Planned Agrarian Credit" system, to be operated through the Argentine National Bank (*Banco de la Nación Argentina*), which was designed to bring about a scientific and gradual relocation of various types of agriculture in the interest of greater efficiency, on the basis of a national ecological map prepared by the government's excellent cartographic service.

With the coöperation of the weather (for the first time in four years), an upturn which promised to become general was well begun in the agricultural sector by the end of 1953. Manufacturers still complained of shortages of equipment, but the basic agricultural economy was on its feet again, with bumper yields reported for some crops and satisfactory yields for almost all others, enough cattle moving to market to prevent another meat shortage, and Argentina's foreign exchange position growing steadily stronger throughout the year. Barring another act of God like the droughts of 1949–1952, the economic prospects of the Perón regime as it moved on into its eighth year were at least fair, if not yet promising. It had learned just in time that it would not do to be in too big a hurry about industrializing Argentina or to be too literal about winning its economic independence; that the rest of the country could not thrive while its agriculture was depressed, and that its national economy was still unalterably international to a high degree and likely to remain so for a long time to come.

In one important respect, Perón's vaunted revolution has left the rural life of Argentina substantially unchanged. That is the concentration of landownership in the hands of a relatively small number of persons and corporations. Since these great estates were the basis of the fortunes of that oligarchy which he has never tired of denouncing, one might have expected him to give top priority to a thoroughgoing agrarian reform aimed at breaking up these so-called *latifundios* and distributing the land among the rural descamisados, as had been done in Mexico since the Revolution of 1910. He has indeed talked a great deal about such a reform, but he has done little about it beyond breaking up a few estates belonging to political enemies of his regime, such as the Patrón Costas whose election to the presidency Perón and the other members of the G.O.U. prevented by the coup of June 1943. He claimed in June 1953 to have redistributed 1.2 million acres to date, but there were that many acres in a single latifundio at the beginning of his regime. While that was the largest latifundio, there were two others of 950,000 and 575,000 respectively, and 2000 landlords were reported to own 135 million acres, or one-fifth of the total area of Argentina.

The regime's failure to do more about the land may be explained on four grounds. First, at the outset the government was too absorbed in its industrialization program to take on any rural problem of such magnitude as a reform of the land system. Secondly, measures taken by Perón to improve the position of tenant farmers appear to have lessened the pressure for a radical program of agrarian reform. In the third place, there soon began the prolonged and severe agricultural crisis, which discouraged interfering with the land system lest that prove an aggravation. Finally, so great a part of Argentina's rural economy was geared to large-scale operations that the fragmentation of it by land reform, however desirable it might seem politically and socially, would be economically wasteful and perhaps even disastrous. This was a warning that Argentines and other Latin Americans, including the Venezuelan revolutionaries of 1945,* took from Mexico's sobering experience with its land reform. To be sure, instead of merely breaking up the great estates into small private properties, the reform might replace them with some kind of coöperative or communal system, but that would be a complicated and difficult operation, and again the parlous state of agriculture discouraged meddling with it for the time being. As a result, while Perón was still promising agrarian reform at the close of 1953, the promise still remained largely unfulfilled.

4. INDUSTRY AND MINING

As pointed out above, the sound development of a diversified economy in Argentina must be based on agriculture. In the short range, the proposition has not always held good. On some conspicuous occasions agriculture's adversity has proved to be the manufacturers' opportunity. This was true during the world-wide depression after 1929, and again when the Perón depression in Argentine agriculture was at its worst, from 1949 to 1952. In both periods Argentina's manufacturing industries were stimulated by the demand made upon them to cover import deficiencies caused by the inability of depressed agriculture to finance the country's requirements of imported goods.

Yet the experience of the latter period proved that in the long run manufacturing was still dependent upon agriculture. After the latter had made a substantial recovery in 1953, manufacturers were still complaining of a shortage of machinery, replacements, fuels, and raw materials. All these were imported goods which in the long run still had to be paid for by the country's basic

---

* A. P. Whitaker, *The United States and South America: The Northern Republics* (Cambridge, Mass., 1948), pp. 208–209.

agricultural exports. Again faulty government policy must share the blame with adverse circumstances. Perón and his advisers, after having come close to wrecking Argentina's agricultural economy by sacrificing it to industry, swung to the opposite extreme after 1950. By sharply curtailing industrial credits and imports of machinery, fuel, and raw materials, they now gave the manufacturers an advance dose of the austerity which was made nation-wide in 1951.

Nevertheless, despite the errors in their basic assumptions and timing, Perón and his advisers were not all wrong. They were right in saying that Argentina had already demonstrated its capacity for extensive industrialization and that further development along this line was necessary in the interest of a better balanced economy and a higher standard of living. In certain respects they were also more nearly right than their critics about the specific direction which further industrialization could and should take. Adequate development of these propositions would require a much more detailed examination of the whole complicated and controversial problem of Argentine industrialization than can be undertaken here.

As shown by the table of gross products on page 182, manufactures had almost caught up with agriculture by 1945, passed it in 1947, and widened their lead to a 2-to-1 ratio in 1952. In 1945, however, they still consisted overwhelmingly of nondurable consumer goods — textiles, boots and shoes, food and beverages — and the government's commitment to the achievement of "economic independence" required their expansion in many directions, including newsprint, vehicles, durable goods, and, above all, a steel industry. The obstacles to be overcome were formidable. Chief among these were the country's deficiencies in natural resources described in an earlier chapter. In addition, for some time before 1947, when the first national census since 1914 was taken, it was widely believed that Argentina's population was not only too small but also too nearly static to provide the expanding market necessary for any considerable industrial growth.

Some of these obstacles, such as shortages of fuel and lack of raw materials, proved to be real enough, though most of them were now reduced in one way or another, as will be shown below. The supposed population handicap, however, turned out to be imaginary. The error is understandable, since no national census was taken between 1914 and 1947, and in the absence of authoritative data it was naturally assumed that population growth must have slowed down because of such unfavorable factors as the Great Depression after 1929 and the rigorous controls imposed on immigration ever since 1930. When fact displaced fancy, it was revealed that, instead of remaining nearly static in this generation, the population of Argentina was in fact growing very rapidly — about as rapidly as that of any other country in the Latin American group, which, demographers tell us, has a rate of population increase greater than that of any other large region of the world. From 7.9 million in 1914, Argentina's population had doubled by the time the next census was taken in 1947. The high rate was maintained under Perón. In 1945, just before his first election, it was estimated to be 15.4 million, and in 1953, 18.5 million; in other words, the nation had gained 3.1 million inhabitants, representing a 20 per cent increase, during Perón's first seven years in power.

To support its industrial program, the government devoted much attention to the fuel and power problem. Its efforts met with a large measure of success, but this was not unqualified. For example, while the discovery of a large new oil field in the northern province of Salta added about 400 million barrels to the country's known reserves, transportation difficulties impaired its usefulness; and oil consumption was increasing three times as fast as domestic production. Again, the volume of electricity generated by public utility companies was increased by 30 per cent from 1947 to 1951 (3576 million kilowatt hours and 4718 million k.w.h., respectively); but the increase came to a halt in 1952, at which time 97 per cent of the total was still generated by steam plants using expensive imported coal and only 3 per cent was hydroelectric. Argentina was lagging behind other South American countries in the production of power. Though four-fifths of its power served only the Buenos Aires and

Rosario areas, even here the supply was so inadequate that some firms installed power plants of their own.

Definitely on the credit side are increases in certain lines of industrial production, the construction of oil and natural gas pipelines, and the discovery of important iron ore deposits in northern and central Argentina and a large deposit of coal in the far south. While there were substantial increases in a great variety of lines, such as chemical products, cement, paper, beer, and diesel and fuel oils, the greatest of all was made by electric motors, of which six times as many were produced in 1952 as in 1946. A natural gas pipeline from Comodoro Rivadavia to Buenos Aires was completed in 1950, and two oil pipelines were under construction in 1953, one of them tapping the Salta field discovered in 1950. The two iron ore deposits were both discovered after 1940. One lies in the rugged Cerro de Zapla in the extreme northwestern corner of Argentina, and yields a medium grade ore. The other and much more accessible one is at Sierra Grande, some 600 miles south of Buenos Aires and close to the Atlantic Ocean, so that its ore (which is said to be of higher grade, approximating that of the rich Brazilian Itabira deposits) can be moved by water almost all the way to Argentina's industrial centers along the River Plate. The coal formation (the only important one so far found in Argentina) contains bituminous coal. It is at Rio Turbio in southernmost Patagonia, and thus at the opposite extremity of Argentina from the Zapla iron mines. But, what is more to the point, like the Sierra Grande iron deposits, it is close to the ocean, so that water transport can be used most of the way in exploiting it.

The discovery that, after all, Argentina did have important coal and iron deposits fired the ambition, which that country shares with most other underdeveloped countries, to build up a steel industry of its own. Aside from these discoveries, there were two facts that gave the design some plausibility in the case of Argentina. In the first place, that country has long had the highest per capita consumption of iron and steel in Latin America, and yet because of the depression and the war its consumption rate since 1931 has been lower (most of the time, much lower) than it was in the preceding decade. As a result, a large backlog of demand for steel has been built up which it has been impossible to supply since the war, first because of shortages of steel available for export in the principal industrial countries, and later because of Argentina's lack of sufficient quantities of foreign exchange to buy all the steel it needed.

In the second place, Argentina has already started an iron and steel industry of its own, so that the only question is how far this can and should be expanded. Down to 1938 all the country's iron and steel requirements were met by imports from abroad. In that year domestic production began with a modest 5000 tons. This grew to 55,000 tons in 1942, the last year before the military coup that started Perón on his way up to the Casa Rosada. By 1946 the figure had been raised to 170,000 tons, at which it remained through 1948. It then moved up again to about 200,000 tons by the beginning of the second Five-Year Plan. While this plan generally stressed agriculture rather than industry, it nevertheless committed the government to Argentina's boldest venture yet in the industrial field, the construction of a combined steel and coking plant at San Nicolás (between Buenos Aires and Rosario) which would increase the country's annual steel production fivefold by 1957.

The discussion of the San Nicolás project brought out some important facts about both the domestic and the international aspects of the economy of Argentina. In 1946, its steel industry consisted of five rolling mills; their principal products were bars, wire, and light structures, and these were made mainly from imported scrap and with imported coking coal. Their total production that year amounted to 170,000 tons, as compared with foreign imports amounting to 437,000 tons. They enjoyed protection both under a tariff act dating from 1916 and a system of import permits dating from 1932.

The San Nicolás project was studied in the light of this experience and of the discoveries of iron ore and coal deposits recently made. The conclusions reached were (1) that its product would have the same delivered costs as imported steel (Sparrows Point was used as the basis of this comparison); (2) that its establishment would therefore be desirable from the Argentine point of view, since it would save about half the foreign exchange that would be required if foreign steel were purchased; (3) that it would be most economical to use iron ore from Sierra Grande, rather than from Zapla or Brazil (Itabira or Corumbá); (4) that coking coal would probably have to be imported, in which case it could be obtained most cheaply from Colombia; but (5) that processes recently developed in France and Yugoslavia suggested the possibility of adapting to this purpose the bituminous coal from Argentina's recently discovered Rio Turbio deposits, which would cost as much delivered to Buenos Aires as imported coal, but which would again save foreign exchange.*

With the experts convinced that steel from the new San Nicolás plant would cost no more than imported steel and that it would save large amounts of foreign exchange and make extensive use of Argentina's newly discovered iron ore, and perhaps of its coal as well, it is no wonder that the project was carried forward under the second Five-Year Plan. Top priority in the plan, however, was given to "development of power production," which pushed even "mechanization and exploitation of agricultural and cattle-raising activities" into second place. These were followed by "exploration of mines and utilization of minerals," "maintenance and re-equipment of the existing installations and productive elements," "industries connected with the transportation and communications plan," and "industries connected with housing."

Specific industrial targets of the second Five-Year Plan were a 25 per cent increase in cement production, which had remained stationary at two million tons since 1940; the doubling of the heavy chemical industry's current production of about 100,000 tons of basic acids and alkalis; the expansion of current tractor production to 50 per cent of domestic requirements, and the beginning of the manufacture of other motor vehicles; the doubling of current newsprint production capacity, which covered

* Economic Commission for Latin America (United Nations), *Study on Iron and Steel Industry* . . . (2 vols., 1953, mimeographed), I, 22–25, "Conclusions Referring to Argentina."

less than one-fourth of current consumption, and increases of about 50 per cent in the production of other types of paper and cardboard, which would bring them above current requirements. These details illustrate the guiding principle of the whole industrial part of the plan, which was to meet the need, demonstrated by the hard experience of recent years, for an increase in basic and production industries.

In conclusion, it should be noted that it is not always easy to distinguish between industry and armaments in the record of these years, for they were often intermingled in a way confusing to outsiders. Thus, the iron mine and blast furnaces at Zapla were operated under Army authority, while the Air Ministry had charge of the production of tractors, automobiles, and motorcycles.

5. TRANSPORTATION AND COMMUNICATIONS

The most striking development in this field was the extremely rapid growth of a large Argentine State Merchant Fleet. Though not established until 1941, it had already passed the million-ton mark by the end of 1951, and in that same year, and for the first time in history, Argentine ships carried a larger share of the country's foreign trade than the ships of any other nation. Only three years earlier the Argentine share had been about half as large as that of the United States and less than half as large as Great Britain's.

To some extent this development was only one more illustration of a world-wide phenomenon of the period since 1939, namely, the growth of sizable merchant marines in countries that had hitherto had very small ones or none at all. Without attempting to explain the general phenomenon, we may note two factors that were of special significance in the case of Argentina. The first was the shipping shortage created by World War II, which was felt most acutely in Argentina because of her exceptionally high degree of dependence upon overseas trade. When the war broke out, there were only 45 merchant ships of 196,000 tons under the Argentine flag, and most of these were owned by foreigners. Hence, when in August 1941 the Inter-American Financial and Economic Advisory Committee recommended the expropriation of foreign-owned vessels tied up in American ports by the war, Argentina for once responded with alacrity to an inter-American call and expropriated 16 Italian ships. With these she established her State Merchant Fleet. The other factor was the rampant nationalism of the Perón regime. Its slogan of "economic independence" committed it to an all-out effort to free Argentina's carrying trade from foreign domination, especially since the largest foreign carriers were the two nations which, in the eyes of the Argentine leaders, were the chief exponents of imperialism, Britain and the United States.

Accordingly, a great expansion of the merchant fleet was made a major feature of the first Five-Year Plan. Most of the ships were built in Britain, the Netherlands, and Sweden. Except for two oil tankers, the program had been completed by the end of 1951, by which time the fleet consisted of 386 motor vessels of 100 gross tons and over, with an aggregate gross tonnage of 1,043,863. Many of these were small freighters, but several were large ships of the combined de luxe passenger and refrigerated cargo type and they entered into competition with the best of the older foreign lines connecting Argentina with Europe and the United States. One of the largest, and the only one not built on government account, was a 22,000-ton whale-factory ship. There were also about a dozen tankers built for the Y.P.F.;* Argentina did not intend to get caught, like Iran, with no tankers on its side in case of a break with the "imperialist" powers. The names of these ships celebrated not only Argentina but more particularly its present regime: there was an *Eva Perón,* an *October 17,* a *Presidente Perón,* and, for good measure, a *Juan Perón* (the whaler). And the government took care of its own, using incentives and pressure to route foreign cargo on Argentine ships — apparently with good results. In the trade from east coast

---

* Yacimientos Petrolíferos Argentinos, a government organization which since 1936 has held a monopoly of the Argentine oil industry, except that private companies previously established (1915–1936) have been permitted to continue to operate.

ports of the United States to Argentina during 1950, Argentine ships carried an average of 3110 tons of cargo as compared to 472 tons for ships of United States registry.

The total tonnage entering Argentine ports fluctuated around nine million tons per year during this period, but Buenos Aires continued to tighten its monopoly as a port of entry. In 1951 it accounted for 84 per cent of the national total, and had a lead of more than ten to one over the country's second largest port, La Plata (renamed Eva Perón just after that lady's death in 1952). Rosario, once the nearest rival of Buenos Aires, had been reduced to insignificance, partly because of the wheat shortage, but also because government policy favored Buenos Aires.

The government also extended its control over river shipping and air transport. In the former field it had begun by acquiring the Dodero fleet, which at the outbreak of the war had dominated river transport on the Plata system. Subsequent additions were made, but on a far smaller scale than in the case of the overseas fleet since Argentina had the river navigation very much to herself.

Control of all domestic air transport was taken over by the government in 1945 and operated through four companies which in June 1950 were consolidated into a single corporation, Argentine Airlines (*Aerolíneas Argentinas*). A foreign branch operated services to Europe and, beginning in March 1950, to New York. Most of the international traffic, however, continued to be carried by foreign companies such as long-established Pan American and a newcomer, Braniff. Since the beginning of the war, travel time between Buenos Aires and New York had been cut from four or five days to one, mainly as a result of improvements in navigation aids which made night flying possible over South America.

Both passenger and freight air traffic increased rapidly through 1950. Then the depression of 1951–52 brought about a sharp drop in passenger traffic on the Argentine Airlines, though the foreign airlines held up well because most of their passengers were foreigners and could travel by whatever line they chose. As a result of the government's policy of routing freight over its own lines, by air as well as by sea, the reverse was true of freight traffic: from 1948 on, the freight tonnage carried by foreign airlines decreased, while that carried by Argentine Airlines increased even during the depression.

Land transport, whether by railroad or highway, was in a generally unsatisfactory and declining state throughout the whole postwar period. National pride was gratified by the "repatriation" of the railroads through purchases from their foreign owners just after the war,* but in equipment and service they continued the deterioration begun during the war by the prolonged shutting off of replacements from abroad and the domestic political crisis. By the time foreign supplies were once more readily available, Perón had used up most of Argentina's wartime accumulation of foreign exchange and gold, much of it in "repatriating" the railroads. New equipment, such as diesel electric locomotives and freight and passenger cars, was purchased and more was on order from the United States, Britain, The Netherlands, Hungary, and other countries. This was authoritatively described in 1951, however, as "only a fraction of requirements," since "the great bulk of Argentine rolling stock" was "both overage and in many cases overworked."

Far from helping, highway transport aggravated the railroads' passenger traffic problem, which was not one of too few passengers, but of too many. The acute fuel shortage forced some curtailment of bus services and a great reduction in the use of private automobiles, of which in any case there were fewer per capita in 1950 than a decade earlier. Since the growing population had to get about somehow, the already overcrowded trains were called on to carry a rapidly increasing burden. In the worst depression year, 1952, the number of their passengers reached its all-time peak of 530 million, as compared with 354 million in 1949. On the other hand, the depression brought a sharp decline in freight traffic, from 50 million tons in 1948 to 39 million in 1952.

Despite the gravity of the problem, the government seemed justified in giving transportation and communications no better

* See below, p. 201.

than fifth place in its list of six priorities in the new Five-Year Plan for 1953–1957. No solution was possible without a restoration of Argentina's basic exports, for, as far ahead as one could see, this would continue to be the only way of building up freight cargoes at home and paying for the railroad equipment and motor fuel that must be bought abroad.

In the field of communications, the two chief developments of the Perón period were the inauguration of television broadcasts in 1951 and a reorganization of radio broadcasting two years later. Television was inaugurated with great fanfare on the sacred October 17, but at the end of the year there were only 1200 sets in operation, as compared with an estimated 2,225,000 radio receiving sets — one for every eight inhabitants. The new organization of radio broadcasting, adopted late in 1953, was another example of the anti-foreign, centralizing policy of the Perón regime. Existing licenses were canceled, new licenses were granted only to native Argentines or to companies having not less than 70 per cent Argentine capital, and the number of broadcasting companies was reduced to three, all of which were either operated or closely supervised by the government.

6. FOREIGN TRADE

Of the many great changes that have taken place in Argentina's foreign trade since 1939, the most striking is the replacement of Great Britain by the United States as Argentina's best customer. There has also been an increase in Argentina's trade with other Latin American countries, particularly her neighbors in South America. The composition of her imports has likewise changed greatly, and these have developed an inelasticity that hampers her internal development and which can be overcome only by sharply reversing the decline that has gone on almost uninterruptedly since 1947 in her basic agricultural exports.

For a brief period after the war Great Britain recovered the predominant position in Argentine export trade that had always been hers from the beginning of Argentine independence to 1939. In 1948 and 1949 she took about one-fourth of all Argentine exports, and her share was nearly three times as large in 1948, and more than twice as large in 1949, as that of the United States, which was Argentina's second best customer. In Argentine imports, however, the United States tightened its prewar hold on first place, taking a 3-to-1 lead over Great Britain in 1948 and dropping behind only once more, in 1949. Then, from 1950 to 1952 (the last year for which substantially complete figures are available), the United States forged ahead of Britain in Argentine exports as well, as the accompanying table shows.

	Argentine Exports (Millions of Pesos) Countries of Destination			Argentine Imports (Millions of Pesos) Countries of Origin		
Year	All	United States	Great Britain	All	United States	Great Britain
1948	5,541.8	537.4	1,535.5	6,189.7	2,286.9	775.2
1949	3,718.9	398.7	848.9	4,641.7	689.5	721.6
1950	5,427.3	1,108.7	973.1	4,821.1	787.3	569.2
1951	6,710.9	1,183.4	1,148.2	10,491.7	2,199.2	787.6
1952	4,392.0	1,114.7	619.5	8,361.2	1,537.0	509.3

The fluctuations in Argentine trade during these years were so wide, and the period so short, that any conclusion drawn from them must be tentative. Nevertheless, for what they were worth, they indicated that the primacy of the United States over Britain was likely to become permanent. This seemed all the more likely since the United States had also replaced Britain as the largest foreign investor in Argentina and had shown its capacity to absorb a large volume of Argentina's basic production for export. This disposed of a cliché which — with good reason in earlier years — had long dominated discussion of relations between the two countries, namely, that the economies of the two countries were so highly competitive that the United States could not provide a market for Argentina's principal products.

Another cliché — that the United States will not buy Argentina's meat — disappears when one looks at the list of things the United States was now buying from Argentina. The list for 1952 was headed by meat; this made up 30 per cent of the total value of United States imports from Argentina. What is more, it

exceeded by 50 per cent the value of the Argentine meat purchased the same year by Great Britain, and by a still wider
margin the value of any Argentine product of farm or range sold
to any other country. To be sure, the meat bought by the United
States was canned, and the "hoof-and-mouth" ban was still in
effect and Argentines were still resentful over it. Nevertheless,
the fact remains that the United States had become one of the
very largest purchasers of those basic agricultural exports which
were bound to remain for a long time to come a decisive factor
in the internal development as well as the foreign trade of Argentina.

As an exporter, Argentina had freed herself of her former
almost exclusive dependence on the European market by developing considerable outlets among her South American neighbors. In fact, in aggregate exports for the four years 1949–1952
she sold more to Brazil alone than to any country in Europe
except Great Britain; and her combined exports to Brazil, Chile,
and Peru exceeded even her exports to Britain. This was something new in the peacetime pattern of Argentina.

On the other hand, Argentine imports showed signs of shaking
down into a geographical pattern somewhat like that of the
prewar period, that is, one in which Europe, if not in first place,
would at any rate have no rival for second place to the United
States. A particularly interesting case was that of Germany.
Virtually nonexistent in Argentina's import list in the first four
years after the war, Germany began a strong recovery in 1950,
and in 1952 passed even Britain, as well as France and Italy,
and was topped only by the United States and Brazil.

A postwar anomaly which was soon eliminated was the
partially successful effort to develop a large-scale trade between
Argentina and her political bedfellow, Franco Spain, under an
agreement initiated in 1944. The success was Spain's. Insignifi-
cant in Argentina's export list before the war, Spain now received
such large shipments of Argentine foodstuffs, financed by Argentine loans, that as late as 1948 she stood fourth from the top of
the list, behind only Britain, Italy, and the United States. Argentina, however, got only a fraction of the raw materials and manu-

factures which should have been sent by Spain in return. The flow of Argentine foodstuffs was accordingly shut off, with the result that by 1950 Spain was again down in her accustomed place in the Argentine export list, about on a par with Austria and below Finland. Economics had proved stronger than ideology.

More extensive than the shift in the geographical distribution of Argentina's foreign trade was the change in the distribution of her imports among the four major categories (consumer goods, raw materials, fuels and lubricants, and capital goods), as shown by the accompanying table.*

ARGENTINE IMPORTS, 1937–1952 (selected years)

(Value in Millions of U.S. dollars at 1948 prices, and per cent of total)

Year	Consumer Goods Value	%	Raw Materials Value	%	Fuels & Lubricants Value	%	Capital. Goods Value	%	Total Imports Value	%
1937–39 average	534.7	40.2	264.7	19.9	109.1	8.2	421.7	31.7	1,330.2	100
1947–49 average	297.4	21.2	342.5	24.4	147.9	10.6	614.1	43.8	1,401.9	100
1950	121.7	11.9	301.3	29.6	174.3	17.1	422.2	41.2	1,019.7	100
1951	145.8	12.3	398.6	33.7	198.1	16.8	440.5	37.2	1,183.0	100
1952	110.8	11.3	328.3	33.5	168.6	17.2	372.4	38.0	980.1	100

As these figures show, the relative shares of the four major categories of imports as they existed in the last three years before the war were profoundly altered in the postwar period. By 1947–1949 consumer goods had been cut to only a little more than half of their prewar share, and by 1952 to just over a fourth of it. On the other hand, by 1952 raw materials and fuel had increased their shares 70 and 100 per cent respectively. Even capital goods, which changed least, had risen 20 per cent above the prewar level. Without pretending to give a full explanation of these sweeping changes, we may note that they were probably due in part to the general decline in the level of imports, but

* Rearranged, but otherwise identical with the table published in Economic Commission for Latin America (United Nations Economic and Social Council), *Economic Survey for Latin America 1951–1952* (New York, 1953), p. 173, Table 21.

that other factors, such as government policy, must be taken into account, since all these changes were well under way during the prosperous period 1947–1949.

However they are to be explained, these changes suggest two important conclusions, one retrospective, the other prospective. The first relates to the charge that, after the war, Argentina and the other Latin American countries wasted their wartime accumulations of gold and foreign exchange in an orgy of luxury spending, instead of concentrating on the replacement of worn-out machinery, rolling stock, and other productive items. So far as Argentina is concerned, the figures in the table seem to refute the charge, and at the very least they show that Argentina's record in this respect was much better in the postwar period than it had been just before the war. At any rate, it compares favorably with that of Brazil. Starting in 1937–1939 with percentages almost identically the same as those of Argentina, Brazil's record in these two categories was as shown in the accompanying table.

PERCENTAGES OF TOTAL BRAZILIAN IMPORTS

	1937–39	1947–49	1950	1951	1952
Consumer Goods	41.9	35.0	35.3	37.9	36.9
Capital Goods	31.5	40.7	39.0	36.5	37.0

The second conclusion, which is prospective, is that by 1952 Argentine imports had become inelastic and were likely to remain so for a long time to come. This conclusion is drawn mainly from the record of the other two categories of imports, raw materials and fuels and lubricants. By 1952 they accounted for half the country's total imports, as compared with just over a quarter in 1937–1939; and they had become indispensable. Capital goods for progress, as well as consumer goods for comfort, must be sacrificed in a pinch for raw materials and fuel, without which the new economy of Argentina could not operate. This inelasticity made the further economic development of Argentina depend upon an increase in the country's capacity to import in order to provide a wider margin for the purchase of capital goods. Since capacity to import was limited by capacity to export (we assume, of course, that the terms of trade remained unchanged), this situation underlined the urgent need for raising the level of Argentina's basic agricultural exports.

7. FOREIGN INVESTMENTS

In the 1940's Argentina proceeded more rapidly with the formation of domestic capital than any other Latin American country, granted loans or credits to several countries in Europe as well as America,* and for a time seemed on the point of passing from a debtor to a creditor position on general balance. This development, reinforced by Perón's political clamor for economic independence, led to extensive changes in the pattern of foreign investments in Argentina.

In this respect, as in Argentina's trade with foreign nations, the most striking development of the postwar period was the replacement of British leadership by that of the United States. Here, too, the change meant the end of a preponderance which was as old as Argentine independence, and which was greatly increased during that economic revolution in Argentina brought about by British capital and enterprise between 1880 and 1914. Even when the United States began to appear as a serious commercial competitor in the two interwar decades after 1918, Britain's primacy in the Argentine investment field seemed unchallengeable. In 1940, according to estimates prepared by the Institute of Economic Studies in Transportation, total foreign investment in Argentina amounted to about $2264 million, of which Great Britain accounted for $1380 million or 60 per cent, the United States (which ranked next), $350 million, and Belgium (in third place), $250 million.

After a decade of war, postwar readjustment, and Argentine nationalization, the total foreign investment had been cut to one-third the 1940 figure, the United States had risen to first place, with about one-fourth of all foreign investments, and Britain had dropped to second place, with about 18 per cent of the total. In 1950 the principal United States investments in Argentina were: manufacturing, $146 million; public utilities and transportation,

* For details, see below, p. 227.

$77 million; petroleum, $48.5 million; and trade, $35 million. Its replacement of Great Britain at the top had come about through a sweeping reduction in the amount of British investments, not through an increase in those of the United States. In fact, the unfavorable climate created by Perón had led to a falling off of the latter from $380 million in 1943 to $355 million in 1950, in contrast to an increase of nearly one billion dollars in United States investments in the rest of Latin America from 1947 to 1950.

The British shrinkage was due much less to her wartime liquidations than to the postwar pressure of Perón's program of nationalization. The most important result of this pressure was the Argentine government's purchase of various foreign-owned properties in the field of transportation and communication, such as the French-owned railroads and the United River Plate Telephone Company (1946), a subsidiary of the International Telephone and Telegraph Company, a United States corporation.

Much the largest operation of this kind, however, was the purchase by the Treaty of the Andes (February 1948) of the British-owned railroads, whose mileage (18,000) was 70 per cent of the nation's total. The railroads were vitally important for transportation in and out of the great pampas region, the nation's economic heartland. To Perón, this was his most signal victory in his campaign for Argentine economic independence. It was won not by expropriation, as Mexico had won its fight with the foreign oil companies in 1938, but by purchase for about $600 million. The terms of the purchase were arrived at by juggling Argentina's wartime sterling balance and renegotiating her meat and wheat agreement with Britain, and the price paid was regarded by many as just, if not indeed rather generous. So, too, was the price ($94 million) paid for the North American telephone company mentioned above.

This avoidance of extreme measures such as expropriation in dealing with the imperialists is one of the surprising features of a regime which went to the greatest verbal extremes in attacking them. Perhaps Perón was keeping an anchor to windward; perhaps he was following his usual tactics of giving the screw another turn from time to time; perhaps he was afraid that more drastic action might wreck the Argentine economy. At any rate, until 1953 he gave the impression of calculating just how much the "capitalist-imperialists" would stand, and stopping just short of the limit.

Within this limit he made life very unpleasant for them. So far as foreign investors were concerned, the two worst features of his system were that it severely limited, and at times shut off, both remittances of profits and withdrawals of capital. Not all foreign enterprises were treated alike in this respect. For example, a pharmaceutical company supplying essential drugs was in a stronger bargaining position than a rayon manufacturer; but foreign enterprises of the former type were relatively few. The result was that after 1946 remittances were small both in proportion to total investment and also in comparison with other Latin American countries, and they were reduced still further when Argentina's brief postwar boom came to an end. On their total investment of about $350 million, United States investors received net payments on income averaging only $21 million in 1946–1949, and this was reduced to $7 million in 1950 and $17 million in 1951. In the two latter years Argentina stood eighth among the Latin American countries in this respect, and of the total Latin American payments it accounted for only 1.2 per cent in 1950 and 2.3 per cent in 1951.

In their operations inside Argentina, according to an analysis published by the United States Department of Commerce in April 1953, foreigners were in most respects not unduly discriminated against, receiving substantially the same treatment as Argentines in such matters as taxation and social welfare regulations. But both foreign and domestic enterprise had many things to complain of, mainly in relation to government policy. First and foremost were the repeated general wage increases, averaging 56 per cent per year from 1946 to 1952, which were believed to be the basic factor in Argentina's accelerating postwar inflation. As a result, wage cost per unit of production more than doubled in this period; and in addition, fringe benefits increased the cost by another 40 to 50 per cent. As if this were not enough, all employers were "solicited" from time to time for contributions to quasi-official charitable and social organizations.

Finally, the government limited the field for foreign investment by reserving to itself public utilities and the development of natural resources, and by increasing its participation in heavy industry and fostering increased participation by Argentines in other branches of manufacturing; and local interests already controlled most agricultural and livestock enterprises. Accordingly, the Department of Commerce analysis of April 1953 concluded that Argentina offered only limited opportunity for new investment of foreign private capital; that this opportunity seemed to lie in the introduction of "specialized products, or technologically advanced processes developed in the more highly industrialized economies"; but that "any appreciable movement of capital to Argentina" was unlikely "until the ability to remit profits and withdraw capital is assured."

Before the year was out, Perón's government had given assurances on both points. The bitter experience of the past two years had driven home the lesson that the collaboration of foreign "capitalist-imperialists" must be obtained if the recovery and further development of the Argentine economy were not to be indefinitely postponed pending the restoration of its key agricultural sector to something like its prewar state of health. That would be a slow process, for this sector had already been in a decline for several years before Perón nearly wrecked it. In the meanwhile Argentina could not even share in the limited aid to development provided by the International Bank for Reconstruction and Development, since it was not a member of that organization. The only aid received from the United States Export-Import Bank, a $125 million credit granted in 1950, had no direct bearing on this situation; it merely facilitated the payment of long overdue commercial accounts in the United States.

Accordingly, on August 26, 1953, Perón's government promulgated a law designed to attract new foreign capital investment in industrial and mining projects in Argentina. The main attractions offered were the permission, first, to remit profits up to 8 per cent per annum to the country of origin, and second, to withdraw the principal amount of the investment after ten years in annual quotas of 10 to 20 per cent as authorized. Also, in individual cases, the government would provide subsidies and other aid and grant exemption from customs duties. "Industry" was broadly interpreted to include "all activity in the transformation of products" and even public works.

Important restrictions, however, were still imposed by this law. New investments were to be confined to industrial and mining enterprises, and must serve the purposes of the economic development programs under the second Five-Year Plan. Each investment must be approved in advance by the government and made the subject of an agreement which, among other things, would determine the rate at which a particular enterprise might make future withdrawals of principal under the new general rule. Finally, two highly important questions were not clarified. These were the rates of foreign exchange and the treatment to be accorded foreign capital already invested. On the first question the law was silent and a subsequent official gloss merely gave a strong general assurance that investors would be treated fairly. On the second point the same gloss only referred to existing regulations regarding profit remittances.

On balance, the new foreign investment law seemed likely to mark a turning point in Perón's policy, and the turn was towards the right. The law still maintained his Third Position between collectivism and capitalism, but it moved this closer than ever before to the latter. It was particularly significant because its concessions were made to foreign capital, which in the Peronista lexicon had always been capitalism at its worst. To be sure, the law was so flexible that unfriendly enforcement might reduce these to mere paper concessions, but for a variety of reasons that seemed unlikely.

8. LABOR AND LIVING STANDARDS

These two topics are treated together here for two reasons. First, the living standards of the laborers and their families are the living standards of the great majority of the Argentine people. At the end of 1951 the Argentine labor force was estimated at 7 million, or 39 per cent of the total population; and 70 per cent of these laborers, or about 5 million, were unionized. In the second place, measures taken by the government for the benefit of labor have affected — usually adversely — the living standards of the rest of the population.

Despite her mounting economic troubles after 1948, Argentina still had the highest standard of living in Latin America in 1952. Venezuela's booming oil business gave her people a slightly higher per capita income, but this was offset by higher prices. Statistics of per capita consumption are one indication of Argentina's primacy in this respect, and also of her great weight in the economy of Latin America as a whole. In 1952 the per capita consumption rate for all Latin America, including Argentina, was $205, whereas when Argentina was excluded it fell to $182. In this respect she had fully maintained her lead since 1945, when the corresponding figures were $172 and $153.

The central question, and a highly controversial one, is the extent to which the Perón regime benefited labor by giving it a larger share of the statistical national income, that is, by raising its standard of living. Some of the regime's critics assert that labor has received no benefit, and even that it is worse off because of shortages of meat, wheat, clothing, and other consumer goods; but the available evidence (which admittedly leaves much to be desired) indicates that labor has gained to the extent of getting a larger share of what is available than it did before 1943 and that the main question is the extent of the benefit.

The evidence on some of the chief points at issue was summarized early in 1953 in a study published by the United States Department of Commerce, a source which, in view of the political atmosphere prevailing at that time, cannot be regarded as unduly favorable to the Perón regime. This showed that in 1949, when real wages reached their peak in Argentina, they were 34 per cent above the 1943 level; that by early 1952 rapidly rising prices had cut real wages to 13 per cent below 1943; that thereupon another general wage increase was granted, but that this too was wiped out in the next six months by soaring prices, so that by the end of 1952 "real wages for the unskilled groups were hardly any higher than in 1943." Somewhat the same story is told by the Argentine government's own statistics for the city of Buenos Aires, but with the important difference that according to these the unskilled (that is, the more numerous) group fared better than the skilled group. This difference suggests that even within the labor group the government was discriminating on the basis of its rule, "the greatest good to the greatest number of voters." On the basis 1943 = 100, the index numbers for wages and cost of living are given herewith.

	Wages		
Year	Skilled	Unskilled	Cost of Living
1948	228.1	246.8	180.4
1950	337.6	376.7	296.9
1952	498.0	577.3	562.9

Even for the unskilled workers, who were still contriving to keep ahead in the nation-wide race between wage increases and inflation, there was not much to show in these figures for nearly a decade of crusading for Justicialism. But the figures do not tell the whole story. As the same Department of Commerce study shows, the Argentine workers were also benefiting by their employers' social security contributions and other fringe benefits, which added up to about 40 to 50 per cent of wage costs, and almost all of which the workers had gained since 1943. They also shared in certain other, more general, benefits not designed especially for them, such as the growing domestic consumption of meat (down to the shortage of 1951–52), and the lowered cost of a university education; though in these cases it is even more difficult to measure the extent of the benefit.

On the whole, it appears that the material condition of the Argentine workers improved very considerably from the coup of 1943 down to 1950, and that though a large part of the improvement was wiped out in the economic crisis of the next two years, they still were somewhat better off at the end of 1952 than a decade earlier. But did they think they were better off? Was

Perón justified in claiming (as he did, for example, in his May Day message of 1952) that under his regime the workers had acquired a new sense of dignity and security? To these crucial questions we can give no firm answer.

On the other hand — and this is one of the most striking facts in the whole history of Argentina's descamisado decade — the profits of private corporate enterprise were maintained at a high level throughout its course. An unofficial study of the record of 150 companies listed on the Buenos Aires Stock Exchange shows that their dividends rose from an average of 9.92 per cent in 1940–1945 to 17.71 per cent in 1946–1949, and even in the deepest depression year, 1952, eased off only slightly, to 16.7 per cent. While the latter figure included a considerable proportion of stock dividends to offset inflation, it was still well above the level for the six years just preceding Perón's first inauguration. The same study shows that even in the relatively depressed agricultural-pastoral-forestry sector, the limited number of companies listed on the Stock Exchange likewise increased their dividends from an average of 9.21 per cent in 1940–1945 to 14.47 in 1946–1949. In other words, the chief beneficiaries of Perón's regime seem to have been the two extremes — private corporate enterprise, which he denounced but whose help he needed in running the country's economy, and the descamisado masses, whose votes he must have to keep him in office.

The middle class was less fortunate. Indeed, its members — except for the relatively small number who rose to positions of power under Perón — were the forgotten men of his regime. As just noted, even in the ranks of organized labor, which was the chief object of his solicitude, more was done for the unskilled masses than for the skilled laborers who formed the lower fringe of the middle class. Those higher up in that class, from tradesmen to doctors and lawyers, were left to shift for themselves in the successive waves of inflation brought on mainly by the repeated general wage increases which organized labor received as a reward for supporting Perón. Just what happened to the middle and upper groups of the middle class in these circumstances we have no sure way of knowing, for it is about these groups that reliable data are most difficult to obtain. What evidence is available, however, indicates that most of these individualists in a corporate age fared badly in the mad scramble to keep up with inflation; and trained social scientists thought they observed a distinct deterioration of middle-class morale under the Perón regime.

As Perón reoriented his policy under the impact of the deep depression of 1951–52 and Evita's death in the latter year, the easy generosity he had formerly shown towards her "dear descamisados" began to disappear. When a clamor was set up for another general wage increase in 1953, he at last took a stand against it. The time had come, he said, to break the cycle of inflation, wage increase, and more inflation; labor must work harder, produce more, and make the sacrifices necessary to put the nation's economy back on a sound basis as a preparation for renewed economic development under the second Five-Year Plan, which would provide a higher standard of living for all.

This was something new for Perón. It strengthens the impression produced by other developments between Evita's death and the end of 1953 — his purging of her henchmen, his tightening of his hold over the General Confederation of Labor, followed by his splitting of the labor movement, and his encouragement of new foreign investment and business enterprise — that he had begun to lead a Thermidorian reaction within his own regime. He had none of the proletarian fanaticism that would have enabled Evita to sustain indefinitely a struggle as ruthless as that waged by the Soviet leaders in the generation after 1917. He had never been one for extensive bloodletting, and now that she was gone, he was impatient to put austerity behind him, even if he had to let the imperialist powers lend him a helping hand. Which of these but the United States had the means to do so?

9. How Perón Took a Third Position between Washington and Moscow

We have had much to say about Argentina's economic relations with the outside world from the point of view of their impact upon her domestic economy. Here they will come into the discussion again, but from the point of view of Argentine foreign policy and as only one of several factors — political, military, cultural, and psychological, as well as economic — that shaped the course of Argentina's relations with the United States from Perón's formal advent to power as President of Argentina in June 1946 down to the end of 1953.

1. OLD AND NEW POLICY STRANDS

For Argentina, as for the rest of the world, this period was dominated by the rift between the communist and noncommunist powers, which was primarily a rift between Moscow and Washington. By a singular coincidence, the split became wide-open and a threat to world peace on the eve of Perón's first inauguration in June 1946, and consequently exerted a decisive influence upon Argentina's international position and his foreign policy from the very beginning of his administration.

This explains why the central theme of his foreign policy throughout the period was his Third Position, as he came to call it — a position, or better a "middle way," between "collectivism" (that is, communism) and capitalism. By taking a middle way, he hoped to increase Argentina's bargaining power in dealing with the core problem facing Argentina in the postwar period, namely, the problem of obtaining a place in the world commensurate with her capabilities and aspirations. An increase in her bargaining power was sorely needed, for, in a sense, pro-Axis Argentina was defeated along with Italy and Germany in World War II, which left her bereft of strong friends and almost completely isolated. As Perón saw it, the East-West split provided him with a heaven-sent opportunity to extricate Argentina from this situation by playing off one side against the other. Neither of the other alternatives — a firm commitment to one side or the other — was acceptable, for such a commitment, whether to Washington or to Moscow, would have been incompatible with the ardent national-ism which was one of the two chief features of his regime and a major source of his popular support among the Argentine people.

One must, however, distinguish sharply between his Third Position and the systematic neutralism which flourished among other peoples of the "in-between" world during these years. Perón himself made the distinction. As we have noted earlier, he described his Third Position as a philosophy and denied that it committed Argentina to an iron-clad policy of neutrality — a policy which he unsparingly condemned. This is one time when we may believe that he meant just what he said, for in foreign as well as domestic policy he was ever the opportunist. His govern-ment flirted with both sides, but did not marry the Argentine nation to either.

His task was made easier by the state of policy and public opinion in the United States. After the fiasco of the "Blue Book on Argentina" in February 1946, Washington seemed to have no interest in further "crackdowns" on Perón such as those at-tempted with so little success by Secretary of State Hull in 1944 and by Assistant Secretary Braden in 1945–46. During the next seven years, Washington followed a policy which has been labeled "appeasement" by its critics. The term seems hardly ap-propriate, however, if only because of the great disparity in size and strength between the United States and Argentina. The policy is better described as one of intermittent conciliation for limited objectives. The two major objectives were, first, to obtain Argentina's coöperation in strengthening the military defenses of the free world against the communist threat, and second, to pro-mote the economic interests of the United States in Argentina.

This policy left so many important questions untouched and was carried out so sporadically and with so many evident mis-givings and so little sustained vigor that it hardly deserves to be dignified by the name of policy; and it was only partially success-ful. Moreover, it was strongly opposed in certain quarters in the United States, particularly among intellectuals and in labor circles, with the persuasive argument that military and economic convenience did not justify the United States in seeking to con-ciliate a quasi-totalitarian tyranny which was actively engaged in stirring up Yankeephobia throughout Latin America. Yet the state of opinion, both in Washington and in the nation at large, was such that this policy, if it may be so called, remained in effect to the end of the period. A major factor in producing this state of opinion was the general shift of attention away from Latin America to other parts of the world, which were generally re-garded as much more important in the postwar period. The inattention of the nation at large made it easier for those who were interested in Argentina for military and economic reasons to have their way; and the general approach to the Argentine problem was dominated by the feeling that, since crackdowns had failed, conciliation should be given a try, especially since the replacement of the Axis threat by the Moscow menace had fundamentally altered the terms of the Argentine problem.

While there were many new factors in the situation after 1946 — these included, besides the East-West split, the new United Nations organization and its specialized agencies, and a rein-vigorated Inter-American system — there was nevertheless a high degree of continuity with the earlier period in the policies and attitudes of both governments. As for the United States, all its various attitudes towards the Perón regime from 1946 on had been anticipated in the period 1943–1945. Moreover, its major complaint against Argentina after 1946 — that she was not doing her duty as a member of the Inter-American System — had been made time and again for many years past against Argentine gov-ernments of the old regime on whose ruins Perón rose to power.

In Argentina, the element of continuity was so strong that in most respects the Perón regime continued policies and attitudes that were already traditional in that country. These included a strong preference for bilateral over multilateral arrangements, and for Spanish Americanism over Pan-Americanism, as well as pretensions to leadership in Latin America, especially in the River Plate area. For a time after 1943, Perón and his associates also continued the traditional orientation of Argentina towards Western Europe, though they substituted Spain, Italy, and Germany for Britain and France as the chief orientation points; but the substitutes were eliminated one by one and had not been fully replaced up to the end of 1953. A partial replacement was effected through Perón's recurrent flirtations with Moscow, which carried on Argentina's traditional balance-of-power policy of playing off a strong non-American power or group of powers against the United States.

Recognition of this element of continuity in Perón's policies and of the long-range nature of his basic problem as defined above should not be permitted to obscure the fact that he also had short-range problems and policies. One such problem was created by Argentina's uncertain economic prospects and her need for foreign capital. A foreign policy factor which turned out to be of much shorter range than anyone expected in 1946 was the influence of the strongly Yankeephobe Evita; her death in 1952 removed a chief obstacle in his own regime to an accommodation with the United States.

2. PROBLEMS FACING THE NEW PRESIDENT

If we begin with an estimate of the main elements of strength and weakness in the international position of Perón's government at the time of his inauguration in June 1946, we shall be better able to understand the nature of his problems and the reasons for his choice of policies.

Among the elements of strength, none was more important than the fact that Argentina was now a member in good standing, at least technically, of the two international organizations which were of greatest moment to her, the Inter-American System and the United Nations. It was no mean achievement to have gained these positions. So recently as the early months of 1945 she had been excluded from the Inter-American Conference on Problems of War and Peace at Chapultepec (Mexico City) and had gained admission to the United Nations Conference at San Francisco in the face of strong opposition led by the chief delegate of the Soviet Union, Foreign Minister V. M. Molotov. So far as this achievement depended upon Argentine action, Perón was given the major credit for it, since, as pointed out in an earlier chapter, he was mainly responsible for the changes in Argentine policy (notably the eleventh-hour declaration of war on Germany and Japan) which opened the way for his country in both organizations.

Other elements of strength were Argentina's favorable financial and commercial position in the world at large, the recent improvement of her power position in South America, and the prestige Perón had won, both at home and in other Latin American countries, by his victory in his recent "duel" with Washington. The first element included Argentina's large wartime accumulation of gold and foreign exchange and the booming postwar market for her foodstuffs. The second related mainly to Brazil, the only neighboring country strong enough to cause Argentina any concern. It consisted in the fact that Argentine rearmament, facilitated by the termination of the war, was rapidly restoring the South American balance of power, whose upset in Brazil's favor had been one of the major causes of the military coup of 1943 in Buenos Aires.

As for Perón's victory in his duel with Washington, he had achieved that by winning the election of February 24, 1946 in the face of a long campaign against him by the State Department, climaxed by the publication of the "Blue Book" on the eve of the election.* Two days after the election, the United States Government accorded Perón's victory a measure of recognition both by sending an ambassador to Buenos Aires, where, as a sign of its displeasure with the regime, its embassy had been

---

* See above, Chapter 7, p. 148.

left in the hands of a mere chargé d'affaires since Spruille Braden's return to Washington in August 1945; and also by choosing as its new ambassador George Messersmith, a veteran Foreign Service officer who was known to be out of sympathy with Braden's "tough" policy and in favor of trying to get along with Perón. In the eyes of many Latin Americans, the latter's victory in this encounter made him a David to the Goliath of Yankee imperialism.

Nevertheless, the United States still had reservations about Perón; and that, in the situation which faced him at his inauguration, was one of the major elements of weakness. Braden, his head bloody but unbowed, stayed on for more than a year as the State Department's chief policymaker in the Latin American field, and if his differences with Ambassador Messersmith created confusion in the United States, he still had enough influence left to block any major concessions to Perón. Moreover, so long as he remained in the Department, there would always be the danger of more harassments like the Rodríguez Larreta Doctrine of late 1945. This "doctrine," named for the Uruguayan foreign minister who proclaimed it, was in effect a proposal of multilateral, inter-American enforcement of "the essential rights of man," and it was generally regarded as aimed against the violation of the rights of man by the government of Argentina. Allegedly inspired by Washington and certainly applauded by Washington as soon as it was published, the doctrine found too little support in Latin America to make its adoption possible; but it found enough support there to make it a hindrance to Argentine leadership in Latin America, to which Perón, like many of his predecessors, aspired.

By the time of Perón's inauguration, the Rodríguez Larreta Doctrine was a dead issue; but another issue of 1945, on which Braden still blocked Perón, was still very much alive. This was the negotiation of a permanent inter-American defense treaty, as provided for by the Chapultepec Conference in March 1945. A conference for that purpose at Rio de Janeiro, Brazil, had been arranged for the following October; but at the last minute it was postponed under pressure from the United States, which was just at that moment bringing its campaign against Perón to a climax and was unwilling to sit down at a conference table with the military dictatorship (as it then was) which he was known to dominate. Perón's electoral victory and Messersmith's appointment to Buenos Aires the following February put the matter in a new and more favorable light from the point of view of Washington. In Buenos Aires, too, the attitude of the authorities towards the projected conference, while mixed, was favorable on balance, and it was typically Argentine: they had no enthusiasm for multilateral military arrangements, but they were unwilling to be left out. Yet month after month passed and still the conference was delayed — presumably through Braden's influence. The question was still in suspense when Perón took office.

The uneasy truce with Washington was only one of many elements of weakness in the Argentine government's international position at this time. The truth is that it had almost no friends anywhere. Even under the Conservative Churchill, Britain had followed the lead of the United States in taking a censorious attitude towards the military government from which Perón emerged. When the Labor Government took office in July 1945 the attitude of London became even more censorious, and it had not perceptibly relaxed after Perón's sweep the following February. In France and Italy the elements brought to power by the postwar reaction against Nazi-Fascism looked with no favor on what they regarded as an American offshoot of that diabolical system. Hardly a year had passed since the Soviet Union had flung the book at the Nazi-Fascist dictators of Buenos Aires during the San Francisco conference; and the Argentine Communist Party had joined the coalition against Perón in the February elections of this year. In Brazil, the Vargas dictatorship, from which Perón had learned useful lessons and which seemed to be moving towards a rapprochement with him in 1945, had been replaced by a democratically elected government that was cool towards him. Indeed, among all the powers of any consequence whatever, the only friendly one was Franco Spain, and that friendship was more of a liability than an asset.

In this situation, membership in the United Nations and the

inter-American system yielded limited satisfaction. It was like belonging to all the right clubs and being cut by most of the members; but the consequences were likely to be more serious for a government bitterly detested by many of its own people. Yet membership in both organizations must be kept up, for important developments were expected to take place in both in the near future.

Consequently, the most urgent problem in foreign relations that faced Argentina at Perón's inauguration was neither economic nor military, but political. It was not economic because the country seemed to be doing well in that respect. Many details of sale and purchase needed attention, but for the time being Argentina's basic foreign trade problem was already solved for her by the hunger of the postwar world. The problem was not military, because there was no threat of armed aggression from any quarter, and, despite much loose talk to the contrary, there is no evidence that at that time Perón planned armed aggression against Argentina's weaker neighbors in the River Plate area — much less against any stronger and more remote power. The major problem of the moment was political, and the political problem was twofold: to consolidate Argentina's position in the two international organizations, and, in her bilateral relations, to win friends or at any rate play off unfriendly nations against each other. Nor must we forget that, along with this, and sometimes overriding sound policy, was the pressure of the Argentine people, who wanted their country to make a noise and attract attention in world affairs.

3. PERÓN SKETCHES HIS FOREIGN POLICY

In his inaugural address of June 4, 1946, Perón began his discussion of foreign policy with a reassertion of Argentina's traditional devotion to the principle of national sovereignty and ended by raising the question (which he did not attempt to answer) whether the Act of Chapultepec and the United Nations Charter "converge or conflict with the traditional way of life established in our Magna Carta [the Constitution of Argentina]." On the first point, he summed up "the very simple philosophy which has guided and will continue to guide our international relations" in the statement that "Argentina respects all other countries, but this respect must be reciprocal. No one, great or small," he continued, "can be permitted to interfere, openly or covertly, in matters that affect our sovereignty." Then, with a side glance at the victorious Great Powers, he reaffirmed the historic Argentine doctrine, "Victory does not give rights," and deduced from this "spiritual position" Argentina's historic devotion to the prevention or peaceful settlement of disputes by negotiation.

This led him on to a defense of Argentina's record of compliance with international obligations. "Exercising the freedom of choice that befits a free country, we have chosen the path in international affairs that best serves our national interests; but once the choice has been made, we have followed a straight line." Our critics, he complained, have misrepresented the facts to our discredit; but the wrong done us is being righted and "it will not be long until all peoples recognize that no nation has gone further than we have in complying with international obligations contracted within the limits of our constitutional and legal system." Finally, after remarking (to applause from the galleries) that a nation faced with an international agreement not in accord with its constitution could either reject the agreement or alter its constitution, he closed with the statement that he would later seek the advice of Congress on the question whether the Act of Chapultepec and the United Nations Charter accorded with "our Magna Carta."

Before consulting Congress, he promptly followed up these rather Delphic generalities with a specific and less equivocal act: the opening of diplomatic relations with the Soviet Union by formally receiving its ambassador two days after his inauguration. As little as eighteen months earlier, this friendly gesture towards Moscow would have had no special significance, for from the dissolution of the Comintern in 1943 to the eve of the San Francisco Conference in 1945, most of the Latin American countries that did not already have diplomatic relations with Moscow opened them with encouragement from the United States. Argentina was an exception and, as already noted, the antagonism between the Buenos Aires authorities on the one hand and Moscow and the Argentine Communist Party on the other continued through Perón's election in February 1946.

Almost at once, however, the rift between East and West was made notorious by the crisis over Iran and by June all Latin America was discussing the danger of an early war between the Soviet Union and the United States.

This was the moment that Perón chose to reverse Argentina's stand by opening diplomatic relations with the Soviet Union. The timing of his act conjured up visions of Argentina's becoming the American citadel of communist intrigue in a new conflict, as it had been the citadel of Nazi-Fascism in the late war. These fears were not to be fulfilled, but the incident did mark the beginning of Perón's Third Position diplomacy.

It is possible, therefore, to regard his inaugural address as a bid for accommodation with the United States on a "forget and forgive" basis, and his friendly gesture towards the Soviets as an effort to acquire a trump card for his negotiation with Washington. At any rate, the beauty of the Third Position is that it enables one to work both sides of the street, and after his gesture to Moscow Perón lost little time in balancing it with a move in the opposite direction. On June 26 he submitted the Act of Chapultepec and the United Nations Charter to the Congress for confirmation of the decrees of the *de facto* government in 1945 adhering to the former and ratifying the latter. Such confirmation of all but the most routine legislative acts of a *de facto* government was necessary in accordance with the then generally accepted interpretation of that peculiarly Argentine thing which we may call the constitutional law of revolutions. Perón himself accepted the prevailing view at this time, and accordingly held that Argentina was not bound by the decrees of 1945 and that Congress was entirely free to accept or reject the two pacts in question as it saw fit.

Ostensibly, Perón took a neutral stand on this question. In his message of June 26 transmitting the pacts, he merely formulated the problem in more precise terms, stating that there were really two questions before Congress: first, whether the pacts were constitutional, and second, whether they accorded with the interests of Argentina. Congress was to decide these questions as it saw fit, and its decision would be definitive.

Actually, however, the unanimity with which the Peronista members of Congress supported both pacts can be taken only as reflecting Perón's own strong support of them. The Senate's action was particularly interesting. Solidly Peronista, it voted unanimously in favor of both instruments after a single speech, that of the chairman of the Foreign Relations Committee, Diego Luis Molinari. No questions were asked and there was no debate.

In view of the submissiveness of Congress to Perón, of Molinari's important committee assignment in the Senate, and of the Senate's unanimous approval of his committee's report in favor of the pacts, we can be almost as certain that this speech represented Perón's views at the time as if he had delivered it himself. While he flirted with the Soviet Union, he moved to consolidate Argentina's position both in the Inter-American System, which Moscow had tried (with some success during the war) to hamstring, and in the United Nations, which Moscow was even then crippling by the lavish use of its veto power.

As for Argentina's bilateral relations, which were soon to take first place in his diplomacy, Perón's initial policy in this matter was not made clear in his public addresses and must therefore be inferred from his subsequent actions. With Spain, Argentina's only friend at the moment, there was no change in the close relationship dating from 1944. With regard to Britain, there was an effort to take advantage of her distresses in two directions, economic and territorial — to recapture the British-owned railways in Argentina and get a higher price for Argentine beef, and to oust the British from the Falkland Islands and keep them out of the segment of Antarctica claimed by Argentina.

4. FOLLOW-UP, 1947–1949

With the same vigor and opportunism that he showed in domestic affairs, and with a considerable measure of success in the next three years, Perón addressed himself to the task of strengthening Argentina's position both in the two international organizations and in her bilateral relations. Developments abroad favored him greatly. Hardly six months had passed since his inauguration when the deepening world crisis improved his situation with respect to both of the great powers that were most important to Argentina and least friendly towards his regime, Britain and the United States. The touchstone was provided at the beginning of 1947 by the situation in Greece. Communist guerrillas supported by the neighboring Soviet satellites threatened to overturn the pro-Western government of that country; weakened Britain, forced to cut her commitments, withdrew the support she had long given that government; and the United States, hurriedly replacing Britain, announced the Truman Doctrine. This marked the beginning of a new and graver phase of the East-West rift and an open effort on the part of the United States to unite the noncommunist nations and build up their military strength against the threat of war with the Soviet Union.

All this was grist to Perón's mill. The United States was now eager to consolidate the Western Hemisphere defense system, but could hardly do so without Argentina's coöperation; and Great Britain's declining power as reflected in the Eastern Mediterranean could hardly fail to find a reflection in the River Plate area as well. Likewise, the deepening world crisis gave Perón an opportunity to develop his Third Position and on that basis to play a stellar role in United Nations affairs.

As a result, at the end of his first year in office, Perón was already able to claim, as he did in an exultant speech on June 18, 1947, that he had "emerged triumphant" from the grave situation that faced Argentina in her foreign relations at the beginning of his administration. The achievement to which he pointed with "the greatest pride and the purest satisfaction" was that he had commanded universal respect for "our independence and our sovereignty, both political and economic." Three weeks later, on the anniversary of Argentina's declaration of political independence (July 9, 1816) and in the same place (Tucumán), he had a representative assembly of "the governmental, popular, and laboring forces" of the nation adopt a formal Declaration of Economic Independence (July 9, 1947). The express purpose of the act was "to consummate [Argentina's] economic emancipation from the foreign capitalist powers which have exercised tutelage, control, and dominion over her . . ."

5. RIO DEFENSE PACT

A major source of satisfaction to Perón at this time was the decision of the United States to resume and push to a rapid conclusion the plans for an inter-American conference to draw up a permanent Western Hemisphere defense treaty. Since the postponement of the conference in October 1945 had been a slap at Perón, the holding of it now was a victory for him since he had made no important concession in order to bring it about. What had changed was the attitude of the United States government. The change signified the final abandonment of the Argentine policy of Assistant Secretary of State Braden, who accordingly resigned in June 1947, as also did his antagonist, Ambassador Messersmith.

Washington had decided that, in view of the growing threat of another world war, it would after all include Perón's government in the Hemisphere defense treaty rather than have no treaty at all. And such a treaty was important not only in itself but also as a precedent for similar arrangements subsequently made with other parts of the world, notably the North Atlantic Defense Treaty (1948), with a view to filling the security gap created by the failure of the United Nations. A step in this direction had already been taken when the United States–Canada Joint Defense Board initiated technical military coöperation between the countries in February 1947. That step was quick and easy, since it involved only two countries. It was another matter to arrange for military coöperation among the twenty-one states comprised in the Inter-American System; and the conference did not finally assemble at Rio de Janeiro until August 1947.

Argentina played a leading role in the conference. Her most spectacular contribution was a visit paid it by the fabulous Eva

Perón, who was returning from a highly publicized trip to Europe. More substantial, if equally unwelcome, contributions were made by Argentina in connection with the two major questions that came before the conference. One of these, not on the agenda, was economic. By this time the Marshall Plan for Europe was taking shape, and south of the border there was a rising demand that the United States also launch a Marshall Plan for Latin America. The demand was echoed at the Rio conference, where the Latin Americans argued that it was germane to the purpose of the conference, since economic defense was inseparable from military defense, their own contribution in case of another war would again have to be mainly economic, and the best defense against communist infiltration would be to raise the standard of living. The United States, pointing out that economic problems would be taken up at the approaching general conference in Bogotá, insisted successfully upon adhering to the strictly military agenda of the Rio Conference. The Argentines, of course, did not let pass this chance to champion the Latin American cause against the pinch-penny plutocrats north of the Rio Grande.

The other major question, and the only one properly before the conference, was resolved by the adoption (September 2, 1947) of the Inter-American Treaty of Reciprocal Assistance, which is usually referred to as the Rio Defense Treaty. In its major outlines the treaty only made permanent the wartime stipulations of the Act of Chapultepec in favor of mutual assistance against aggression, whether from an American or a non-American source. There were some important innovations, however, and these were designed to make the system more effective. They included new procedures and machinery, an exact delimitation (with map) of the Western Hemisphere defense zone, and the provision that a three-fourths majority vote should be binding in all decisions taken under the treaty, except that no nation could be obligated to use armed force without its own consent. Argentina had tried, but failed, to restrict the scope of the treaty by excluding from its purview an attack on United States forces stationed outside its own territory, for example, in China, Germany, or Greece.

All this was distasteful to the Argentines. They had accepted the Act of Chapultepec reluctantly, and now the principle of that act was made permanent and the unwelcome features of it were strengthened. In fact, the new treaty completed the process by which, beginning in 1936, the loose-jointed, pacific inter-American association was transformed into a fairly compact regional security system. Argentina had resisted this trend from the start, so that her resistance to it at Rio de Janeiro is another instance of the high degree of continuity between Perón's foreign policy and that of his predecessors.

At Rio her resistance was particularly tenacious on the question of voting; on this point she illustrated her devotion to the principle of national sovereignty by insisting upon the rule of unanimity, which in effect would have given each of the twenty-one governments a veto. Overruled on this and other questions, she nevertheless signed the treaty; but then another three years passed before she ratified it under the circumstances and with the negative results that will be described below. Here again Perón followed long-established rules of Argentine foreign policy: never be left out; resist effective regionalism; when resistance fails, accept the results nominally, but fail to ratify or enforce.

Finally, again following precedent, Argentina took advantage of the Rio meeting to reassert her long-standing claim to the Falkland Islands, and she now added her claims in the Antarctic. An Argentine meteorological station had recently been established in the latter area; report had it that Buenos Aires was less interested in the meteorology than the mineralogy of the region, and hoped to find uranium there.

Perón's definition of Americanism in his speeches of these years was flexible enough to allow his opportunistic foreign policy full play. Speaking on the anniversary of Argentine independence, July 9, 1947, the month before the Rio Conference, he described all America as a "community" of nations, whose unity was not only sketched by geography and elaborated by the "material deeds" of their people, but also bound together by "a single body of ideas and doctrines" fused by their common history, "the forge of the continent itself." At the same time, probably in order to insure Argentina's inclusion in the Rio Conference, he went so far as to say that in case of war between the United States and the Soviet Union, Argentina would be on the side of the United States. On the other hand, in an address delivered on October 16, 1948, just over a year after his representatives signed the Rio Defense Treaty, he followed up a similar Pan-American sentiment with important qualifications: "The crisis through which humanity is passing . . . has enabled us to define unequivocally what our participation in the general tasks must be. Our civilization was not achieved for war or destruction." Since the Rio Treaty did contemplate the possibility of war, this was not reassuring to the other parties to the treaty, and the significance of his statement was increased by the fact that the Soviet blockade of Berlin was at this moment under discussion in the Security Council of the United Nations as a threat to peace.

6. UN: BERLIN, SPAIN, HAVANA

The Soviet blockade of Berlin in 1948 provided Argentina with one of her few appearances, all brief, in the headlines of United Nations news. At that time her able Foreign Minister, Juan Atilio Bramuglia, was chairman of the Security Council, and he took a prominent and creditable part as spokesman of its six "neutral" members in an effort to work out a compromise solution which featured the world's news for several weeks towards the end of the year.

Perón had little zeal for the United Nations, however, and one of the main reasons was brought out by his opposition to the resolution of 1946 recommending that the member states withdraw their chiefs of mission from Madrid. Perón is reported to have explained that "Franco stuck by me when I needed friends and I won't desert him now"; but he also based his action on broader grounds — that the United Nations was failing to respect national sovereignty, was throwing fuel on the fire of domestic disputes, and was seeking to establish "an impossible ideological uniformity."

Both Argentina and the world organization had changed greatly in the dozen years since Foreign Minister Saavedra Lamas had worked with the League of Nations harmoniously and with distinction. Now, the United Nations was characterized by a more democratic spirit and an internationalism that impinged more strongly upon that national sovereignty of which Perón was the jealous guardian. Moreover, one of the chief attractions of the League of Nations for Argentina — the absence of the United States from it — was gone; in the United Nations, Buenos Aires was bumping into Washington at every turn. In short, Perón was almost as completely out of step with the new world-wide organization as Saavedra Lamas had been in step with its predecessor. Accordingly, Perón confined Argentina's participation in the United Nations largely to those organs in which prestige required her presence and in which she could cut a figure on the world stage and her representatives could hold a watching brief for her national interests. He did not make Argentina a member of most of the subsidiary and related organs, such as the Food and Agriculture Organization, the International Bank for Development, the International Monetary Fund, and UNESCO, in which less glory was to be won and Argentine sovereignty might be limited in practical matters or offended by policies of which he did not approve.

The same nationalistic approach characterized Argentina's action at the United Nations Conference on Trade and Employment, held at Havana from November 1947 to March 1948 on the basis of plans prepared in a conference just held at Geneva in which Argentina had not taken part. There was general agreement at Havana on the major objective of raising living standards by removing excessive barriers to the international flow of trade and productive capital; but on the question of how to bring this about, four widely different solutions were proposed. One extreme was represented by the United States, which favored free private enterprise as well as a rapid reduction of barriers; the other extreme, by the countries (including Argentina) which conducted state trading operations. In between were the two other groups: the underdeveloped countries (again including Argentina, together with the rest of Latin America), which demanded special rights to use various protectionist devices in forwarding their development programs, and the advanced countries of Europe, which also leaned toward government trade control and also demanded special rights, though for different reasons, such as their balance-of-payments difficulties and existing systems of imperial preference.

Argentina thus belonged to two of the four groups, but at Havana her chief delegate, the same Diego Luis Molinari whom we have already encountered in other connections, identified her mainly with the underdeveloped nations. He thereby achieved the maximum degree of solidarity with the other Latin American nations. Some of them were partially or wholly committed to private enterprise, but all of them clamored for special rights as an aid to their development programs. There was nothing new about their stand. They had taken it very strongly at the Chapultepec Conference in 1945 and several of them had already adopted it in the interwar period or even earlier. Consequently, Molinari struck a familiar and popular Latin American note when he denounced the proposal by the United States for a rapid reduction of barriers as a thinly disguised device of economic imperialism by which it would prevent the industrialization of the Latin American countries and keep them in a state of colonial servitude. In order to establish Argentina's position of leadership in the resistance to Yankee imperialism, he announced that his government would provide five billion dollars for the economic development of Latin America — an offer later repeated and developed by Argentina's economic czar at that time, Miguel Miranda, on a visit to Caracas, but never carried out.

Molinari used the Havana Conference as a sounding-board for a reply to the widespread charge that Argentina had compounded her refusal to coöperate in international relief and rehabilitation by profiteering at the expense of a war-torn and starving world.

In a speech on December 2 he gave detailed figures in United States dollars, which showed, in the first place, that in 1940–1946 Argentina had donated $94 million worth of beef, wheat, and other articles to Finland, Norway, Greece, France, the Holy See, Italy, Luxembourg, the Red Cross, and the international wheat pool; and, in the second place, that under Perón, Argentina had contributed $1151 million to the economic reconstruction of the world in the form of credits and long-term loans through Argentine institutions, IAPI and the Central Bank, to Belgium, Bolivia, Chile, Czechoslovakia, Finland, France, Italy, Romania, and Spain.

Not satisfied with the concessions on economic developments and other points obtained during the conference, Molinari refused in the name of his government to sign the completed Charter of the International Trade Organization. To the end of 1953 the United States had not ratified the charter. However, it was a party to an earlier and less ambitious measure in the same field, the General Agreement on Tariffs and Trade (October 1947), but in this case, too, Argentina abstained. Bilateralism was still her watchword, and it was on this basis that her trade with the United States was regulated. The two chief instruments in effect at this time were the century-old general treaty of commerce of 1853 and a more limited trade agreement of 1941 which was highly favorable to her.

7. OAS: BOGOTÁ

On the heels of the United Nations trade conference at Havana came the general Inter-American Conference at Bogotá, Colombia. Begun in March 1948, the conference was rudely interrupted by an insurrection in that city, but resumed and completed in April. The economic issues debated at Chapultepec and Havana were raised again at Bogotá; the same divergence of policy between the United States and Latin America emerged; again the Argentine delegation exploited it vigorously, and again, as at Chapultepec, agreement could be obtained only on generalities which could — and did — mean different things to different people, and for which in any case no effective means of enforcement were provided.

The two chief products of the Bogotá Conference were the Charter of the Organization of American States (a new name for the Inter-American System) and the Pact of Bogotá, which dealt with the peaceful settlement of disputes and was largely a codification of measures adopted by previous conferences. These two instruments, together with the Rio Defense Treaty adopted six months earlier, rounded out the reorganization of the regional system contemplated in the Act of Chapultepec of 1945.

The more important of the two Bogotá agreements was the Charter. It was the first ever adopted since the American regional system began to take shape in 1890. While in the main it merely formalized practices and institutions that had grown up over the years, it made some important innovations. The result was a more rational, more compact, and better rounded organization.

Argentina was, of course, on hand at Bogotá — nothing could have induced her to stay away; but her distaste for American regionalism had not diminished and her participation in the conference was given a typically Peronista twist. As the delegates were getting down to work, Perón blandly told the world (March 24, 1948): "I believe the time is past for conferences, speeches, and Foreign Office dinners. That road leads nowhere. We must react against such practices . . . Our policy is to reach bilateral agreements with all the Latin American countries . . . the policy of San Martín."

Moreover, the composition of the Argentine delegation at Bogotá, which contained none of the big names of the Perón regime, showed a certain lack of esteem for the affair; and when the insurrection occurred, the Argentine delegates were in favor of calling off the conference and going home. Of course, when the other delegates stayed and resumed the conference, the Argentines stayed also.

They took an active part in the debates and, as might have been expected, opposed the strengthening of the regional organization. When the question of a name arose, they flatly refused to agree to "union," "association," or "community" on the ground that these would imply the creation of a "super-state" and thus impinge upon national sovereignty. On the same ground they objected to giving the Council of the Organization any political powers, but were overruled. They also opposed, this time successfully, the establishment of a permanent military agency as one of the organs of the Council. On the positive side, they insisted upon incorporating in the Charter's chapter on principles the nineteenth-century Argentine phrase of which Perón was so proud, "Victory does not give rights." This was finally agreed to, though, in order to avoid misunderstanding, the phrase was tied to the condemnation of aggression, so that the principle as adopted read: "The American States condemn war of aggression: victory does not give rights."

The results of the Bogotá Conference did not change Perón's attitude towards the American regional system. In the month following its adjournment he declared (May 24, 1948) that "The best way to consolidate Pan Americanism" would be to put an end to the "spoliation" of Latin America by capitalist-imperialism and trusts-without-a-country. The significance of this statement lies in the fact that by this time the United States had become, in the Peronista lexicon, the standard-bearer of capitalist-imperialism, and no longer shared that dubious honor even with Great Britain. And nearly a year later (March 1, 1949), Perón could find nothing better to say for "regional pacts and coalitions" than that they were "not altogether objectionable." This was very far from meaning that he had any idea of pulling out of the regional system. On the contrary, he never missed a chance to be on hand when decisions were made; but once they were made, he found one way or another of reasserting his own freedom of action so that he could go on working both sides of every street.

8. SPREADING PERONISMO

In those bilateral relations with the other Latin American states which in his speech of March 24, 1948 were given first place in his diplomacy, Perón continued to emphasize economic agreements of the kind which he negotiated with Chile in December 1946 and which looked to an eventual customs union. Down to 1949 these had borne little fruit; for example, the one with Chile aroused so much opposition in that country that it was not ratified, and the most amenable government, that of General Higinio Morínigo in Paraguay, ruled a country which was already the poorest in South America before it was further impoverished by the civil war of March–September 1947 that brought Morínigo to power with Perón's assistance.

The lesson Perón apparently learned from this experience was that the other Latin American countries needed to be better educated in Peronismo. As a result, he intensified an experiment which was begun early in his administration and which by 1949 had met with so much success in spreading the influence of Peronismo that it caused serious uneasiness in countries where the system was not admired or trusted. This was the sending of specially trained labor attachés (*delegados obreros*) to spread the Peronista gospel in foreign parts. According to Perón, they were to be sent to every quarter of the globe. Actually, they seem to have operated mainly in Latin America, but there they extended their influence not only to Peru, where the government brought in by the military coup of October 1948 favored the pro-Argentine faction of Peruvian labor, but also to relatively democratic Costa Rica, Mexico, and Cuba. Besides employing the usual propaganda devices through press, radio, and personal contact, the Argentine labor attachés used the large funds placed at their disposal to subsidize friendly newspapers and to give likely converts free trips to Buenos Aires, where they were indoctrinated in the Peronista Trade Union School.

Probably less important in the long run, but more spectacular and alarming at the moment, were the military coups allegedly inspired by Perón in several South American countries — Paraguay, Bolivia, Peru, and Venezuela. We say allegedly because the evidence is only circumstantial, and because such evidence as is available is likely to be misleading. All we can be sure of is that none of them produced a regime with the most essential features of Perón's — the combined support of the armed forces and the masses organized in captive labor unions. The outstanding dictatorship which emerged in South America in these years, the one that took shape in Colombia in 1948–49, was not the product of a military coup and it was aimed against the Colombian faction most sympathetic to Perón (the one led by Jorge Eliécer Gaitán until his assassination in 1948) and was dominated by the Colombian counterpart of that Argentine oligarchy to which he had sworn eternal hostility.

It is hard to believe that Perón, who had studied the history of that part of the world, could have placed any real reliance on the establishment of friendly regimes by military coups in the kaleidoscopic South American countries. It is not suggested that he never intervened, but only that when he did so, it was with some limited and temporary objective, or simply to increase his nuisance value in the great theater of world affairs, where his own and his country's interests largely lay. For the long pull in South America, his main reliance was probably on the proselytizing efforts of his labor attachés on behalf of Peronismo and its Third Position.

In Argentina's relations with the nations of Europe, the chief developments of this period were with Britain, Spain, and Italy. In the case of Britain, the high light was the Andes Convention of 1948, an economic agreement which we have already discussed. In a less irenic vein, Argentina made trouble for Britain in the Falkland Islands and Antarctic cases, both directly and through a new inter-American Committee on European Dependencies in America set up by the Bogotá Conference of 1948 despite the opposition of the United States and Brazil, which held that problems involving such dependencies should be handled by the United Nations, not the American regional system.

As for Spain and Italy, Perón in May 1949 chose them for special mention as examples of the great improvement in Argentina's relations with Europe since 1946. Actually, the rapprochement with Spain, already in existence in 1946, was beginning to turn sour at this very time because of Spain's persistent failure to pay up; and the improvement in the case of Italy, lacking the ideological basis that existed in the case of Spain, was due mainly to Argentine financial aid which Buenos Aires was now no longer able to afford and supplies of Argentine foodstuffs which were already being cut down by drought and mismanagement. Germany was just beginning her postwar recovery, and the Soviet Union, whose trade with Argentina was infinitesimal, was useful mainly as a political bogy in developing the Third Position.

9. KOREA: ARGENTINE CRISIS

The outbreak of war in Korea on June 25, 1950 brought on a major crisis in Argentine foreign policy and public opinion. Perón's government, which had just rounded out its fourth year in office, faced the crisis from an international position which was stronger in several respects than in 1946, but weaker in others, and on balance far from satisfactory. He had consolidated Argentina's position in the United Nations and the Organization of American States and had thawed the frigidity that had marked the attitude of most of the principal foreign governments towards his government at the outset.

On the other hand, both the UN and the OAS had developed in ways that were not to his liking, and if he had fewer enemies abroad, he also had no warm friends except in a few minor Latin American countries. Worst of all, he no longer had the fuel to sustain a dynamic foreign policy. That had come mainly from Argentina's big postwar balance of gold and foreign currency, which was now exhausted, and her large export balance, which disappeared in 1949 and had not reappeared up to the end of the period under consideration in these pages. In fact, by June 1950 Argentina's financial position had deteriorated so greatly that it had become necessary to cast about for some means of getting around Perón's pledge that he would not accept a foreign loan.

These circumstances made the outbreak of the Korean war the most important event, from Perón's point of view, that had taken place anywhere in the world since his inauguration four years earlier. It opened up a prospect that held great advantages and perhaps even greater disadvantages for his regime. If the war spread far enough — but not too far — or if, without spreading, it lasted long enough, then Argentina's gathering economic storm would be dispelled by the renewal of a boom market for her produce.

On the other hand, the war faced him with a political problem which was difficult in both its international and its domestic aspects. Both the international organizations to which Argentina belonged had called on their members to join in resisting the North Korean aggression; the UN Security Council had done so explicitly in a resolution proposed by the United States, and the OAS Council had done so implicitly by endorsing that resolution. If Perón did not comply, he might expose his regime to a number of unpleasant consequences, beginning with the refusal of the United States to grant the aid which he now needed. Yet if he did comply, he would be violating his own policies and policies strongly supported by many Argentines of the opposition as well as by his own followers.

Perón's first snap judgment was in favor of some measure of compliance. He actually carried this to the point of at last ratifying the Rio Defense Treaty, and the circumstances indicate that he ratified it in order to further a negotiation already under way with the United States. The Rio Defense Treaty had been submitted to the Argentine Congress in 1948 but there was strong popular resistance to it, and it gathered dust for the next two years. No action had been taken on it when the war in Korea broke out. Several weeks earlier, however, rumors began to circulate that it was going to be ratified, and on May 4 the *New York Times* stated that the United States had made its ratification a *sine qua non* of a financial and economic agreement which Argentina was seeking to conclude. Still nothing happened until hostilities broke out in Korea and gave Perón the excuse he needed to meet the United States' requirement. Three days later (June 28, 1950) his compliant party in the Chamber of Deputies muzzled the opposition (which consisted of a handful of Radicals) and railroaded the ratification through the same day.

But what next? Having at last ratified the treaty, would Perón go on to support the United Nations police action in Korea? His first moves indicated that he planned to do so. To the UN Security Council he sent a message that Argentina was ready to make contact with the UN command in Korea, and in a press conference he applauded the sending of troops to Korea by the United States, declared that Argentina, too, was embarked on a course befitting a member of the community of American nations, and, when asked to specify more clearly what that would be, replied, "Actions speak louder than words."

At the same time, however, he had his Information Office and its agents throughout the country report on the reaction of public opinion to the ratification of the Rio Defense Treaty. If he had in fact planned to carry compliance any further, the results of the survey stopped him in his tracks. Public opinion was strongly opposed to Argentine participation in the fighting, and Perón, accepting the verdict gracefully, said, "I will do what the people wish." Accordingly, Argentina's contribution to the United Nations police action in Korea was limited to a modest gift of foodstuffs.

Yet Perón got what he wanted from the United States. In due course the pending agreement was completed and it included a commercial credit of $125 million from the U. S. Export–Import Bank. Whatever one may think of the merits of the deal, its conclusion is hardly surprising. Perón had met the *sine qua non* condition by ratifying the treaty, and if Argentina did not send troops to Korea, neither did any other Latin American country except Colombia, which sent them a year later. Moreover, the commercial credit was strongly supported in the United States as well as in Argentina, and was indeed earmarked for the liquidation of overdue balances in favor of United States exporters to Argentina.

This fact provided a good deal of justification both for Perón's claim that the transaction did not violate his pledge never to accept a foreign loan, and also for the sharp criticism of the transaction by a North American expert, Simon G. Hanson. Calling it "the Argentine bailout," Hanson wrote:

During the post-war period there had been discussion of the desirability of the [United States] government setting up export-credit insurance . . . Business and government decided against it. Yet, when a particular group of businessmen assumed the risk in the Argentine, a legitimate business risk, and got caught . . . they came to Washington for retroactive coverage on non-existent insurance for which they had never paid the premium.

This does not tell the whole story of the deal (it did not claim to do so), for the attitude of both the government and the public in the United States towards the Buenos Aires regime had changed greatly since the beginning of the cold war. In the new atmosphere, condemnation of the Nazi-Fascist origins and totalitarian character of Perón's government was overborne by the desire not only to do business with Argentina, but also to obtain such military and political coöperation as she would give in meeting the communist threat.

In Argentina one of the most significant facts brought out by the controversy over the Rio Defense Treaty and the Korean crisis was that the bulk of the only important opposition group, the Radical Party, were committed to a foreign policy even more distasteful to the United States than that of Perón himself. While a Radical splinter group favored ratification of the Rio Defense Treaty, this was bitterly opposed by almost all the leaders of the party, including the solid Radical Parliamentary Bloc and the candidates for president and vice-president in the national election of 1951, Ricardo Balbín (now in jail) and Arturo Frondizi.

They began by taunting the Peronistas about the Third Position, "which has been abandoned," declared one of the Radical leaders, Luis Dellepiane, "just when it ought to have been taken." Another described the new Third Position as "kneeling to the United States," and the Peronista majority promptly had his words stricken from the record. Frondizi remarked sarcastically that "The upshot of the 'Braden or Perón' business has been the triumph of Braden." He explained: "The agreements of Chapultepec, Rio de Janeiro, and Bogotá do not provide for the right kind of democratic solidarity, a solidarity in the interest of social progress and national self-determination. They bind us to the destiny of the United States, without any possibility of choice on our part. We shall have war or peace as the statesmen and soldiers of that country decide." And at another point: "The United States insists upon the economic, political, and military unity of the continent [Western Hemisphere] under its own direction, and it is getting its way, while in many nations of the continent dictatorships are maintained, human rights are not respected, and the people are living on a low cultural and economic level." Denying the charge that his group's stand implied solidarity with the communist bloc, he pointed out with perfect truth that they were the very same Radicals who had vainly opposed their party's joining with the Argentine Communist Party in the Democratic Union of 1945–46.

He also denied with perfect truth that his group's opposition to Yankee imperialism signified antagonism to the United States as a whole. "On the contrary," he declared, "we admire the people and free institutions of the United States, and we feel that we are identified with them in their origin and development. Our anti-imperialist position is a position of implacable hatred for the monopolies of that great country."

Nevertheless, the fact remained that this dominant Radical group had also taken a position of uncompromising hostility to a fundamental line of policy, extending from Chapultepec through Rio de Janeiro to Bogotá, to which the government and people of the United States were thoroughly committed; and that the position of the Radicals in this matter was taken not as an incident to their struggle against Perón but in accordance with the time-honored principles of their party, above all as established by its law-giver Irigoyen, whom they quoted time and again in support of their stand.

10. FOREIGN MINISTERS' MEETING

Six months later, the Korean war took a far more serious turn when Communist China entered it in force at the end of November. In the next few weeks there seemed imminent danger that the conflict would become world-wide. Accordingly, an emergency Meeting of American Foreign Ministers (the first of its kind since 1942) was summoned to meet in Washington to concert defense measures against the threat of aggressive international communism. The three-point agenda embraced military and political coöperation, emergency economic coöperation, and coöperation to strengthen internal security.

Because of the circumstances, this promised to be a highly important meeting, but the promise was not fulfilled, for by the time it was held (March 26 — April 7, 1951) a general war no longer seemed imminent. So far as publicity went, the meeting was completely blanketed by the visit to Washington of the President of France, Vincent Auriol, which began on the same day and lasted a week.

The thirty resolutions that were the fruit of this meeting included none of great moment, and the unanimity with which most of them were adopted gave an exaggerated impression of the degree of unity achieved. Actually, the chief division — that between the United States and Latin America — was about as wide at the end as at the beginning on the major issue, which arose from the former's desire to stress military coöperation and the latter's to stress emergency economic coöperation with a view to bolstering up the prices it received for its raw materials and foodstuffs.

The situation was ideal for Argentina, and her delegation made the most of it, but with an unaccustomed moderation counseled by a special circumstance. This was the fact that shortly before the meeting was held, the Perón regime had shocked public opinion, in Latin America as elsewhere, by its thinly disguised seizure of the great Buenos Aires newspaper *La Prensa*. Probably in order to draw a red herring across this trail, just two days before the Washington meeting opened, Perón made the sensational announcement that his government had developed an improved process for the "controlled liberation of atomic energy." The announcement was doubtless designed, among other things, to give the foreign ministers' meeting some-

thing else to talk about, besides *La Prensa,* but the hostile reaction that the latter case provoked in Latin America as well as
the United States evidently convinced Perón that this was no
time for his delegation to play *enfant terrible.* If it did so, it
might only provoke the other delegations to adopt a resolution
condemning the Argentine government's seizure of *La Prensa.*
Such a measure was widely urged outside the meeting, but
never taken up in it; for here the usual Pan-American rule of
official sweetness and light prevailed.

When they chose to, as they now did, the Argentines could
play the game under this rule as well as anyone else. On the
only major issue on which they made serious trouble they had
two other Latin American countries standing shoulder to shoulder
with them; one was the second-largest Latin American country,
Mexico, the other Guatemala. The issue, pointed up by the
attrition of man power in Korea, was that of making armed
forces available for the defense of the Hemisphere and also for
United Nations service, in accordance with the UN General
Assembly's "Uniting for Peace" resolution of 1950. Even after
the resolution had been watered down upon the insistence of
Argentina and her two associates, the former's chief delegate
further stipulated that his country would not send its armed
forces anywhere without the consent of its people in accordance
with its constitution. To preserve Argentine sovereignty intact
and resist anything that smacked of a super-state was still the
keystone of Argentine foreign policy.

11. MAKING UP WITH WASHINGTON

In the period from the close of the Washington meeting in
April 1951 to the end of 1953, Perón first intensified his bid for
Latin American leadership; then, when the results were not
encouraging and death removed the Yankeephobe Evita, he
changed his tactics and began to make up with Washington.

One form taken by his bid for Latin American leadership was
the founding in 1952 of an international labor federation under
his own leadership — the Association of Latin American Labor

Unions, called ATLAS from the initials of its name in Spanish. This was an obvious effort to exploit the putative appeal of Peronismo to the workingmen in Argentina's sister republics. There were already two rival organizations in the field — the Confederation of Latin American Workers (C.T.A.L.), led by a fellow-traveler, the Mexican Vicente Lombardo Toledano, and the Inter-American Regional Labor Organization (O.R.I.T.), which included labor groups in the United States (A.F. of L. and C.I.O.) as well as in Latin America. At the end of 1953 it was still too early to say how ATLAS would fare in competition with these rivals.

On the other hand, it was quite clear by this time that Perón was not going to get much out of the other form that his bid took, which was political interference in individual countries. The point was driven home by the cases of Chile and Bolivia because they were both contiguous to Argentina and therefore presumably most likely to come within any sphere of influence that Perón could set up.

In Chile, the presidential election of 1952 brought into office Perón's personal friend and warm admirer, the seventy-six-year-old General Carlos Ibáñez, who had been aided in his electoral campaign by Argentine funds, propaganda, and influence. The two presidents exchanged visits in 1953 and negotiated a treaty to promote the economic solidarity of the two countries; but that did not make Chile the ally, much less the satellite, of Argentina, and the strength of the opposition in Chile to close coöperation with Perón was so great that the latter seemed likely to derive little advantage from the situation beyond the satisfaction of having a friend in the Chilean presidential chair.

In Bolivia, a revolution rumored to have been aided by Perón brought to power in 1952 a regime headed by Víctor Paz Estenssoro, who had been living in exile in Buenos Aires for the past six years. This seemed to promise well for Argentine influence with the new Bolivian government, but the promise was not fulfilled. Paz Estenssoro followed a domestic policy which in some respects resembled Perón's, but his foreign policy was oriented towards Washington rather than Buenos Aires.

The generally negative results of Perón's Latin American campaign may help to explain why, in the field of foreign relations, the whole mood of his regime seemed to change in the year following the death of Evita. The key to the new mood was furnished by the reversal of his government's attitude towards foreign investment in Argentina. The most striking manifestation of the change was the adoption of a more friendly attitude towards the United States, which was the most likely source of private capital.

The United States was also the best source for the technical skills and know-how called for by many of the projects planned. In this respect, however, Argentina's own resources were more nearly adequate, for she was one of the best developed countries in Latin America.* She had never shared in the Point Four or Technical Assistance programs of the United States (any more than she had shared in Lend-Lease), but she had never seemed to miss them greatly. Foreign capital, on the other hand, she must have, and accordingly Perón now reversed his attitude and promised it fair treatment.

This, however, was only the beginning of a broad policy change, for experience had shown that the political climate, both international and domestic, would have to be made more agreeable to the Yankees. The process was helped along by the able ambassador of the United States, Albert F. Nufer, who held that post from July 1952 to the end of the period covered in these pages. Unlike his predecessors, who were businessmen — James Bruce, vice-president of the National Dairy Products Corporation, Stanton Griffis, partner in Hemphill, Noyes & Co., investment bankers, and Ellsworth Bunker, president of the National Sugar Refining Company — Nufer was a career diplomat. Nevertheless, he probably knew more than did any of them about the economic problems of Argentina, since he had recently (1949) served as chairman of a joint United States–

---

* Eugene Staley, *The Future of Underdeveloped Countries* (New York, 1954), p. 16, places Argentina and four other Latin American Countries in the "intermediate" group, and all the rest in the "underdeveloped" group, by level of economic development.

Argentine commission which had made a thorough study of the whole range of economic relations between the two countries with a view to rewriting their antiquated commercial treaty of 1853.

Accordingly, the announcement in late March 1953 that a new law was in preparation to attract foreign capital was followed up in the summer and autumn by propitiatory measures of broader scope. First, however, following his usual tactics, Perón prefaced his honey with vinegar in order to make the honey taste sweeter. In a May Day address he laid aside the reserve he had maintained since the beginning of the new Eisenhower Administration in Washington and denounced Argentina's imperialist "enemies" with all his former vigor. On the following day the semi-official newspaper *Democracia* cleared up any possible doubt about the allusion by informing its readers that "the name of our enemy [is] the United States of North America." Argentine newspapers thereupon boycotted news provided by United States press services, and on May 12 the ban was made official. Yet only a week later the ban was lifted, and although the boycott continued, from this time on the attitude of the Argentine government towards the United States became first less hostile and then positively friendly.

The climax came with the enthusiastic reception accorded President Eisenhower's brother, Milton Eisenhower, when he visited Buenos Aires briefly in July on a tour of South America. The news boycott was at last lifted, and in August *Democracia* hailed "the new era of friendship with the United States." Perón himself warmed up gradually. In August he said that there were "no problems" between the two governments; on October 5, during a state visit to Paraguay, he praised President Eisenhower as one of the most powerful leaders in the Western World; and in a major address on the famous October 17, he expressed "complete friendship" for the United States. Tangible results of the new attitude were the readmission of sixteen periodicals published in the United States, including the *New York Times* and *Time* and *Life* magazines, which had long been excluded; the arrest of twenty Argentine communist leaders; and the pas-

sage of an amnesty act which, while its terms were unacceptable
to the opposition in Argentina, was expected to produce a good
effect on opinion in the United States.

In addition to these measures and the flow of private capital,
observers expected two other tangible results from the new
rapprochement. One was direct or indirect financial aid from the
United States government. In a widely commented address on
October 14, 1953, John M. Cabot, Assistant Secretary of State
in charge of Latin American relations, who had accompanied
Milton Eisenhower on his recent trip to Argentina and other
South American countries, reported that in their discussions with
Perón the latter had declared there was "no price tag" on his
friendship for the United States. Whatever the precise meaning
of that phrase and the report of it might be, a few small projects
involving United States aid to Argentina were on foot by the
end of the year. It remained to be seen whether these were the
whole story or only the preface; the former hypothesis gained
its main support from the economy mood of the United States
Congress.

The other result expected was the conclusion of a bilateral
military pact like those already entered into by the United States
with Chile, Uruguay, and several other Latin American countries
under authority originally conferred by the Mutual Security
Act of October 1951. The United States had already sold Argentina (as likewise Brazil and Chile — the South American balance
of power must not be upset) two light cruisers from its "moth-
ball fleet." The second of these, the *Boise*, renamed the *9 de Julio*
(Ninth of July) for Argentina's independence day, had been
recommissioned into the Argentine Navy as far back as March
12, 1952. A bilateral military pact, however, was an entirely
different matter since it provided, among other things, for the
standardization of arms and the presence of a United States
military mission to train the recipient country's personnel in the
use of the new arms. Even in more friendly and democratic
Chile and Uruguay the pacts had been concluded only in the
face of strong opposition. In these and other countries the opposition came not only from nationalists and Yankeephobes but

also in many cases from liberals who feared the arrangement would further strengthen the tendency towards military dictatorship in that part of the world.

The latter consideration would hardly have deterred Perón, but he was deterred by the general attitude which he chose to maintain towards the United States until the latter half of 1953. By this time the Argentine Army was reported to be much disturbed by the growing superiority of Brazil. For what the figures may be worth, they show that in 1952 Argentina's navy and air force were slightly superior to Brazil's but that the Brazilian army outnumbered that of Argentina more than two to one. In equipment also, Brazil was said to be superior, though authoritative information on this point is not available.

It may seem astonishing that Brazil's armed forces should have been superior in any way when one recalls that Argentina was under a regime which had been set up by a military coup as far back as 1943 for the very purpose of overtaking Brazil in armaments, and which is known to have lavished large sums upon the armed forces. Much of this money, however, had gone into higher pay and better living conditions for both officers and enlisted men, and much more of it into a variety of activities not directly related to armaments (mining, manufacturing, transportation). Moreover, the economic crisis of 1950–1952, combined with the war in Korea, had made it difficult for Argentina to obtain military equipment from abroad. At any rate, Perón himself in effect admitted these facts in his May Day address in 1952, though he rationalized them by picturing them as a result of the government's decision, in accordance with Argentina's traditional devotion to peace and progress, to concentrate its military expenditures on improving the standard of living of its soldiers and aiding in the development of the nation's economy, rather than on multiplying instruments of destruction.

That view could hardly satisfy the Army for long, and by 1953 Perón found himself drifting towards the situation that had led to Castillo's overthrow ten years earlier. It is not suggested that the Army, which was under his thumb, was likely to rise up against him; but he needed to have the Army strongly with him, and the conclusion of a military pact with the United States would give him at a bargain price many of the things his Army wanted. Though the pact had not been concluded at the end of the year, the conclusion of it seemed likely since a noted visitor to Buenos Aires in November was Lieutenant General Howard A. Craig, U.S.A., chairman of the Inter-American Defense Board, who came away praising Argentina's "positive labor in forging collective security."

This year of returning prosperity was one of intense diplomatic activity on the part of Argentina, and it was featured by the negotiation of bilateral treaties and other agreements, mainly with European and Latin American countries, though an important one was also made with Japan. Most of them, like the three-year $145 million trade agreement signed with France in October, were of a commercial character, but political significance was read into some of them, particularly the one with the Soviet Union in August, which provided for the exchange of Soviet coal, oil, lubricants, machinery, and rolling stock for Argentine wool, hides, linseed oil, and tanning extract, to the value of $180 million. Against this background, there was much speculation regarding the possibility of an alliance between Peronism and communism; but on the whole there was less speculation than a year or two earlier, and less evidence to support it.

Some observers were more troubled by the revival of Perón's open admiration for Germany coincidentally with the recovery of West Germany. On two occasions in May 1952 (one of them was the return of their embassy building to the Germans) he had used such phrases as "our immense debt of gratitude towards our old comrades of the German army" and the "never-denied friendship and affection we have always harbored for the German nation." Statements of this kind seemed to suggest a renewal of the original pro-German bias of his regime and possibly an intention to substitute a revived Germany for the Soviet Union as the counterpoise to the United States in his Third Position game, if for any reason he should be deprived of the services of the Soviets in that role.

12. AIMS OF THIRD POSITION OPPORTUNISM

Looking back over the record of Perón's Third Position performance since 1946, we are inclined to agree with the Radical speaker who, during the Congressional debate over the Korean crisis in 1950, declared that Perón's foreign policy had never been that of a Third Position, but rather that of a pendulum which swung back and forth between the Soviets and the United States. His further statement that, when it came to the pinch of imminent war, Perón always swung to the side of the United States, should be qualified to read "closer to the United States than to the Soviets," for in none of the recurrent war crises — Iran in 1946, Greece in 1947, Berlin in 1948, Korea in June 1950, and Korea again in December 1950 — did Perón make a binding commitment in favor of the United States or the group of nations associated with it. There is more truth in his own assertion that the Third Position was to be understood primarily as a domestic policy, and that it certainly did not mean a rigid neutrality in international affairs; but here too we must enter a reservation, for, rigid or not, his policy in this period did add up to neutrality — but a very flexible neutrality which he kept a free hand to alter or even to discard, as he saw fit.

Though it bore a new label, his foreign policy was as close to his country's traditionally bilateral policy as mid-twentieth century circumstances permitted, and that was essentially a policy of the free hand. The main difference was that he was more opportunistic in applying it. And while his major short-run objectives seem to have been to maintain himself in power and to keep Argentina strong enough to make power worth holding, his long-run objective was the traditional one of winning for Argentina a place in world affairs befitting her capabilities and aspirations. All these objectives could be served by the rapprochement with the United States tentatively begun in the latter half of 1953; and it will be noted that, in this case too, his policy was essentially bilateral.

10. The United States and the Problem of Argentina

All things must come to an end, including Juan Perón's dominion over Argentina. Whether that will come soon or late, and what will follow it, are questions that only a seer could answer. Here we shall venture a few modest projections in various fields, with due attention to the more probable alternatives in the political field and to what they might mean to the United States. These will be described as they appeared at the end of 1953, which is the terminal date of our narrative.

1. PERONISMO AND THE MODUS VIVENDI WITH WASHINGTON

Perón's current six-year term (his second) expires in 1958. His hold on the two principal power groups in Argentina, the armed forces and labor, is so strong that, barring his resignation or assassination, he may be expected to complete his term and, in the next election (1957), obtain the presidency either for himself or for one of his lieutenants. Among the latter there are few likely candidates, since under Perón, leaders who begin to achieve eminence soon find themselves in the discard; witness the case of Foreign Minister Bramuglia, whose success in the United Nations proved his political undoing at home.

The heir apparent at the end of 1953 was Rear Admiral (R.) Alberto Teisaire, who was then in process of being elected to the vice-presidency — a post vacated by the death of Vice-President-elect Quijano. Teisaire was among the very few persons trusted by Perón and he already held, among other important posts, that of chairman of the Executive Council of the Peronista Party. But Teisaire was the strong, silent type, he had no great public following, and he would be sixty-seven by 1958. Different but equally cogent reasons told against all the other potential candidates for the succession.

Perón therefore seemed likely to succeed himself for a third term. His absolute control of the Peronista Party machinery assured him of the nomination if he wanted it. His election if nominated was a virtual certainty in view of his 2-to-1 majority even in the depression election of 1951; especially since he had subsequently tightened the screw on the only large opposition party, the Radicals, and had made converts from other sectors, such as the quondam Socialist Enrique Dickmann, and the former minister of finance under the Conservative Restoration, Francisco Pinedo.

What a third term of Perón would mean for Argentine relations with the United States would of course depend upon the latter as well as upon Perón. The indications were that the United States would do its best to keep relations smooth as long as the Eisenhower administration (which was to continue until 1957) or one like it remained in control at Washington. By the end of 1953 a kind of *modus vivendi* had been reached by the two governments on the three issues that had been the main cause of trouble in the past decade. Washington had reverted to strict nonintervention in terms which meant that it was not going to make any more trouble for Perón on the ground of the Nazi-Fascist, neo-Fascist, or totalitarian character of his regime, as had been done frequently under Roosevelt and in the early part of the Truman administration. Washington had also relaxed its pressure for implementing Western Hemisphere defense except in a form that might now be acceptable to Perón — a bilateral military pact. The third issue had been settled by Perón's concession, made in 1953, in the matter of investments. Apparently this went far towards satisfying Washington; at any rate, shortly thereafter a leading Administration figure, Senator Homer Capehart, talked largely during a visit to Buenos Aires about the coming flow of billions of dollars of United States capital into Argentina.

Most North Americans, knowing their Republican Administration, were convinced that, so far as it was concerned, there was little likelihood that this *modus vivendi* would be upset. The question mark was Perón himself. Many in both countries were quite sure that he was still the opportunist; that his whole purpose in the reconciliation of 1953 was to obtain short-range financial and economic assistance from the United States; and that as soon as he was sure of that, he would renew his Yankee-phobe campaign for its political value at home and abroad. Only a mind reader could be certain that this was not Perón's intention; but the probabilities were against it, since Argentina's needs as revealed by her recent economic crisis were so great that, even with the best will in the world on the part of Washington, they were not likely to be provided for in less than a decade.

Although there appears to be little likelihood of an early change of regime in Argentina, the possibility should not be ruled out of consideration here, particularly since there are many elements of instability in that country, beginning with its large and unhappy middle class. Moreover, so many people in the United States ardently desire the overthrow of the Perón regime that we should give some thought to the alternatives.

Except for a successful revolt, which his strong hold over the Army and labor renders unlikely in the near future, the only plausible alternative to a long continuation of his regime would be a Radical victory in the next presidential election (1957). This is not very plausible in view of the Radicals' 2-to-1 defeat in the last election, 1951, and other circumstances mentioned in the preceding pages; but there is no other opposition party of consequence and the Argentines have never shown much talent for improvising either parties or coalitions. In any case, coalitions are now prohibited.

2. THE RADICALS AS FRIENDS AND CRITICS

What might we expect of the Radicals? They are not merely the only large opposition party in Argentina; they have been a courageous, indefatigable opposition, and in the face of constant persecution they have exhibited the best qualities of the Resistance movements in the Europe of Hitler and Mussolini.

They preach and practice political democracy as it is understood in the United States, including equal opportunity for all political parties, their opponents as well as themselves, and personal liberties such as those of speech, press, and assembly. In other words, if the Radicals came to power, the government of Argentina would be purged of those anti-democratic political features which were a major reason for the "crackdowns" on the Argentine regime undertaken by Cordell Hull and Spruille Braden in 1944–1946 and which have continued down to the present to antagonize a large part of the public in the United States against Perón and all his works.

Nevertheless, the Radicals' soundness on this question now has little if any practical significance for United States–Argentine relations in view of the present determination of the United States not to make an issue of it anyway. But for the demonstrated capacity of the United States for quick and sweeping changes in such matters, this could be described as a settled determination, for it was first implicit in the Argentine policy of the Democratic Truman administration after 1947 and then was made explicit by the Republican Eisenhower administration. It has, therefore, become a bipartisan foreign policy; it is based upon a deliberate rejection of the alternative policy followed by Hull and Braden; and it is in harmony with other policy changes of the same period, such as the shift from condemnation of the Franco regime in Spain to coöperation with it.

At any rate, in the present state of world affairs and public opinion in the United States, no change in the present attitude towards Argentina seems likely to take place in the near future unless the Perón regime becomes identified with aggressive international communism. Efforts so to identify it have recently been made by Spruille Braden and others, but they have apparently failed to carry conviction in Washington or to lessen in any way its desire to promote its military and economic objectives by meeting Perón half way. At the present writing, nothing appears less likely than that Washington will bring on another crisis in its relations with Buenos Aires by again making an issue of the domestic character of the Perón regime, whether that be called totalitarian or neo-Fascist, or simply undemocratic.

On the other hand, there are three other issues which are, and will probably continue to be, of practical significance for the relations between the two countries, and on which the Radicals are firmly committed to positions that might well cause serious trouble with the United States if by any chance they should come to power in Argentina. One is their unconditional rejection of essential features of the Western Hemisphere defense system as built up under Washington's leadership by the Act of Chapultepec (1945), the Rio Defense Treaty (1947), and the subsequent bilateral military pacts between the United States and several of the Latin American countries (not yet including Argentina). The second is the Radicals' insistence upon carrying the nationalization of foreign business enterprises in Argentina even further than Perón has done. This could be, and on occasion has been, carried out in such a way as to avoid international repercussions, that is, by purchase or by expropriation with adequate compensation. On the other hand, it could lead to a controversy like the one begun in 1953 between the United States and Guatemala over the latter's expropriation of property of the United Fruit Company. That the latter alternative is not altogether unlikely is suggested by the Radicals' stand on a third issue, which they describe as Yankee economic imperialism. They define their stand as one of opposition only to Yankee monopolies; but they interpret monopoly so broadly as to include practically all large firms.

In pointing out these possible grounds of friction, we do the

Radicals no injustice, for we merely indicate the probable consequences of policies which their own responsible leaders have stated in print and on careful consideration.* Nor, if we are to believe these leaders, can their statements on these points be explained away as mere by-products of their opposition to Perón which would be forgotten if and when they came to power. On the contrary, they have been at great pains to prove that in these respects they are merely continuing the basic, time-honored policies of the Radical party as established by the greatest of its founding fathers, Hipólito Irigoyen. These policies were followed by Irigoyen when he was in power, and changes that have taken place in Argentina and the world at large since then make it likely that they would be followed even more vigorously by the present Radical leaders if they came to power. Admiration for the latters' courageous fight for freedom in Argentina (an admiration which the present writer feels in the highest degree) should not be permitted to blind one to their antagonism towards certain current policies and interests of the United States. If they were in control in Argentina, the avoidance of serious trouble between the two countries might not be possible without extensive modification of the current policies of the United States.

All told, the Radicals go even beyond Perón in their Yankee-phobia. He heaped unmeasured abuse upon the United States as a matter of tactics; their attacks on this country's policies, though less virulent, are based on principle. Since his recent shift to a rapprochement with Washington has already given encouragement to further "economic penetration" of Argentina by United States capital and business enterprise, and seems likely to bring about closer military coöperation as well, the prospect is that by 1957 there will be even more ground for Radical attacks on "Yankee imperialism," and even more likelihood that these would embroil a Radical government of Argentina with the United States, than is the case at the present time. Conse-

* See particularly Arturo Frondizi, *El tratado de Rio de Janeiro* (1947). *Recopilación de antecedentes. Posición internacional de la Unión Cívica Radical* (Buenos Aires, 1950).

quently, so long as the United States adheres to its present policies, the ousting of Perón would probably result not in an improvement but in a deterioration of relations between the two countries.

From what has been said above, it should be clear that "after Perón" seems to be a good many years in a dim future, at least if we include in the phrase not only the man himself but also the system he has produced. It lies so far ahead that, as regards politics, even the soberest and most carefully considered projections cannot be carried to that distance without being accompanied by so many qualifications and provisos as to render them futile. Hence the choice of nearby 1957–58 as the stopping point for the political forecast ventured above.

3. IN THE LONG RUN

On the other hand, it seems possible to extend the range for the slower-moving processes of economic, social, and cultural change. Thus, Perón's social welfare system and great extension of the powers of the national government are probably here to stay for some time. Similar measures in the United States and Great Britain have survived sweeping political alterations, and there is no reason to think that this will not be the case in Argentina, especially since even among Perón's opponents the majority now endorse his changes in principle, though not in many of their current applications. It is also unthinkable that labor will revert to the unorganized state it was in before the advent of Perón, who found the proportion of union members to total labor force less than 10 per cent and has raised it to over 70 per cent. Culturally, Perón's regime has made so little impact upon the Argentine people that there would be little occasion for change in this respect after the end of his regime, except to correct such absurdities as the requirement of Eva Perón's ghost-written *La razon de mi vida* as a text in schools and universities and the return of the latter and the newspapers back to the hands of persons who have better qualifications than that of being loyal Peronistas.

Finally, it is difficult to believe that in the present generation, at any rate, an Argentine government of whatever complexion will repeat the excesses carried out in the name of industrialization and economic independence in Perón's early years in power. On the positive side, it seems likely that in this generation the majority of Argentines will remember the lesson Perón himself has learned from that sad experience — that, however little they may like it, the development of Argentina's economy must be based for a long time to come upon the fact of its interdependence with the economies of other countries.

Among these other countries the United States now holds first place, and to all appearances will become as firmly entrenched in that place as Great Britain was from the beginning of Argentine independence to World War II. But times have changed and the terms of the new relationship will doubtless be quite different from those that prevailed when Argentina was known to many people both at home and abroad as one of the British dominions. Whatever the exact terms, the relationship between the United States and Argentina is likely to retain the general character of an uneasy truce for a long time to come, if only because there are deep divisions of opinion on policy in both countries. Not very much can be done by international organizations to bring about a more stable adjustment. In the OAS, the United States is so preponderant that, in matters of deep concern to it, that organization normally either acts as Washington wishes or does not function at all; and the United States apparently is developing the will, and has the power, to prevent effective action by the UN in Western Hemisphere matters of the same kind. Consequently, unless the conditioning factors change greatly, the problem of the relations between the United States and Argentina will probably long remain, as it has always been despite the façade of multilateral relations built up around it, essentially a bilateral problem between the two countries.

Appendix.   Suggested Reading

There has been more and better writing about Argentina than about any other Latin American country, with the possible exception of Mexico, if we consider writings in both English and Spanish on all the principal aspects of the nation's life — political, social, cultural, economic, military, diplomatic — both past and present. The reader who wishes to follow up almost any topic discussed in this volume is therefore likely to find the literature abundant, though for the Perón period much of it is widely scattered and strongly biased. Since he will need to know both languages if he is to get the best that is available, works in Spanish as well as English are included in the following suggestions. It need hardly be added that these give only a sampling of the very extensive literature of the subject.

1. LAND AND PEOPLE

There is an excellent 90-page chapter on the human geography of Argentina, with maps and illustrations, in Preston E. James, *Latin America* (2nd ed.; New York, 1950). The most comprehensive economic study, now out of date in some respects but still valuable, is A. E. Bunge, *La economía argentina* (Buenos Aires, 1928–1930; 4 vols.). Much briefer but more up-to-date is Carlos Moyano Llerena, *Argentina social y económica* (Buenos Aires, 1950). On the most important region in recent times, the pampas, there are two excellent studies: Mark Jefferson, *Peopling the Argentina Pampa* (New York, 1926), and Carl C. Taylor, *Rural Life in Argentina* (Baton Rouge, 1948), the latter of which covers not only the pampas but the rest of Argentina as well and is one of the best books in English on that country. Statistics on population, natality, and mortality, at various periods from 1900 to 1943, are brought together, with maps and charts, in *Argentina, Summary of Biostatistics*, prepared by the United States Department of Commerce, Bureau of the Census, in coöperation with the Office of the Coördinator of Inter-American Affairs

(Washington, 1945). Works on particular aspects, such as the natural resources and their use, Indians, immigration, social classes, urbanization, and cultural development, are listed below in appropriate sections.

2. HISTORICAL BACKGROUND: GENERAL

In English, good one-volume surveys are F. A. Kirkpatrick, *A History of the Argentine Republic* (New York, 1931), and Ysabel F. Rennie, *The Argentine Republic* (New York, 1945). Ricardo Levene, *A History of Argentina* (Durham, N. C., 1937), deals mainly with the colonial period and the independence movement. Two compact accounts of the national period are the section on Argentina by J. Fred Rippy in A. C. Wilgus, ed., *Argentina, Brazil and Chile since Independence* (Washington, 1935), and "Part Two: Argentina" in Harry Bernstein, *Modern and Contemporary Latin America* (Philadelphia, 1952). The period since 1930 is stressed in Felix J. Weil, *The Argentine Riddle* (New York, 1944), and John W. White, *Argentina, the Life Story of a Nation* (New York, 1942). A broader view of the national development of Argentina along with that of other South American countries, and including a chapter on River Plate rivalries, is given in C. H. Haring, *South American Progress* (Cambridge, Mass., 1934). Most readers will probably find the foregoing adequate for the colonial and national periods, but for the Indian background, both before and after the Spanish conquest, the interested reader should consult appropriate sections of the monumental *Handbook of South American Indians*, edited for the Bureau of American Ethnology by Julian H. Steward (Washington, D. C., 1946–1950; 6 vols.).

In Spanish, the literature is abundant and generally of high quality for, in the century since Bartolomé Mitre pioneered the way, the Argentines have shown a special proclivity and talent for historical writing. The most recent comprehensive work is the coöperative *Historia de la Nación Argentina* (Buenos Aires, 1936–1942; 10 vols.), edited by Ricardo Levene. As noted in the text, Juan Perón was to have contributed to the military history section of this work, but was diverted by other interests.

No reader should overlook the travelers' accounts, which often give the flavor of the times better than any formal study. To mention only a few such works written in English and since 1800, these include H. M. Brackenridge, *A Voyage to South America* (2 vols.; London, 1820), Francis Bond Head, *Rough Notes Taken During Some Rapid Journeys across the Pampas and Among the Andes* (London, 1826), Charles Darwin, *Voyage of the Beagle,* James Bryce, *South America:*

Observations and Impressions (London and New York, 1912), and Philip Guedalla, *Argentine Tango* (London, 1932). Valuable eyewitness accounts of another kind include Domingo F. Sarmiento, *Life in the Argentine Republic in the Days of the Tyrants* (New York, 1868, translated from *Facundo*), W. H. Hudson, *Far Away and Long Ago* (New York, 1918), and Francis Herron, *Letters from the Argentine* (New York, 1943). See also E. M. Nelson, *The Argentine Republic as Seen by Noted Travelers* (San Francisco, 1915), Alexander W. Weddell (ambassador to Buenos Aires), *Introduction to Argentina* (New York, 1939), and the Argentine part of Frederic J. Stimson, *My United States* (New York, 1931), by a former ambassador to Buenos Aires.

3. HISTORICAL BACKGROUND: SPECIAL TOPICS

Economic and Social: In addition to the works cited above in Section 1, there are many more specialized studies, notable among which are Miron Burgin, *Economic Aspects of Argentine Federalism, 1820–1853* (Cambridge, Mass., 1946); E. Tornquist and Co. *The Economic Development of the Argentine Republic in the Last Fifty Years* (1919); Adolfo Dorfman, *Evolución industrial argentina* (Buenos Aires, 1942); Vernon L. Phelps, *The International Economic Position of Argentina* (Philadelphia, 1938), mainly on the period 1910–1934; Simon G. Hanson, *Argentine Meat and the British Market* (Palo Alto, Cal., 1938), a comprehensive history of the subject; Madaline W. Nichols, *The Gaucho* (Durham, N. C., 1942); Edward Larocque Tinker, *The Cult of the Gaucho and the Creation of a Literature* (Worcester, 1947); Kathleen B. Tappen, *The Status of Women in Argentina* (Washington, 1944); A. E. Bunge, *Una nueva Argentina* (Buenos Aires, 1940); Gino Germani, *La clase media en Buenos Aires* (Buenos Aires, 1942); and José Ingenieros, *Sociología Argentina* (Buenos Aires, 1946). The history of the cities of Argentina (mainly colonial, some nineteenth-century) is discussed in Amilcar Razori, *Historia de la ciudad argentina* (Buenos Aires, 1945; 3 vols.), and Romulo Zabala and Enrique de Gandía, *Historia de la ciudad de Buenos Aires* (Buenos Aires, 1936).

Much valuable information on Argentina will be found in works of broader geographical scope, notably D. M. Phelps, *Migration of Industry to South America* (New York, 1936), George Wythe, *Industry in Latin America* (New York, 1945), Lloyd J. Hughlett, ed., *Industrialization in Latin America* (New York, 1946), Wendell C. Gordon, *The Economy of Latin America* (New York, 1950), Simon G. Hanson, *Economic Development in Latin America* (Washington,

1951), H. Foster Bain and T. T. Read, *Ores and Industry in South America* (New York, 1934), Francis Violich, *Cities of Latin America* (New York, 1944), Cleona Lewis, *America's Stake in International Investments* (Washington, 1937), Royal Institute of International Affairs, *The Republics of South America* (London, 1937), and George Soule, David Efron, and N. T. Ness, *Latin America in the Future World* (New York, 1945).

Cultural: In English the fare is meager except for sections relating to Argentina in works of broader scope, such as W. Rex Crawford, *A Century of Latin American Thought* (Cambridge, Mass., 1944), Arturo Torres-Rioseco, *The Epic of Latin American Literature* (New York, 1942), Pedro Henríquez-Ureña, *Literary Currents in Hispanic America* (Cambridge, Mass., 1945), J. T. Lanning, *Academic Culture in the Spanish Colonies* (New York, 1940), J. Lloyd Mecham, *Church and State in Latin America* (Chapel Hill, N. C., 1934), and Lincoln Kirstein, *The Latin American Collection of the Museum of Modern Art* (New York, 1943). The extensive literature in Spanish is well represented by Carlos Octavio Bunge, *Nuestra América* (Barcelona, 1903), J. V. González, *La tradición nacional* (3rd ed.; Buenos Aires, 1930), Ricardo Rojas, *La literature argentina* (Buenos Aires, 1924; 2 vols.), and *Las provincias* (Buenos Aires, 1927), Juan B. Justo, *Educación pública* (Buenos Aires, 1930), Rafael Alberto Arrieta, *La literature argentina y sus vínculos con España* (Buenos Aires, 1948), Juan Rómulo Fernández, *Historia del periodismo argentino* (Buenos Aires, 1943), and (again a work of broader scope, by a Mexican) Leopoldo Zea, *Dos etapas del pensamiento en Hispanoamérica: del romanticismo al positivismo* (Mexico, D. F., 1949). See also the books on the gaucho by Nichols and Tinker cited in the preceding paragraph.

Political and International: Most of the works cited above, under "Historical Background: General," deal mainly with these topics. In addition, three works in English that have special value because they were written on the eve of the Perón revolution are C. H. Haring, *Argentina and the United States* (Boston, 1941), Austin F. Macdonald, *Government of the Argentine Republic* (New York, 1942), and Santos P. Amadeo, *Argentine Constitutional Law* (New York, 1943). In connection with the last-named topic, mention should be made of Helen Clagett, *A Guide to the Law and Legal Literature of Argentina 1917–1946* (Washington, D. C., 1948). Some of the more important works in Spanish are José Luis Romero, *Las ideas políticas en Argentina* (Mexico, D. F., 1946), Victor Lascano, *América y la política argentina* (Buenos Aires, 1938), Ismael Bucich Escobar, *Historia de los presidentes argentinos* (Buenos Aires, 1934), Segundo V. Linares Quintana, *Los partidos políticos* (Buenos Aires, 1945), and the same author's *Gobierno y administración de la República Argentina* (Buenos Aires, 1946; 2 vols.), L. M. Moreno Quintana, *La diplomacia de Irigoyen* (La Plata, 1928), Enrique Dickmann, *Recuerdos de un militante socialista* (Buenos Aires, 1949), and Rodolfo A. Fitte and E. F. Sánchez Zinny, *Génesis de un sentimento democrático* (Buenos Aires, 1944), more than half of which is devoted to an account of *Acción Argentina, 1940–1943.*

Biographical works in English on any period of Argentine history are scanty. Notable exceptions are Ricardo Rojas, *San Martín, Knight of the Andes,* translated by Herschel Brickell (New York, 1945), and Allison W. Bunkley, *The Life of Sarmiento* (Princeton, 1952), which will guide the reader to the principal books on Sarmiento in Spanish: those by Alberto Palcos and Ricardo Rojas (both sympathetic), Leopoldo Lugones (critical), and Manuel Gálvez (hostile). The last-named is also the author of the best biography of Irigoyen. Collected works are numerous; two items of special value for twentieth-century politics and diplomacy are Federico Pinedo, *En tiempos de la República* (Buenos Aires, 1946–1948; 5 vols.), and Mariano J. Drago, *Luis M. Drago, discursos y escritos* (Buenos Aires, 1938; 3 vols.).

The increasing importance of Argentina in inter-American affairs is reflected in Samuel F. Bemis, *The Latin American Policy of the United States: An Historical Interpretation* (New York, 1943); its citations will guide the reader to the principal works on the subject published before 1943. Subsequently, noteworthy additions on the period shortly before 1943 have been made by Alexander DeConde, *Herbert Hoover's Latin American Policy* (Stanford, Cal., 1951), Edward O. Guerrant, *Roosevelt's Good Neighbor Policy* (Albuquerque, N. M., 1950), *The Memoirs of Cordell Hull* (New York, 1948; 2 vols.), Sumner Welles, *The Time for Decision* (New York, 1944) and *Seven Decisions That Shaped History* (New York, 1950), and Laurence Duggan, *The Americas* (New York, 1950). O. Edmund Smith, Jr., *Yankee Diplomacy: U. S. Intervention in Argentina* (Dallas, 1953), is based mainly on printed works in English. New documents on German activities in Argentina are contained in vol. V (1953) of the United States State Department's series *Documents on German Foreign Policy, 1918–1945,* and the State Department's "Blue Book" of 1946 (see below) is an exposé of pro-Axis activities of the Castillo Administration, 1940–1943, as well as of the military dictatorship of Perón and company, 1943–1945. Documents relating to Argentina are included in James W. Gantenbein, ed., *The Evolution of Our Latin American Policy: A Documentary Record* (New York, 1950). A manuscript study of the triangle Argentina–Great Britain–United States by Donald B. Easum is ready for publication;

I am much indebted to the author for the loan of it during the
preparation of the present volume.

4. THE PERÓN PERIOD

In large part the great mass of material that has been published on
this period is not only ephemeral but also biased. In most cases the
direction of the bias has been determined by the country of origin.
All kinds of publications in the United States — books, articles, newspaper reports — have been overwhelmingly anti-Perón, whereas in
Argentina since 1946 they have become, under compulsion, unanimously pro-Perón, except for an occasional clandestine publication.
Most of the important materials (except the works of Argentine exiles)
have come out of these two countries; and most of those produced
elsewhere have been similarly biased according to the author's liking
or dislike for the Perón regime. Objective analysis based on adequate
information is rare. This should not surprise anyone, for it is hard to
be objective about such a regime and it has itself made information
difficult to obtain and free discussion impossible among the people
best qualified to analyze and judge the regime — the people of
Argentina. The pitfalls are so numerous that no one could hope to
avoid all of them.

Nevertheless, there are three recent books in English, all of broad
scope, that can be recommended for their special virtues: Robert J.
Alexander, *The Perón Era* (New York, 1951), is particularly good on
organized labor; George I. Blanksten, *Perón's Argentina* (Chicago,
1953), contains the best analysis to date of Peronista ideology; and
James Bruce, *Those Perplexing Argentines* (New York, 1953), the
work of a former American Ambassador to Argentina (1947–1949),
written with the aid of Ray Josephs (see below), discreetly skirts controversial questions but otherwise gives an exceptionally comprehensive, well-informed, and lively account of life and manners in Perón's
Argentina. All three were very useful in the preparation of the present
work, though none of them stresses the historical background or the
contemporaneous international environment as does the last mentioned.

Three other recent books in English shed many sidelights on the
Peróns and others: Fleur Cowles, *Bloody Precedent* (New York, 1952),
the precedent being the tyranny of Rosas; Virginia Prewett, *Beyond
the Great Forest* (New York, 1953), the work of an experienced
journalist; and Stanton Griffis, *Lying in State* (New York, 1952), the
work of a businessman-diplomat, which deals in part with Argentina.

There is no biography of Perón in English and no complete biography in Spanish. A semi-official account of his life to the eve of his rise to power is contained in Enrique Pavón Pereyra, *Perón, 1895–1942* (Buenos Aires, 1952). Eva Perón's career is described with no love in María Flores, *Woman with the Whip* (New York, 1952). Her own *La razón de mi vida* (Buenos Aires, 1951), was ghost-written and tells very little about her life; it is now available in English translation.

Older books dealing with the early period of Perón's rise include those by Ysabel F. Rennie and Felix J. Weil cited in the preceding section, and also Ray Josephs, *Argentine Diary* (New York, 1944), a running eyewitness account by an alert journalist, and Ruth and Leonard Greenup, *Revolution before Breakfast* (Chapel Hill, N. C., 1947). The United States State Department's "Blue Book" on Argentina (1946) is identified in the text; but it should be added here that while this exposé backfired politically, it contains valuable information, much of which was drawn from then recently captured German documents. Accounts by Argentine opponents of Perón, most of whom had to go into exile, include the work by Enrique Dickmann cited above; Santiago Nudelman, *El radicalismo al servicio de la libertad* (Buenos Aires, 1947); Silvano Santander, *Técnica de una traición* (Montevideo, 1949); and Ernesto Enrique Sammartino, *La verdad sobre la situación argentina* (2nd ed.; Montevideo, 1951). The chief official report of the crucial election of 1946, which is of course pro-Perón but is copiously documented, is contained in a two-volume work published by the Ministerio del Interior, under the significant title, *Las fuerzas armadas restituyen el imperio de la soberanía popular* (Buenos Aires, 1946).

The history of the period since 1946 has to be written very largely from sources too numerous to detail, such as newspapers, periodicals, government reports, and press releases, supplemented by personal observation and interviews. First and foremost are the careful studies of Latin American, including Argentine, economic problems prepared by the Economic Commission for Latin America, a United Nations organ (under the Economic and Social Council); its most useful study to date, which includes a special study of Argentina in a critical period, is its *Economic Survey for Latin America, 1951–1952* (New York, 1953; mimeographed). The Pan American Union has published a convenient compilation of statistics, *The Foreign Trade of Latin America since 1913* (Washington, D. C., 1951), which contains a separate section on each country. Two items of exceptional value on problems that are both economic and social are Carl C. Taylor's *Rural Life in Argentina,* already cited, and three articles on the middle class in Argentina in the Pan American Union's *Materiales para el estudio de la clase media en la América Latina,* No. 1 (Washington, 1950). An analysis of the amended Constitution (1949) by an outstanding

Argentine authority, Rafael Bielsa, is contained in vol. II of his *Compendio de derecho público*. The text of this constitution and a table of organization of the Peronista Party are brought together with a topically arranged selection of Perón's pronouncements to 1951 on almost every conceivable question in both domestic and foreign affairs in Presidencia de la Nación, Subscretaría de Informaciones, *Doctrina Peronista* (Buenos Aires, n.d.).

In addition to her book mentioned above, Eva Perón is represented by *Mi obra de ayuda social* (Buenos Aires, 1949) and *The Writings of Eva Perón* (Buenos Aires, 1950), collected speeches and articles in an English translation. Two works by present Radical Party leaders are Ricardo Balbín, *Hacia la realización de una democracia responsable* (Montevideo, 1951), and Arturo Frondizi, *El tratado de Rio de Janeiro (1947)* (Buenos Aires, 1950), a brief but very valuable exposition and defense of Radical foreign policy as defined by the party's majority group at that time.

Recent biographical dictionaries for Argentina include Ronald Hilton, ed., *Who's Who in Latin America: Vol. 4, Argentina and Chile* (Stanford, 1950), and *Personalidades de la Argentina: diccionario biográfico* (3rd ed.; Buenos Aires, 1948).

The maximum dispersion of materials in English exists in the field of diplomatic relations between the United States and Argentina. For the years 1943–1946 there is valuable information, presented from widely different points of view, in the works by Cordell Hull and Sumner Welles cited above; and major developments of each year are described in Arthur P. Whitaker, ed., *Inter-American Affairs: An Annual Survey* (New York, 1942–1946; 5 vols.). After 1945 the Council on Foreign Relations resumed publication (interrupted during the war) of its invaluable annual surveys, *The United States in World Affairs*, and these provide some thread of continuity, as well as bibliographical aid, for the later period, though the amount of space devoted to Argentina in this global work is necessarily small. Some official documents on the inter-American regional system are included in Francis O. Wilcox and T. V. Kalijarvi, *Recent American Foreign Policy: Basic Documents, 1941–1951* (New York, 1952), and Argentine data are included in W. S. and E. S. Woytinsky, *World Population and Production: Trends and Outlook* (New York, 1953). Except for occasional works of this kind, the reader will have to range far and wide through a host of fragmentary sources.

5. CURRENT DEVELOPMENTS

Each issue of the monthly *Hispanic American Report* (Stanford University, edited by Ronald Hilton) devotes three or four well-filled pages to Argentina. Fuller reports of outstanding events are often given in newspapers, particularly the *New York Times, New York Herald-Tribune,* and *Christian Science Monitor.* The weekly *Time* magazine frequently reports on Argentina; so does *The Economist* (London), despite the sharp decline of British trade and investment in Argentina in recent years. Occasional articles will be found in *The Atlantic Monthly, Current History, Foreign Affairs, The Yale Review,* and other periodicals, and in various publications of the Foreign Policy Association. The quarterly *Inter-American Economic Affairs* is indispensable in its field. The annual survey, *The United States in World Affairs* (recent volumes written by Richard P. Stebbins), has been mentioned above in another connection. Another annual, *South American Handbook,* regularly devotes a long article to Argentina.

Government publications are particularly useful for economic development, statistical data, and official documents. Among United States Government agencies, the most productive are the Commerce Department (its annual survey of economic conditions in Argentina is particularly useful) and the State Department (particularly through its *Bulletin;* it also distributes on a limited basis monitored radio broadcasts, which frequently give valuable material not available elsewhere). Among United Nations agencies, the steadiest stream of significant material comes from the Economic Commission for Latin America (Economic and Social Council). The Organization of American States and its secretariat, The Pan American Union, likewise produce publications, both regular and special, which often contain significant information on noncontroversial questions; for obvious reasons, controversial questions are avoided.

An excellent guide to current publications is provided by the annual *Handbook of Latin American Studies,* though this is usually some two or three years in arrears.

Index